THE LAST MAN — Girl on Girl

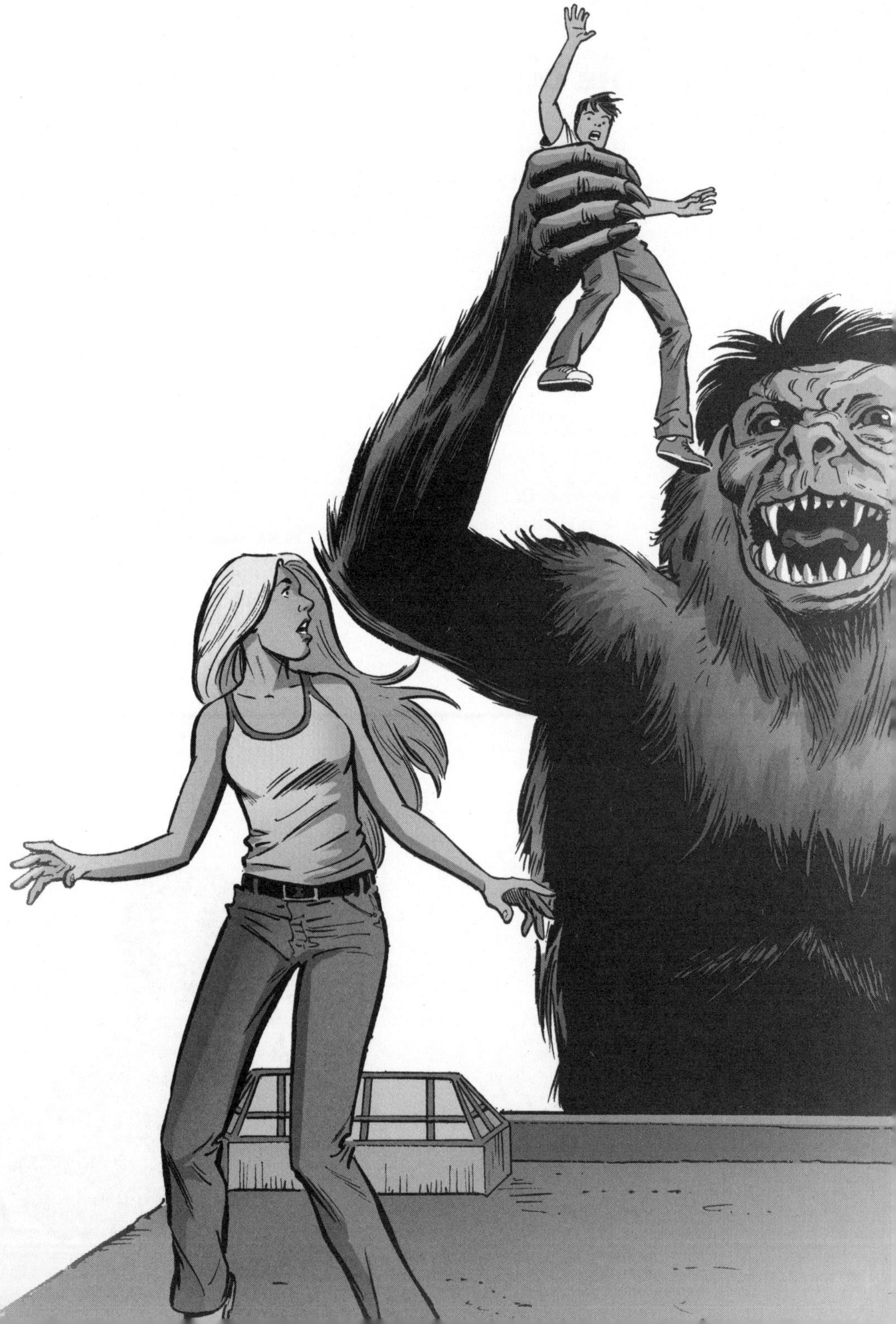

Y: THE LAST MAN – Girl on Girl

Brian K. Vaughan
Writer

Pia Guerra
Goran Sudžuka
Pencillers

José Marzán, Jr.
Inker

Zylonol
Colorist

Clem Robins
Letterer

Massimo Carnevale
Original series covers

Y: THE LAST MAN created by Brian K. Vaughan and Pia Guerra

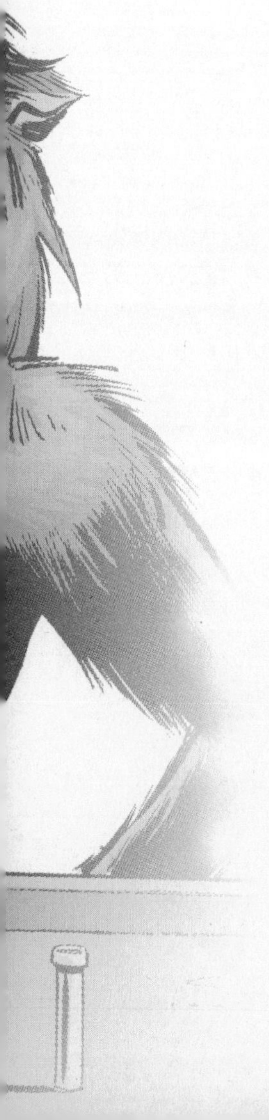

Y: THE LAST MAN — GIRL ON GIRL

DC Comics, 1700 Broadway, New York, NY 10019
A Warner Bros. Entertainment Company.
Printed in Canada. First Printing.
ISBN: 1-4012-0501-1
Cover illustrations by Massimo Carnevale.
Logo designs by Terry Marks.

Y: THE LAST MAN – Contents

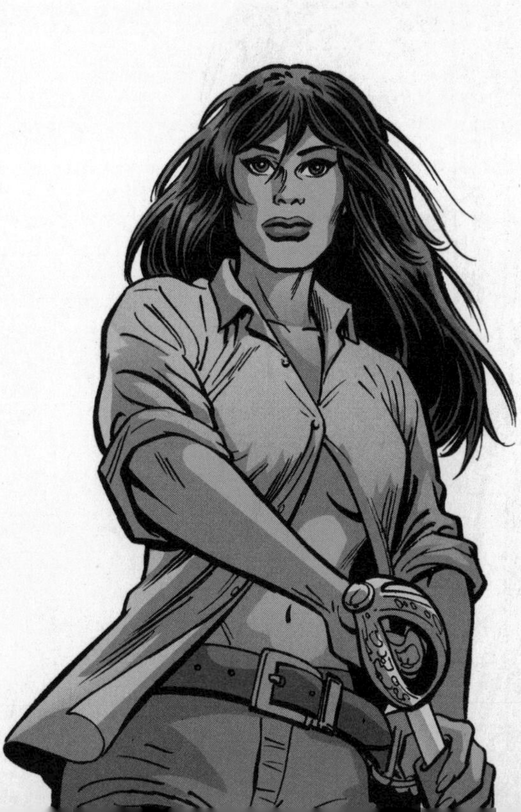

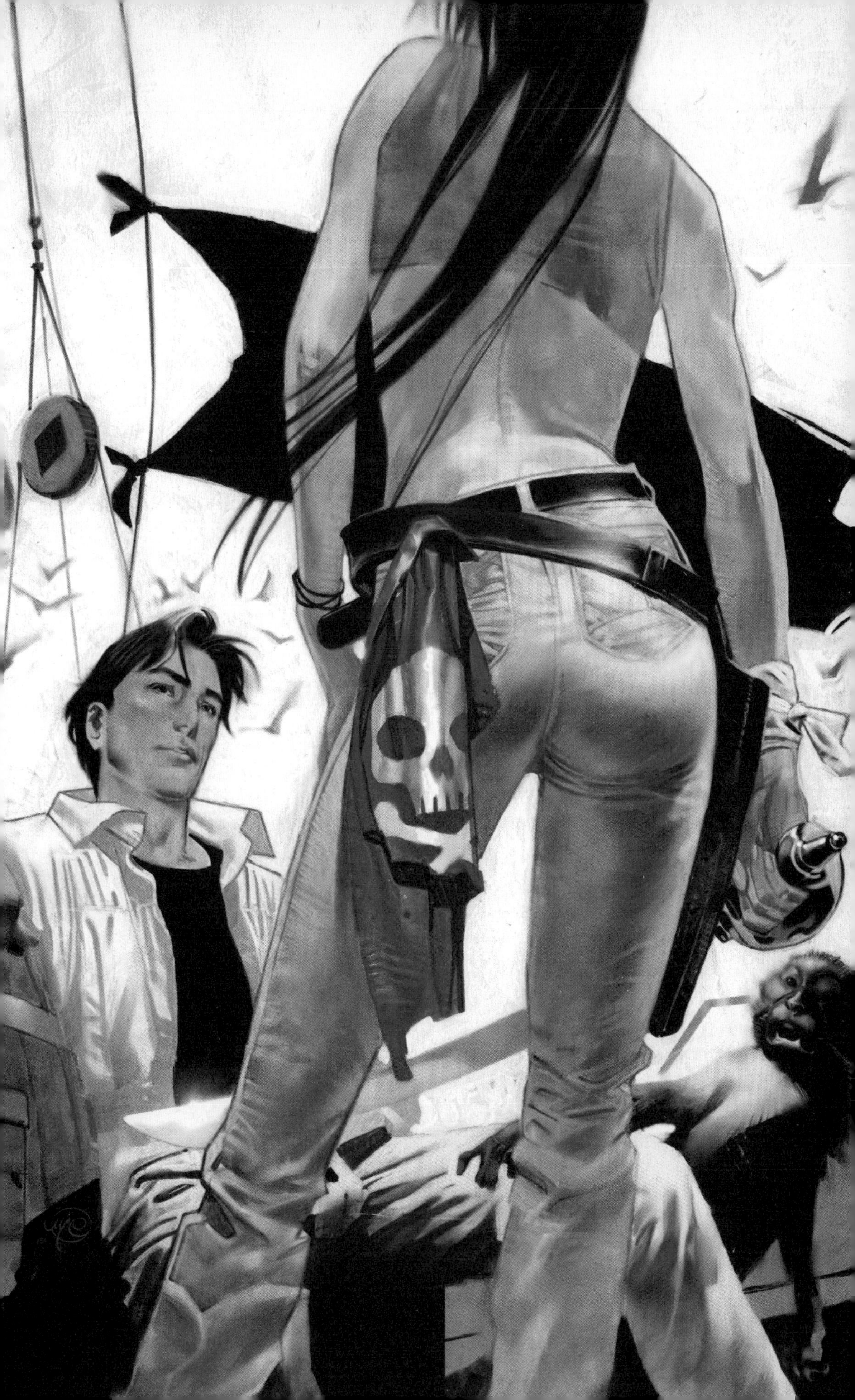

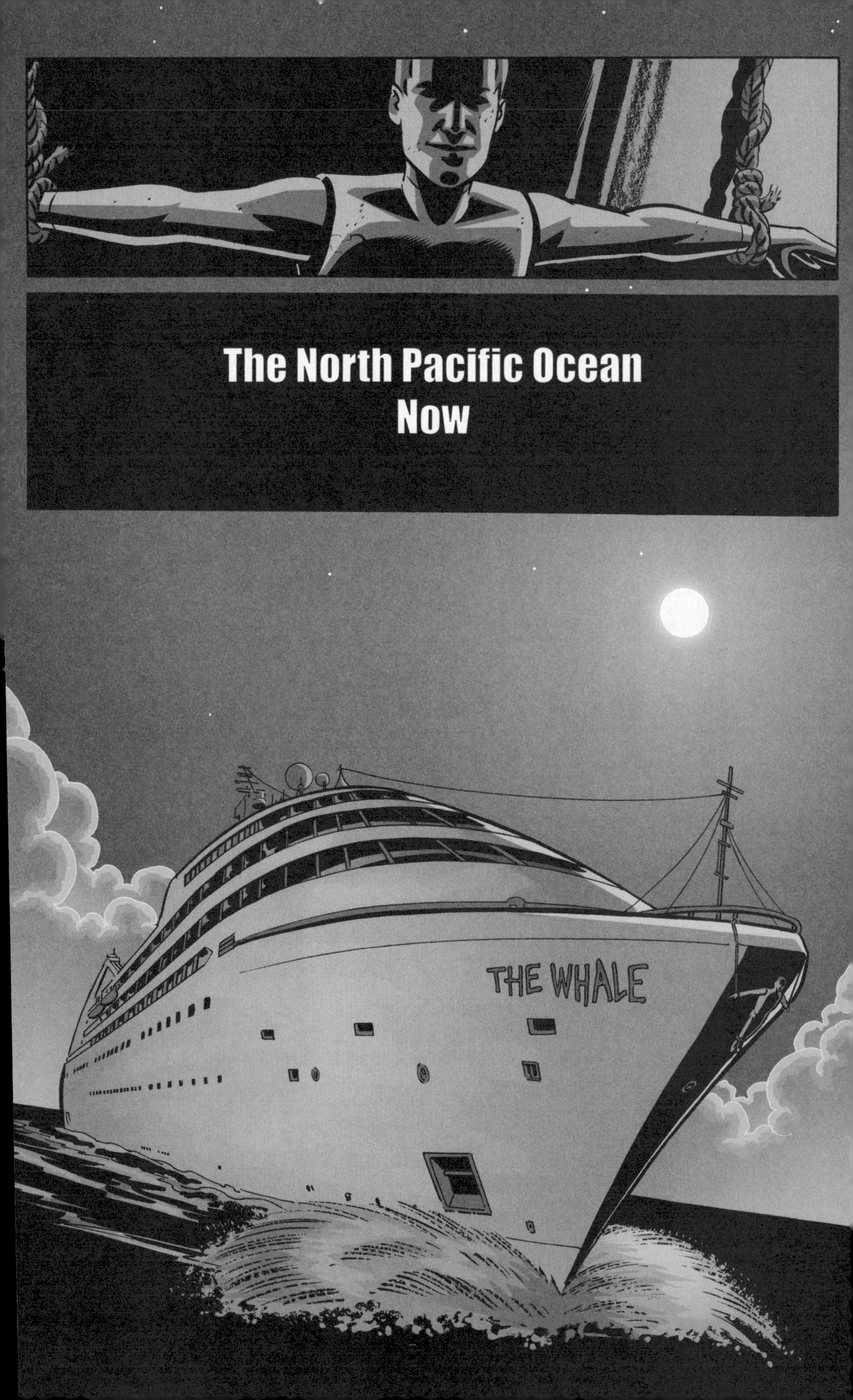
The North Pacific Ocean
Now
THE WHALE

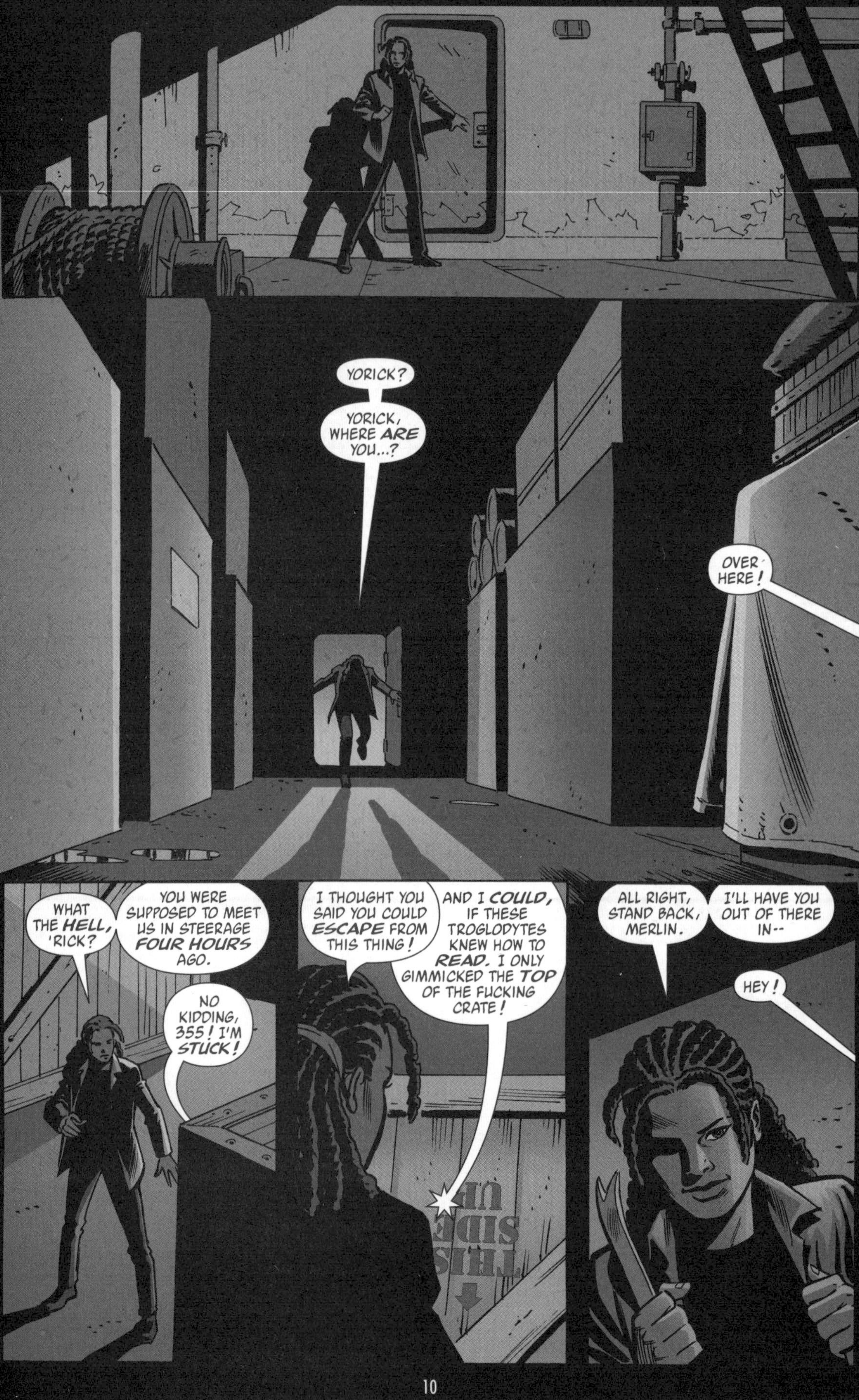
YORICK?
YORICK, WHERE **ARE** YOU...?
OVER HERE!
WHAT THE **HELL,** 'RICK?
YOU WERE SUPPOSED TO MEET US IN STEERAGE **FOUR HOURS** AGO.
NO KIDDING, 355! I'M **STUCK!**
I THOUGHT YOU SAID YOU COULD **ESCAPE** FROM THIS THING!
AND I **COULD,** IF THESE TROGLODYTES KNEW HOW TO **READ.** I ONLY GIMMICKED THE **TOP** OF THE FUCKING CRATE!
THIS SIDE UP
ALL RIGHT, STAND BACK, MERLIN.
I'LL HAVE YOU OUT OF THERE IN--
HEY!

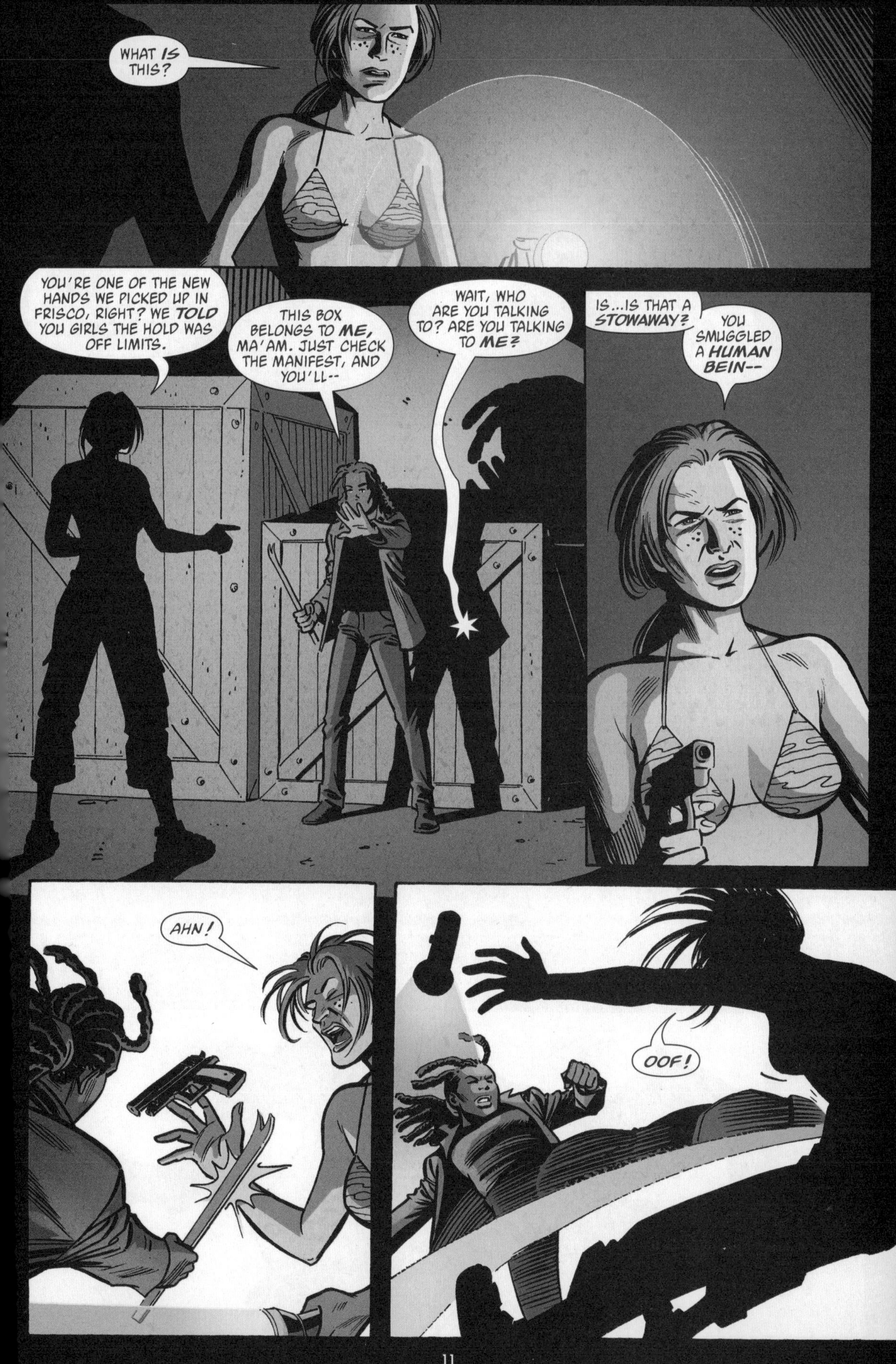
WHAT IS THIS?
YOU'RE ONE OF THE NEW HANDS WE PICKED UP IN FRISCO, RIGHT? WE TOLD YOU GIRLS THE HOLD WAS OFF LIMITS.
THIS BOX BELONGS TO ME, MA'AM. JUST CHECK THE MANIFEST, AND YOU'LL--
WAIT, WHO ARE YOU TALKING TO? ARE YOU TALKING TO ME?
IS...IS THAT A STOWAWAY?
YOU SMUGGLED A HUMAN BEIN--
AHN!
OOF!

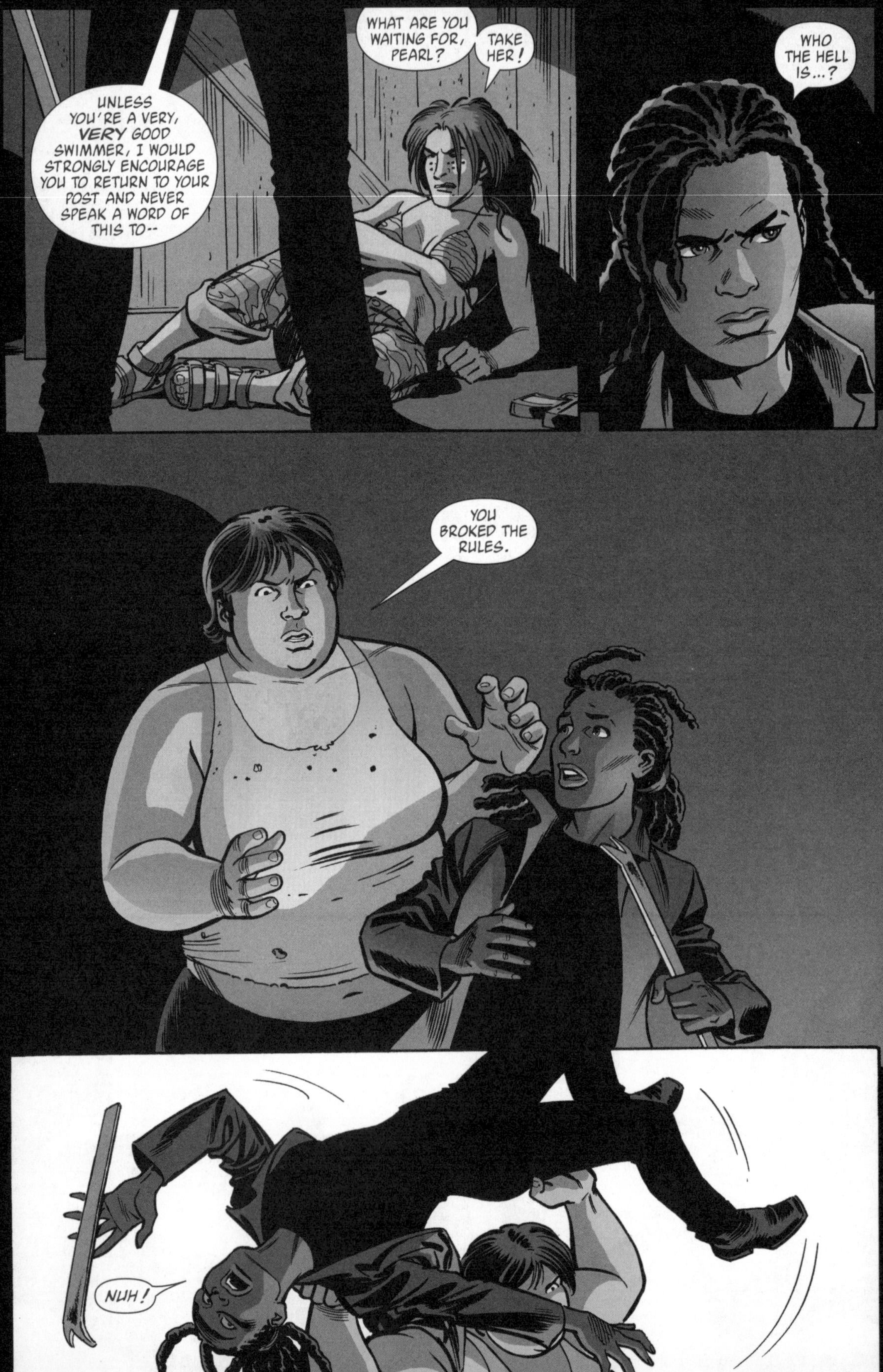
UNLESS YOU'RE A VERY, VERY GOOD SWIMMER, I WOULD STRONGLY ENCOURAGE YOU TO RETURN TO YOUR POST AND NEVER SPEAK A WORD OF THIS TO--
WHAT ARE YOU WAITING FOR, PEARL?
TAKE HER!
WHO THE HELL IS...?
YOU BROKED THE RULES.
NUH!

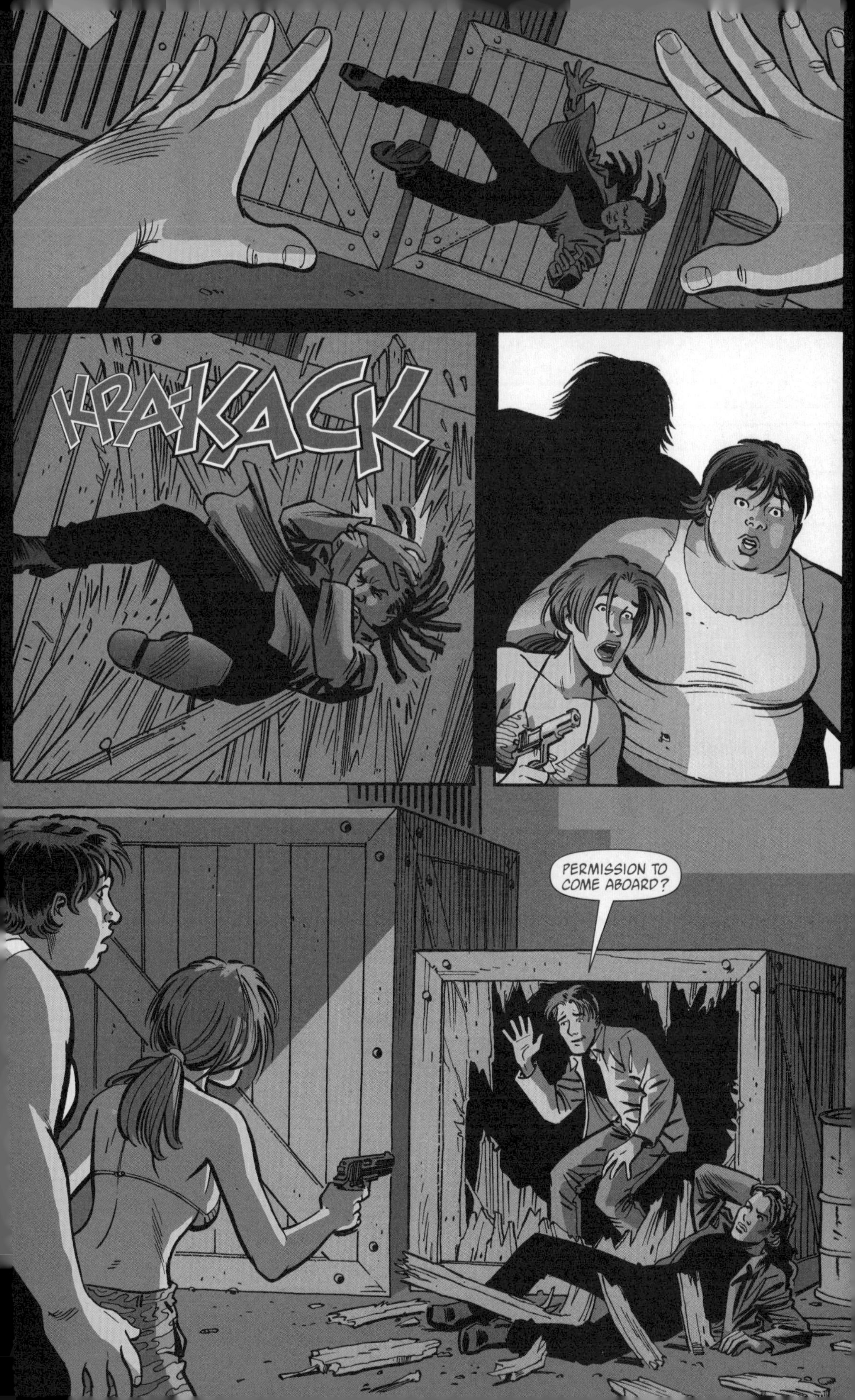
KRA-KACK
PERMISSION TO COME ABOARD?

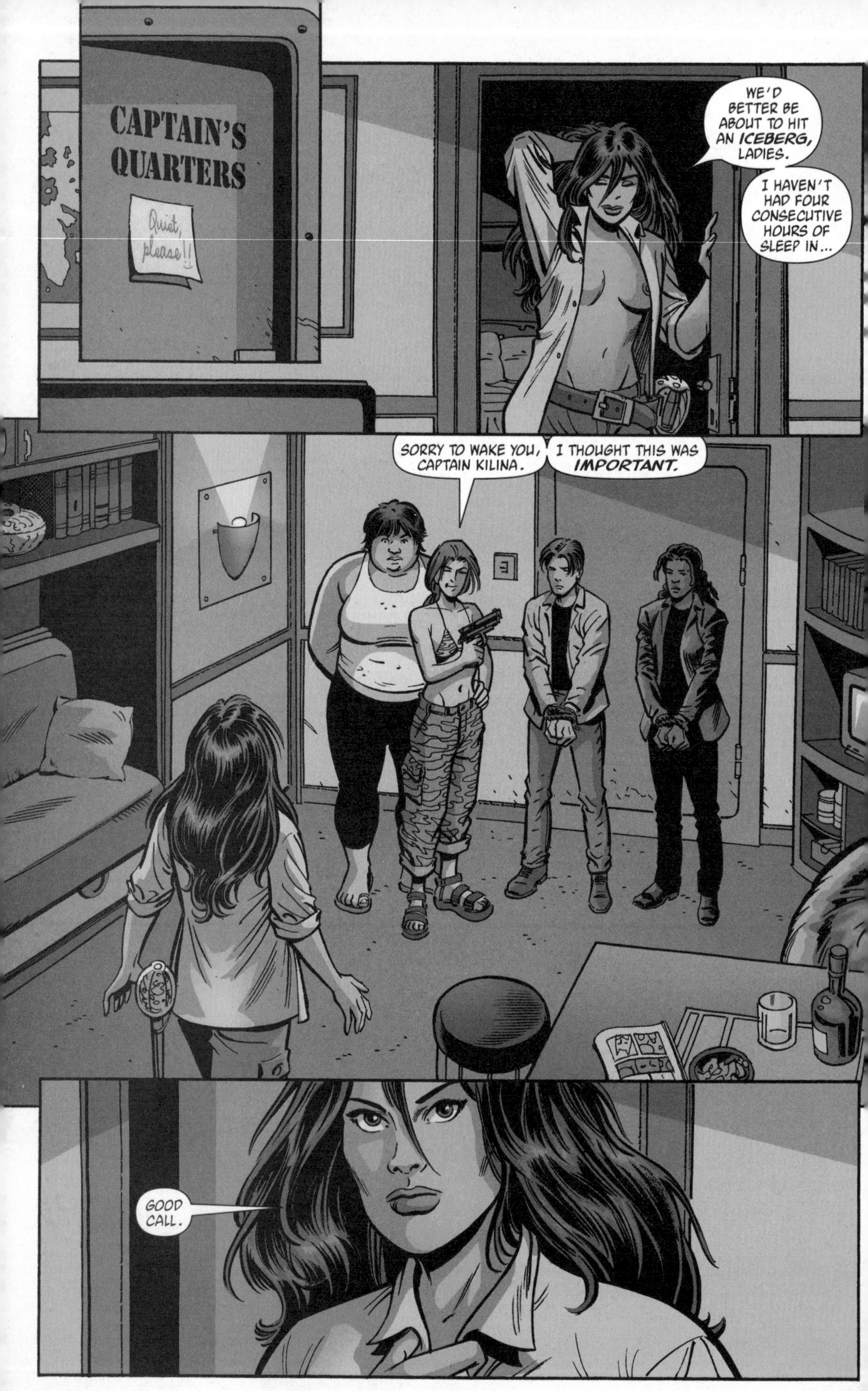
CAPTAIN'S QUARTERS
Quiet, please!!
WE'D BETTER BE ABOUT TO HIT AN *ICEBERG,* LADIES.
I HAVEN'T HAD FOUR CONSECUTIVE HOURS OF SLEEP IN...
SORRY TO WAKE YOU, CAPTAIN KILINA.
I THOUGHT THIS WAS *IMPORTANT.*
GOOD CALL.

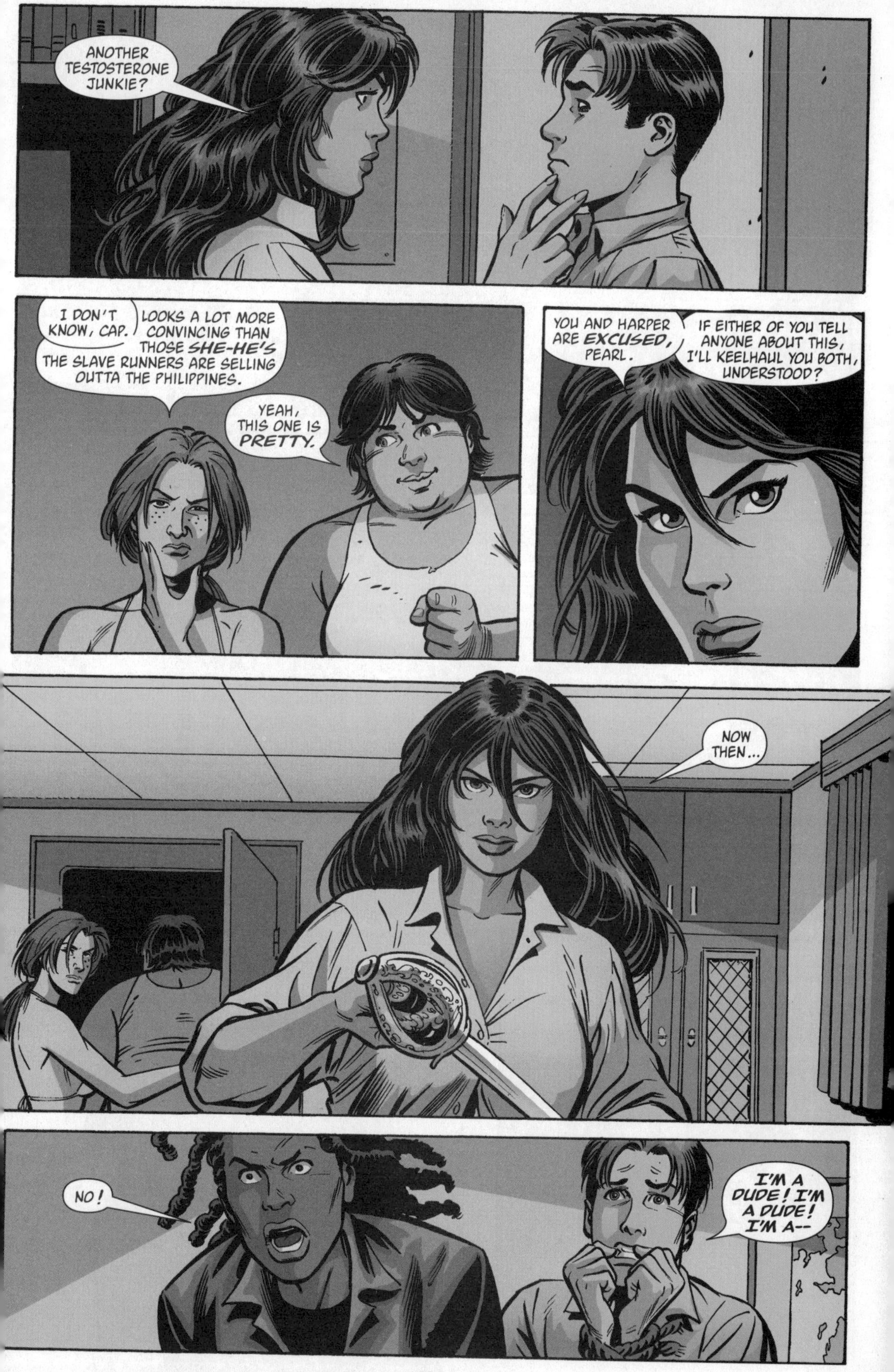
ANOTHER TESTOSTERONE JUNKIE?
I DON'T KNOW, CAP.
LOOKS A LOT MORE CONVINCING THAN THOSE SHE-HE'S THE SLAVE RUNNERS ARE SELLING OUTTA THE PHILIPPINES.
YEAH, THIS ONE IS PRETTY.
YOU AND HARPER ARE EXCUSED, PEARL.
IF EITHER OF YOU TELL ANYONE ABOUT THIS, I'LL KEELHAUL YOU BOTH, UNDERSTOOD?
NOW THEN...
NO!
I'M A DUDE! I'M A DUDE! I'M A--

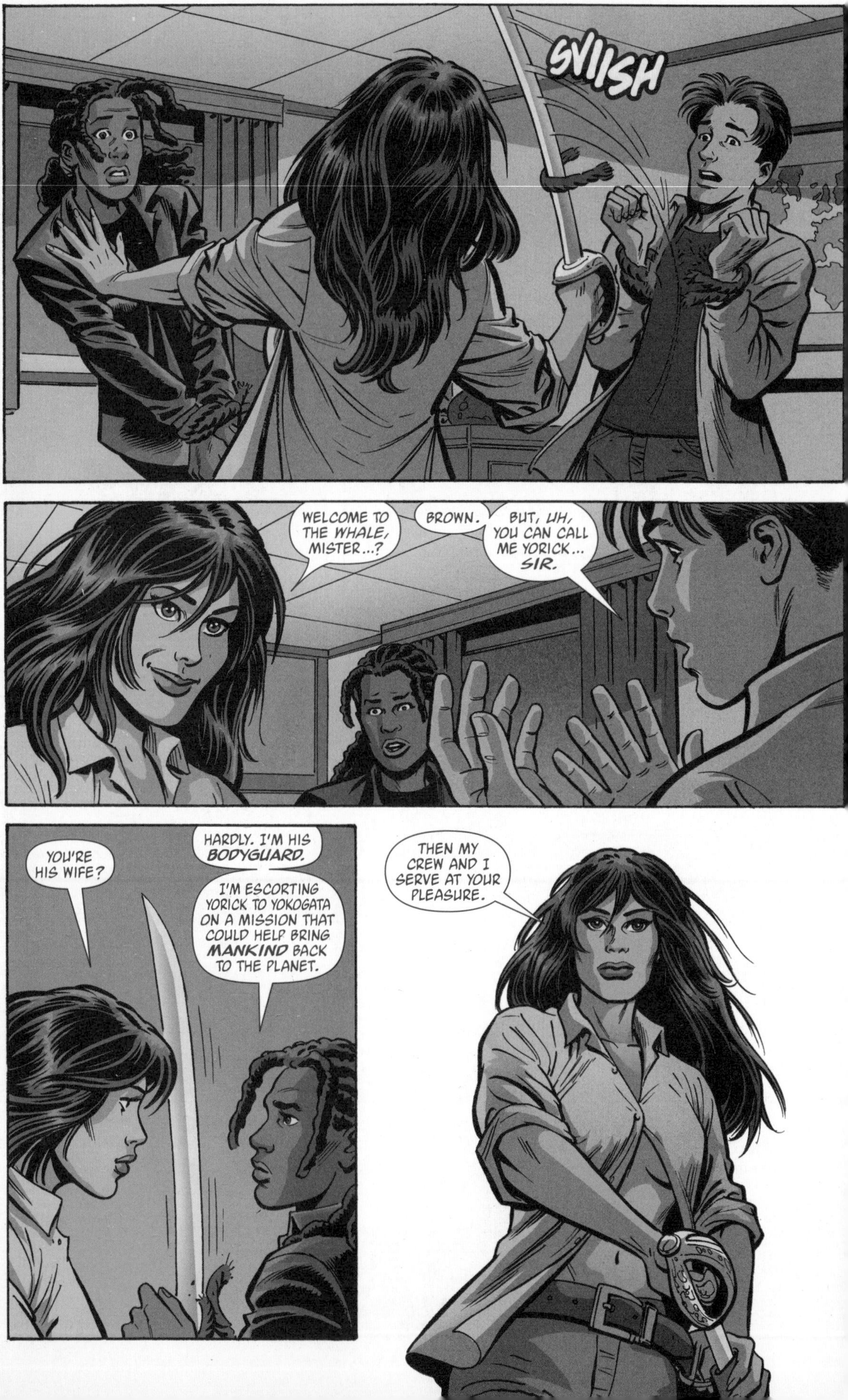
SVIISH
WELCOME TO THE WHALE, MISTER...?
BROWN.
BUT, UH, YOU CAN CALL ME YORICK... SIR.
YOU'RE HIS WIFE?
HARDLY. I'M HIS BODYGUARD.
I'M ESCORTING YORICK TO YOKOGATA ON A MISSION THAT COULD HELP BRING MANKIND BACK TO THE PLANET.
THEN MY CREW AND I SERVE AT YOUR PLEASURE.

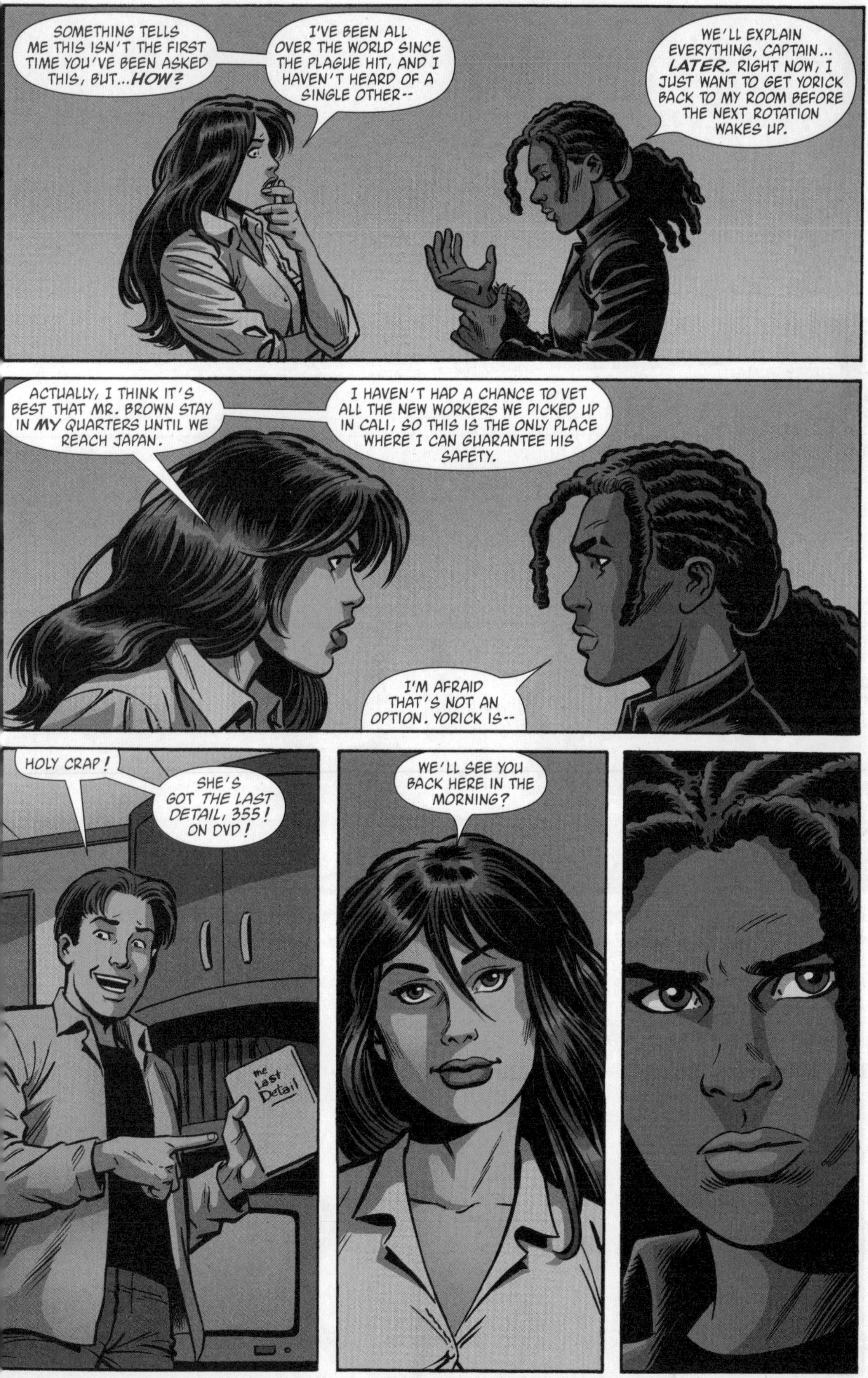
SOMETHING TELLS ME THIS ISN'T THE FIRST TIME YOU'VE BEEN ASKED THIS, BUT...HOW?
I'VE BEEN ALL OVER THE WORLD SINCE THE PLAGUE HIT, AND I HAVEN'T HEARD OF A SINGLE OTHER--
WE'LL EXPLAIN EVERYTHING, CAPTAIN... LATER. RIGHT NOW, I JUST WANT TO GET YORICK BACK TO MY ROOM BEFORE THE NEXT ROTATION WAKES UP.
ACTUALLY, I THINK IT'S BEST THAT MR. BROWN STAY IN MY QUARTERS UNTIL WE REACH JAPAN.
I HAVEN'T HAD A CHANCE TO VET ALL THE NEW WORKERS WE PICKED UP IN CALI, SO THIS IS THE ONLY PLACE WHERE I CAN GUARANTEE HIS SAFETY.
I'M AFRAID THAT'S NOT AN OPTION. YORICK IS--
HOLY CRAP!
SHE'S GOT THE LAST DETAIL, 355! ON DVD!
the Last Detail
WE'LL SEE YOU BACK HERE IN THE MORNING?

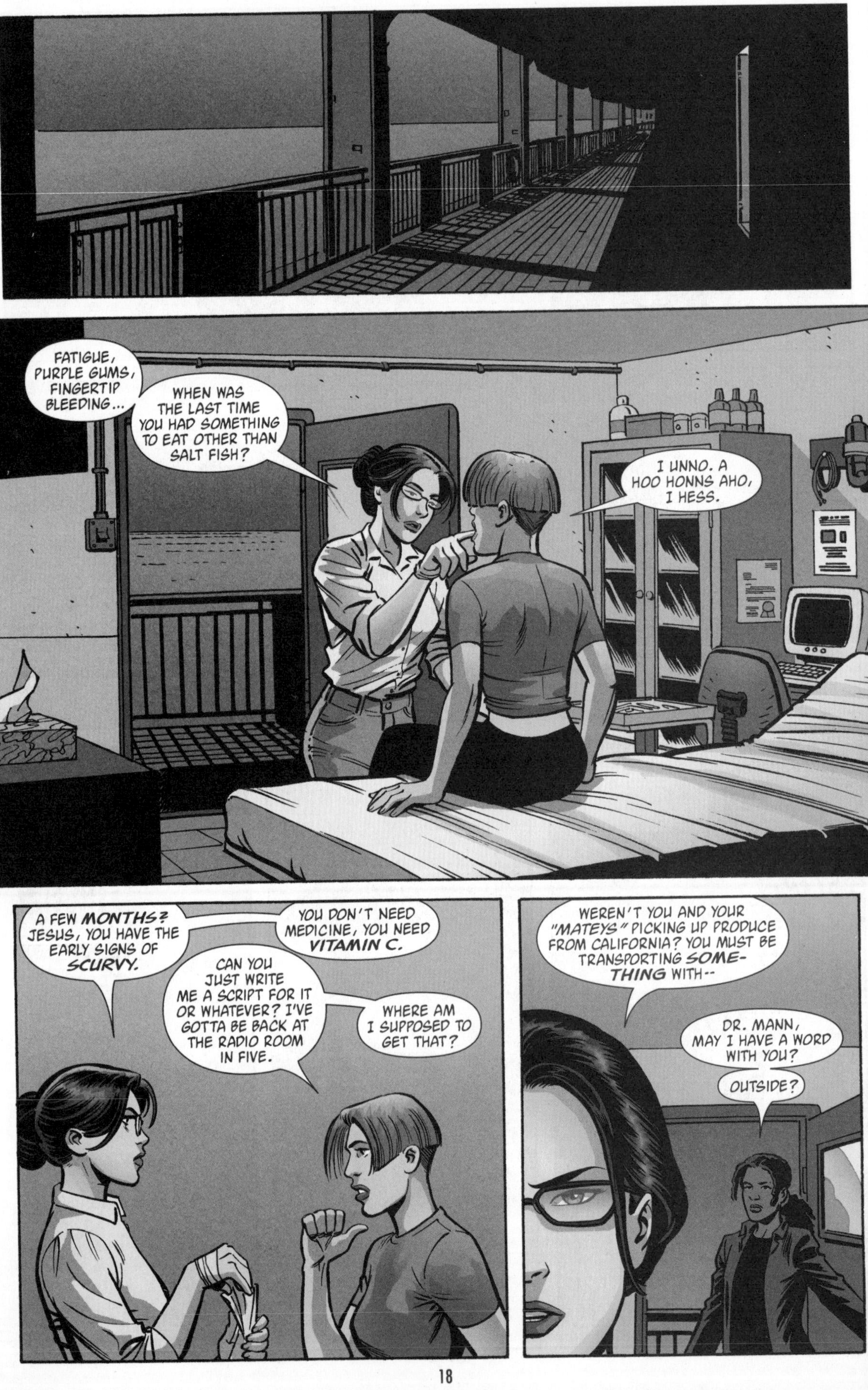
FATIGUE, PURPLE GUMS, FINGERTIP BLEEDING...
WHEN WAS THE LAST TIME YOU HAD SOMETHING TO EAT OTHER THAN SALT FISH?
I UNNO. A HOO HONNS AHO, I HESS.
A FEW MONTHS? JESUS, YOU HAVE THE EARLY SIGNS OF SCURVY.
YOU DON'T NEED MEDICINE, YOU NEED VITAMIN C.
CAN YOU JUST WRITE ME A SCRIPT FOR IT OR WHATEVER? I'VE GOTTA BE BACK AT THE RADIO ROOM IN FIVE.
WHERE AM I SUPPOSED TO GET THAT?
WEREN'T YOU AND YOUR "MATEYS" PICKING UP PRODUCE FROM CALIFORNIA? YOU MUST BE TRANSPORTING SOME-THING WITH--
DR. MANN, MAY I HAVE A WORD WITH YOU?
OUTSIDE?

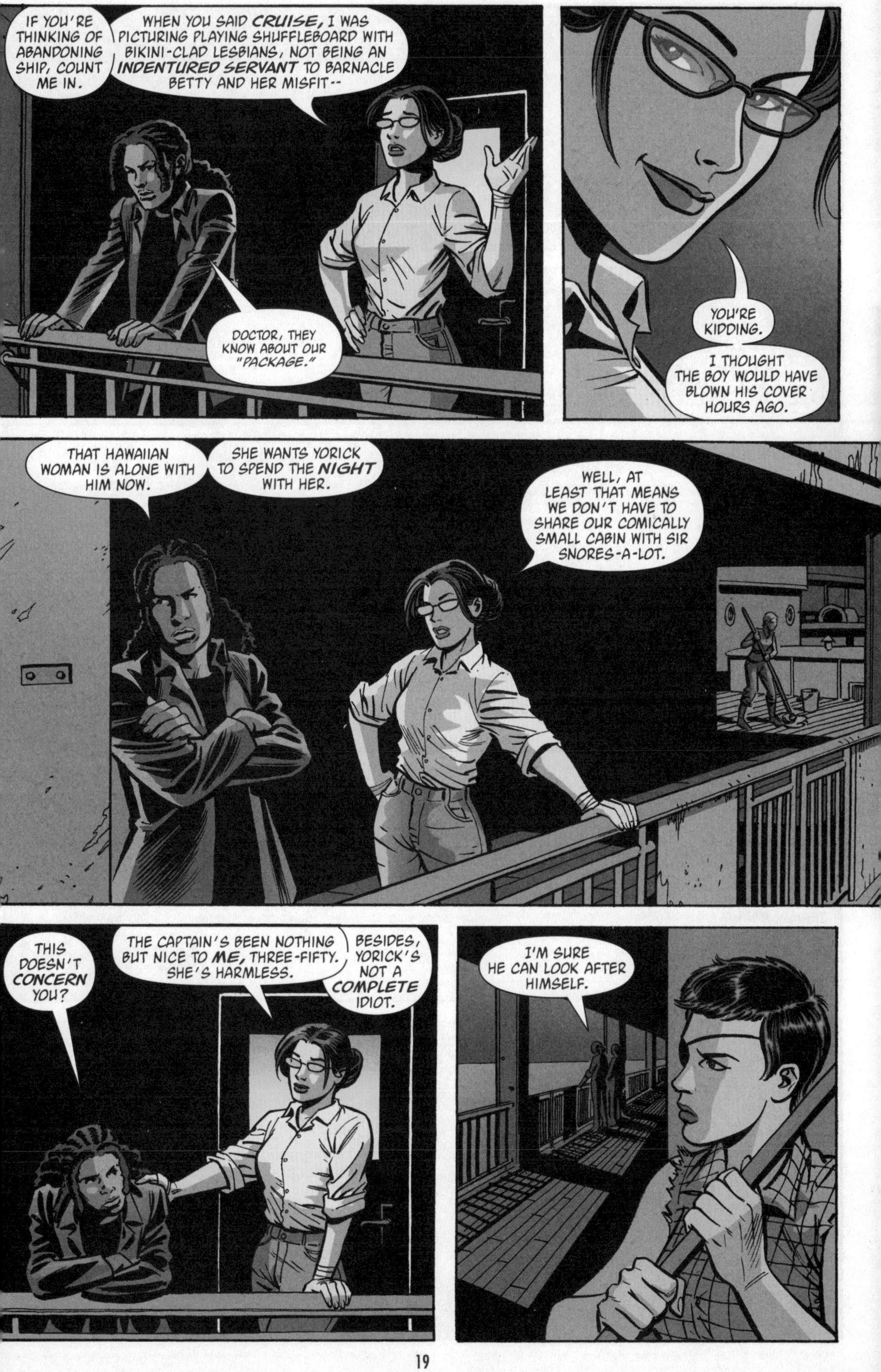
IF YOU'RE THINKING OF ABANDONING SHIP, COUNT ME IN.
WHEN YOU SAID CRUISE, I WAS PICTURING PLAYING SHUFFLEBOARD WITH BIKINI-CLAD LESBIANS, NOT BEING AN INDENTURED SERVANT TO BARNACLE BETTY AND HER MISFIT--
DOCTOR, THEY KNOW ABOUT OUR "PACKAGE."
YOU'RE KIDDING.
I THOUGHT THE BOY WOULD HAVE BLOWN HIS COVER HOURS AGO.
THAT HAWAIIAN WOMAN IS ALONE WITH HIM NOW.
SHE WANTS YORICK TO SPEND THE NIGHT WITH HER.
WELL, AT LEAST THAT MEANS WE DON'T HAVE TO SHARE OUR COMICALLY SMALL CABIN WITH SIR SNORES-A-LOT.
THIS DOESN'T CONCERN YOU?
THE CAPTAIN'S BEEN NOTHING BUT NICE TO ME, THREE-FIFTY. SHE'S HARMLESS.
BESIDES, YORICK'S NOT A COMPLETE IDIOT.
I'M SURE HE CAN LOOK AFTER HIMSELF.

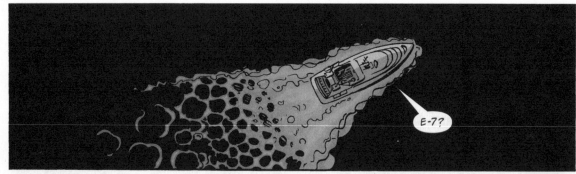

E-7?

CRAP, YOU SUNK MY DESTROYER.

I WOULD TELL YOUR *CARRIER* TO START MANNING ITS LIFEBOATS, TOO.

ANYWAY, YOU WERE SAYING ABOUT THE ASTRONAUT'S *BABY...*?

OH, RIGHT. I MIGHT BE THE LAST MAN ON EARTH, BUT CIBA'S SON IS THE *FIRST BOY.*

AND IF THERE'S EVER GOING TO BE ANY MORE OF US, MY FRIENDS AND I HAVE TO FIND AMPERSAND.

SORRY?

HE'S WHAT SAVED MY LIFE, BELIEVE IT OR NOT.

AMP'S MY PET--

GLEEE!

BA-*FUCK!*

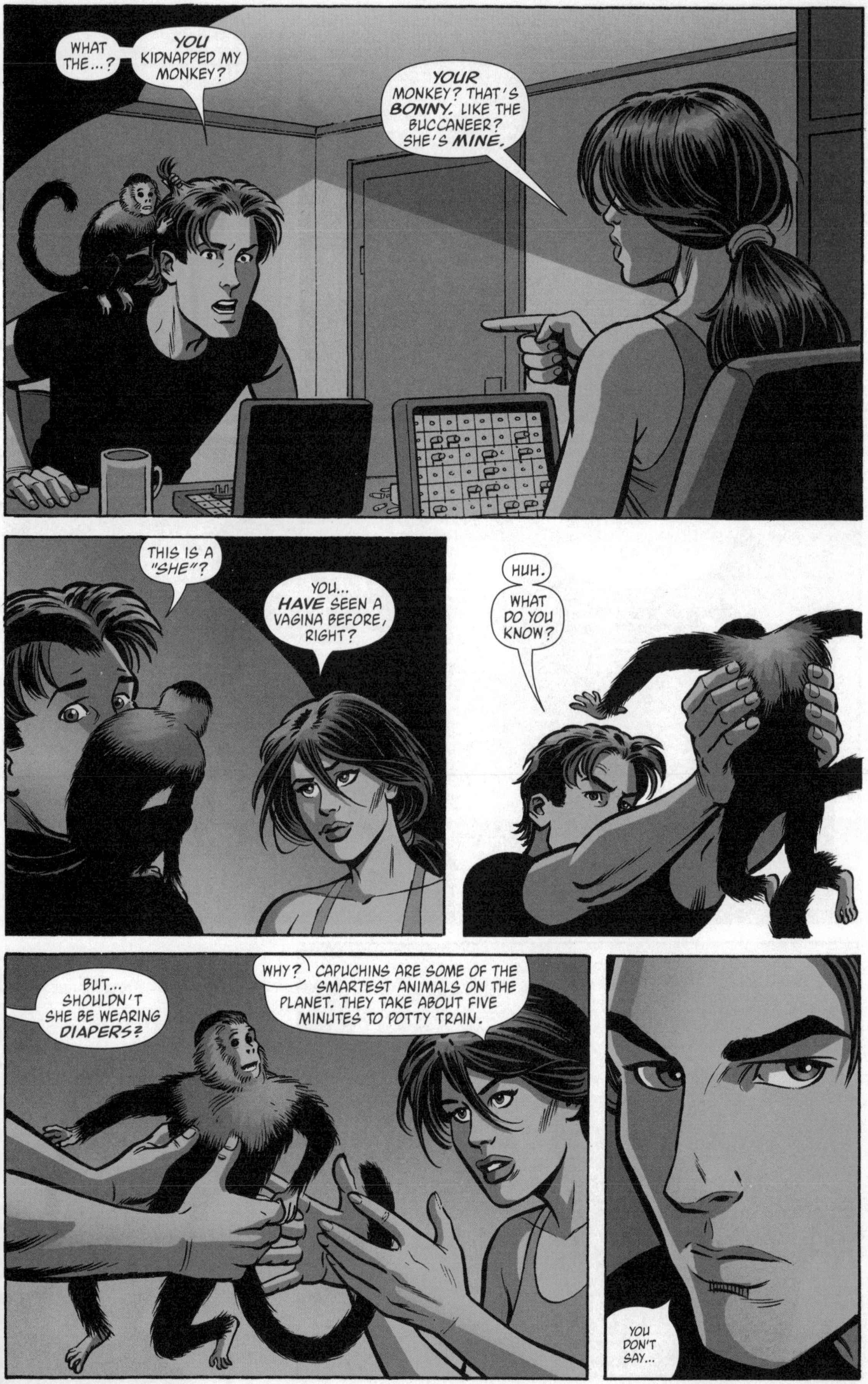
WHAT THE...?
YOU KIDNAPPED MY MONKEY?
YOUR MONKEY? THAT'S BONNY. LIKE THE BUCCANEER? SHE'S MINE.
THIS IS A "SHE"?
YOU... HAVE SEEN A VAGINA BEFORE, RIGHT?
HUH.
WHAT DO YOU KNOW?
BUT... SHOULDN'T SHE BE WEARING DIAPERS?
WHY?
CAPUCHINS ARE SOME OF THE SMARTEST ANIMALS ON THE PLANET. THEY TAKE ABOUT FIVE MINUTES TO POTTY TRAIN.
YOU DON'T SAY...

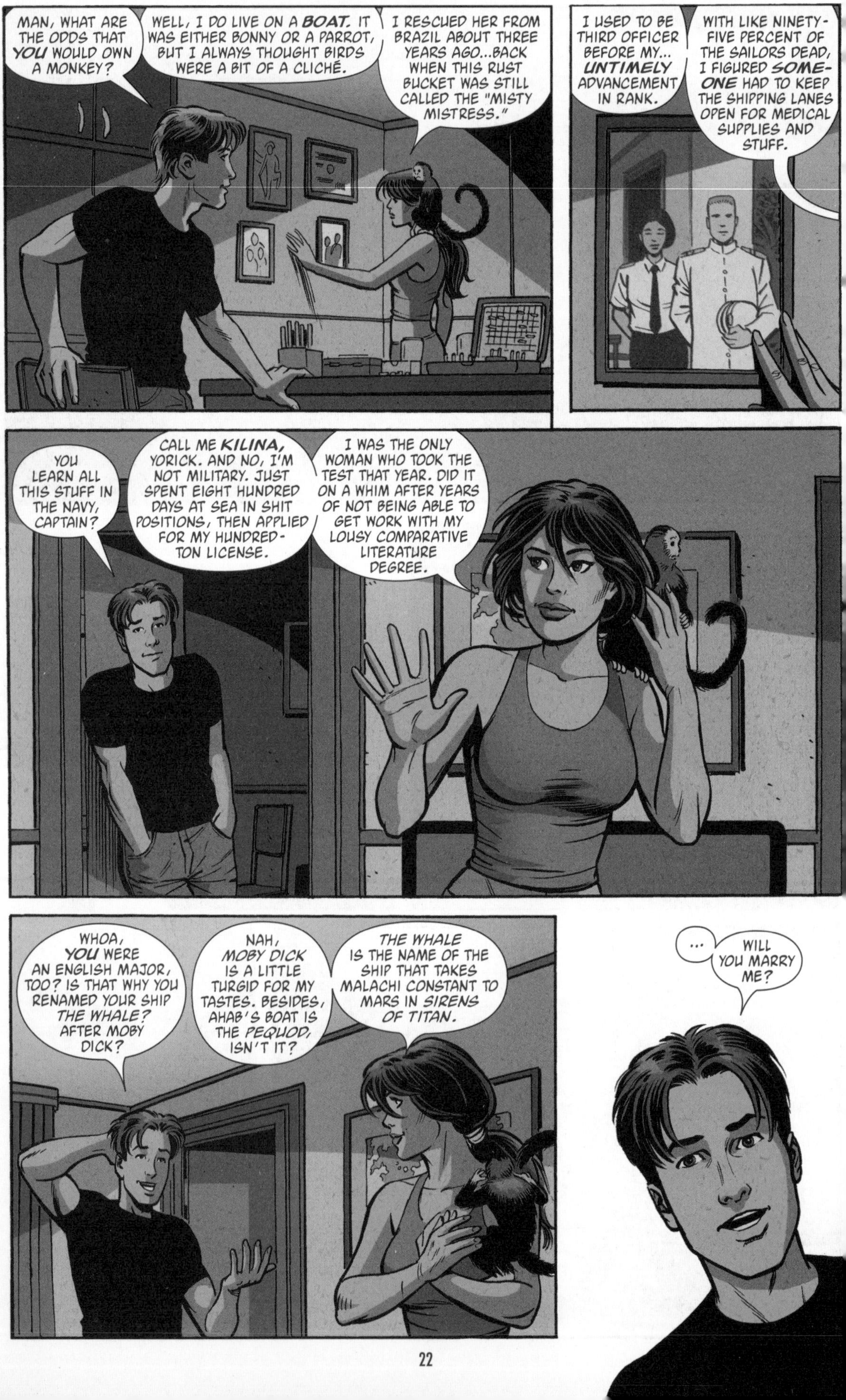

MAN, WHAT ARE THE ODDS THAT YOU WOULD OWN A MONKEY?
WELL, I DO LIVE ON A BOAT. IT WAS EITHER BONNY OR A PARROT, BUT I ALWAYS THOUGHT BIRDS WERE A BIT OF A CLICHÉ.
I RESCUED HER FROM BRAZIL ABOUT THREE YEARS AGO...BACK WHEN THIS RUST BUCKET WAS STILL CALLED THE "MISTY MISTRESS."
I USED TO BE THIRD OFFICER BEFORE MY... UNTIMELY ADVANCEMENT IN RANK.
WITH LIKE NINETY-FIVE PERCENT OF THE SAILORS DEAD, I FIGURED SOME-ONE HAD TO KEEP THE SHIPPING LANES OPEN FOR MEDICAL SUPPLIES AND STUFF.
YOU LEARN ALL THIS STUFF IN THE NAVY, CAPTAIN?
CALL ME KILINA, YORICK. AND NO, I'M NOT MILITARY. JUST SPENT EIGHT HUNDRED DAYS AT SEA IN SHIT POSITIONS, THEN APPLIED FOR MY HUNDRED-TON LICENSE.
I WAS THE ONLY WOMAN WHO TOOK THE TEST THAT YEAR. DID IT ON A WHIM AFTER YEARS OF NOT BEING ABLE TO GET WORK WITH MY LOUSY COMPARATIVE LITERATURE DEGREE.
WHOA, YOU WERE AN ENGLISH MAJOR, TOO? IS THAT WHY YOU RENAMED YOUR SHIP THE WHALE? AFTER MOBY DICK?
NAH, MOBY DICK IS A LITTLE TURGID FOR MY TASTES. BESIDES, AHAB'S BOAT IS THE PEQUOD, ISN'T IT?
THE WHALE IS THE NAME OF THE SHIP THAT TAKES MALACHI CONSTANT TO MARS IN SIRENS OF TITAN.
...
WILL YOU MARRY ME?

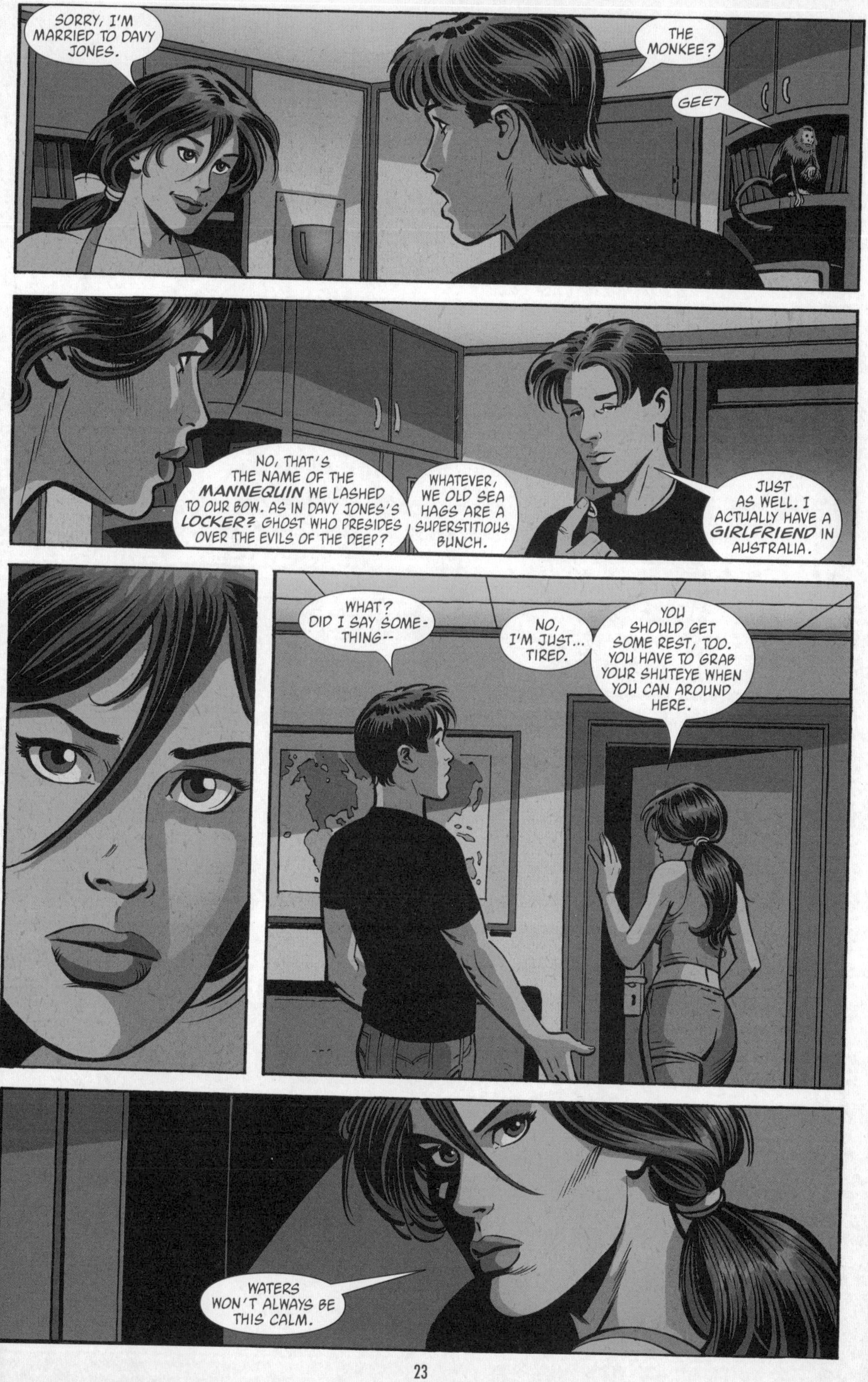
SORRY, I'M MARRIED TO DAVY JONES.
THE MONKEE?
GEET
NO, THAT'S THE NAME OF THE **MANNEQUIN** WE LASHED TO OUR BOW. AS IN DAVY JONES'S **LOCKER?** GHOST WHO PRESIDES OVER THE EVILS OF THE DEEP?
WHATEVER, WE OLD SEA HAGS ARE A SUPERSTITIOUS BUNCH.
JUST AS WELL. I ACTUALLY HAVE A **GIRLFRIEND** IN AUSTRALIA.
WHAT? DID I SAY SOME-THING--
NO, I'M JUST... TIRED.
YOU SHOULD GET SOME REST, TOO. YOU HAVE TO GRAB YOUR SHUTEYE WHEN YOU CAN AROUND HERE.
WATERS WON'T ALWAYS BE THIS CALM.

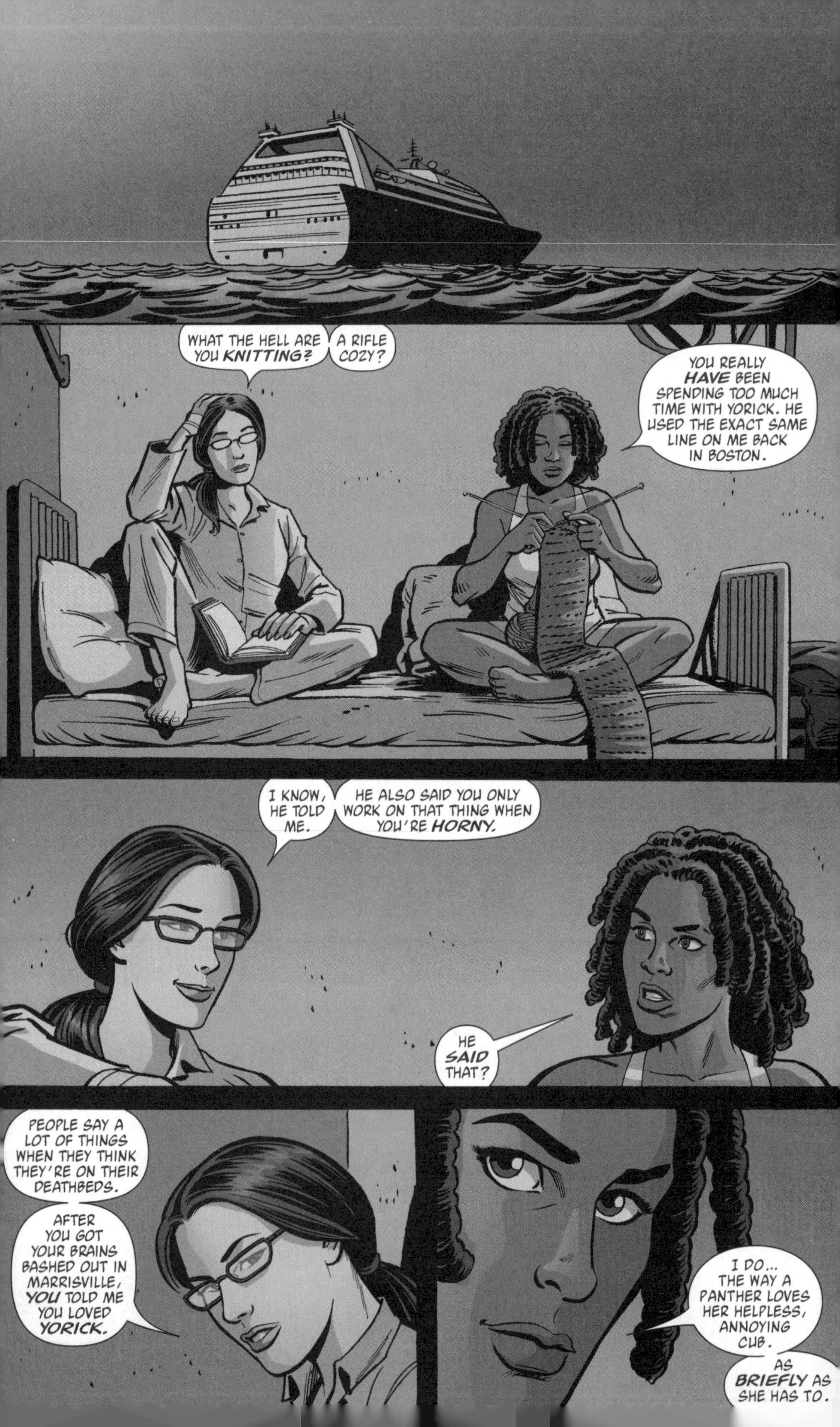

WHAT THE HELL ARE YOU KNITTING?
A RIFLE COZY?
YOU REALLY HAVE BEEN SPENDING TOO MUCH TIME WITH YORICK. HE USED THE EXACT SAME LINE ON ME BACK IN BOSTON.
I KNOW, HE TOLD ME.
HE ALSO SAID YOU ONLY WORK ON THAT THING WHEN YOU'RE HORNY.
HE SAID THAT?
PEOPLE SAY A LOT OF THINGS WHEN THEY THINK THEY'RE ON THEIR DEATHBEDS.
AFTER YOU GOT YOUR BRAINS BASHED OUT IN MARRISVILLE, YOU TOLD ME YOU LOVED YORICK.
I DO... THE WAY A PANTHER LOVES HER HELPLESS, ANNOYING CUB.
AS BRIEFLY AS SHE HAS TO.

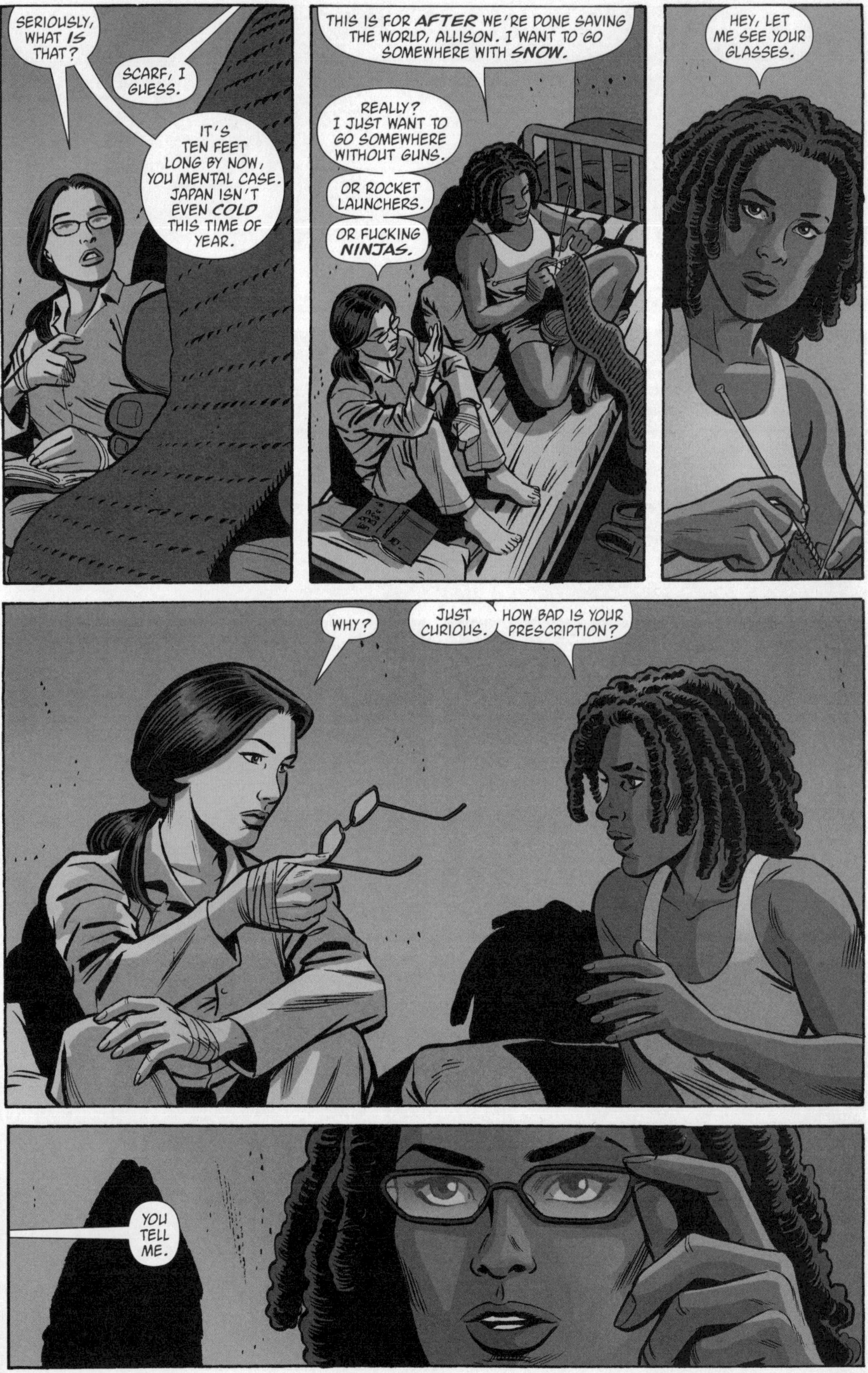
SERIOUSLY, WHAT IS THAT?
SCARF, I GUESS.
IT'S TEN FEET LONG BY NOW, YOU MENTAL CASE. JAPAN ISN'T EVEN COLD THIS TIME OF YEAR.
THIS IS FOR AFTER WE'RE DONE SAVING THE WORLD, ALLISON. I WANT TO GO SOMEWHERE WITH SNOW.
REALLY? I JUST WANT TO GO SOMEWHERE WITHOUT GUNS.
OR ROCKET LAUNCHERS.
OR FUCKING NINJAS.
HEY, LET ME SEE YOUR GLASSES.
WHY?
JUST CURIOUS.
HOW BAD IS YOUR PRESCRIPTION?
YOU TELL ME.

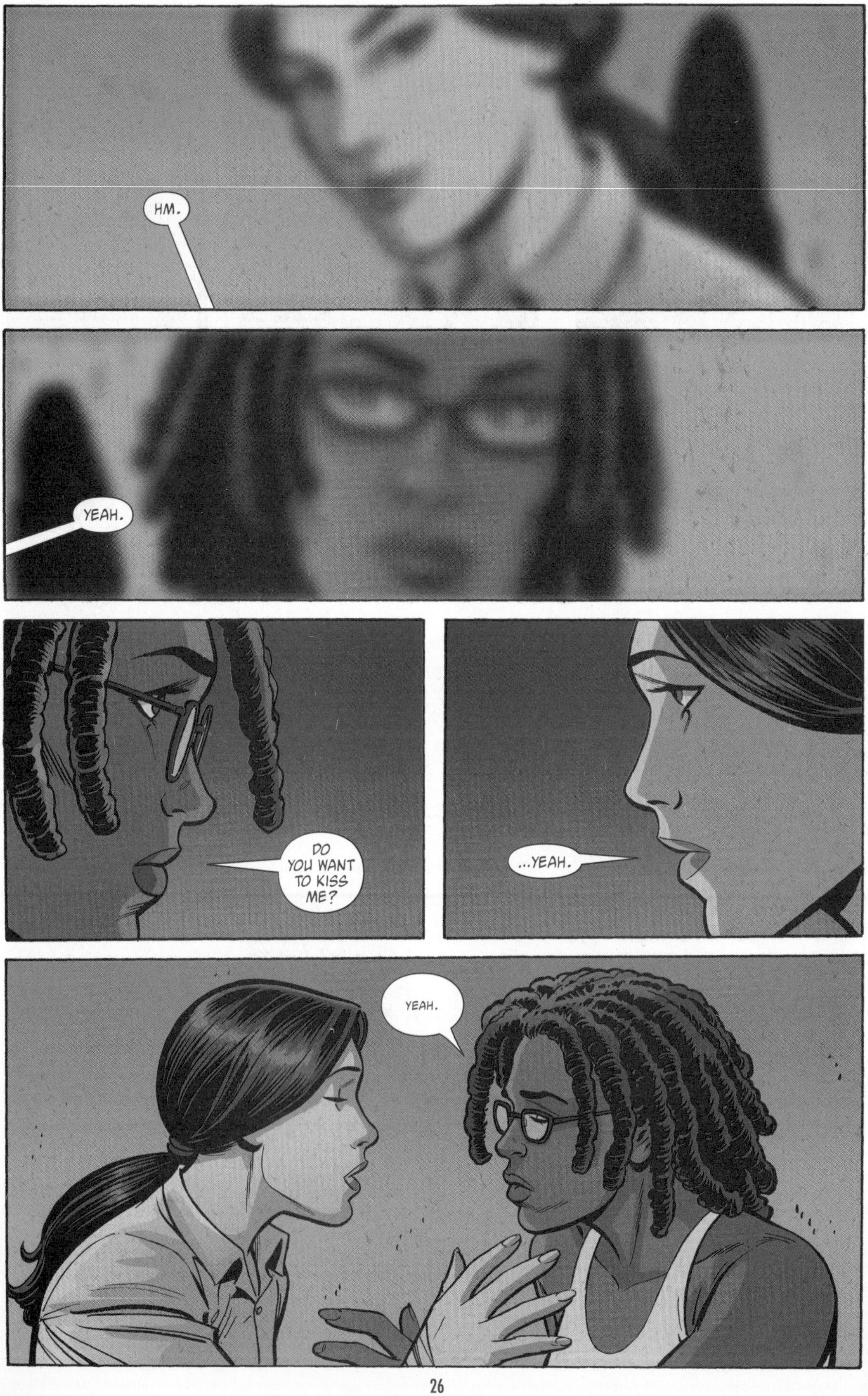
HM.
YEAH.
DO YOU WANT TO KISS ME?
...YEAH.
YEAH.

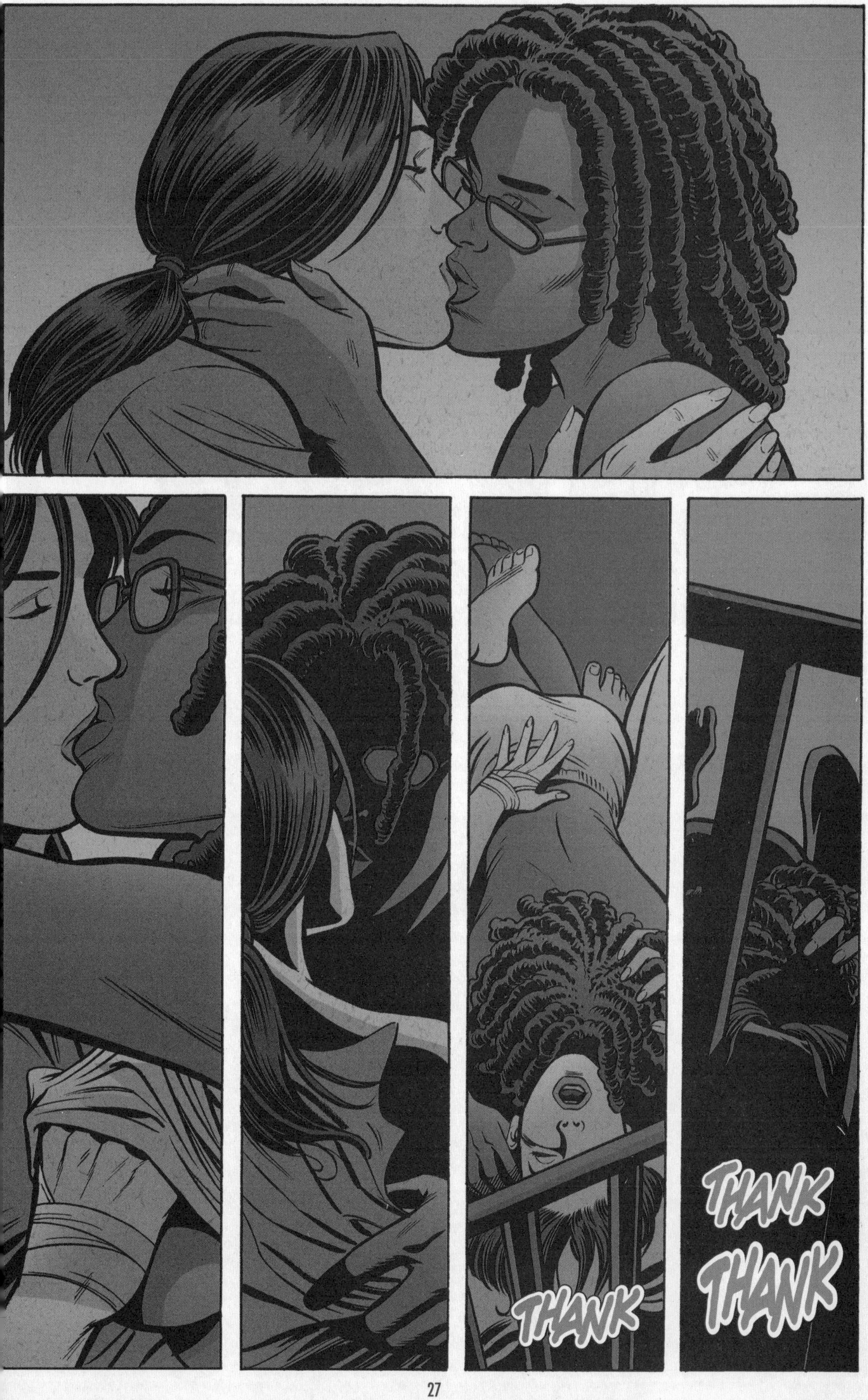
THANK
THANK
THANK

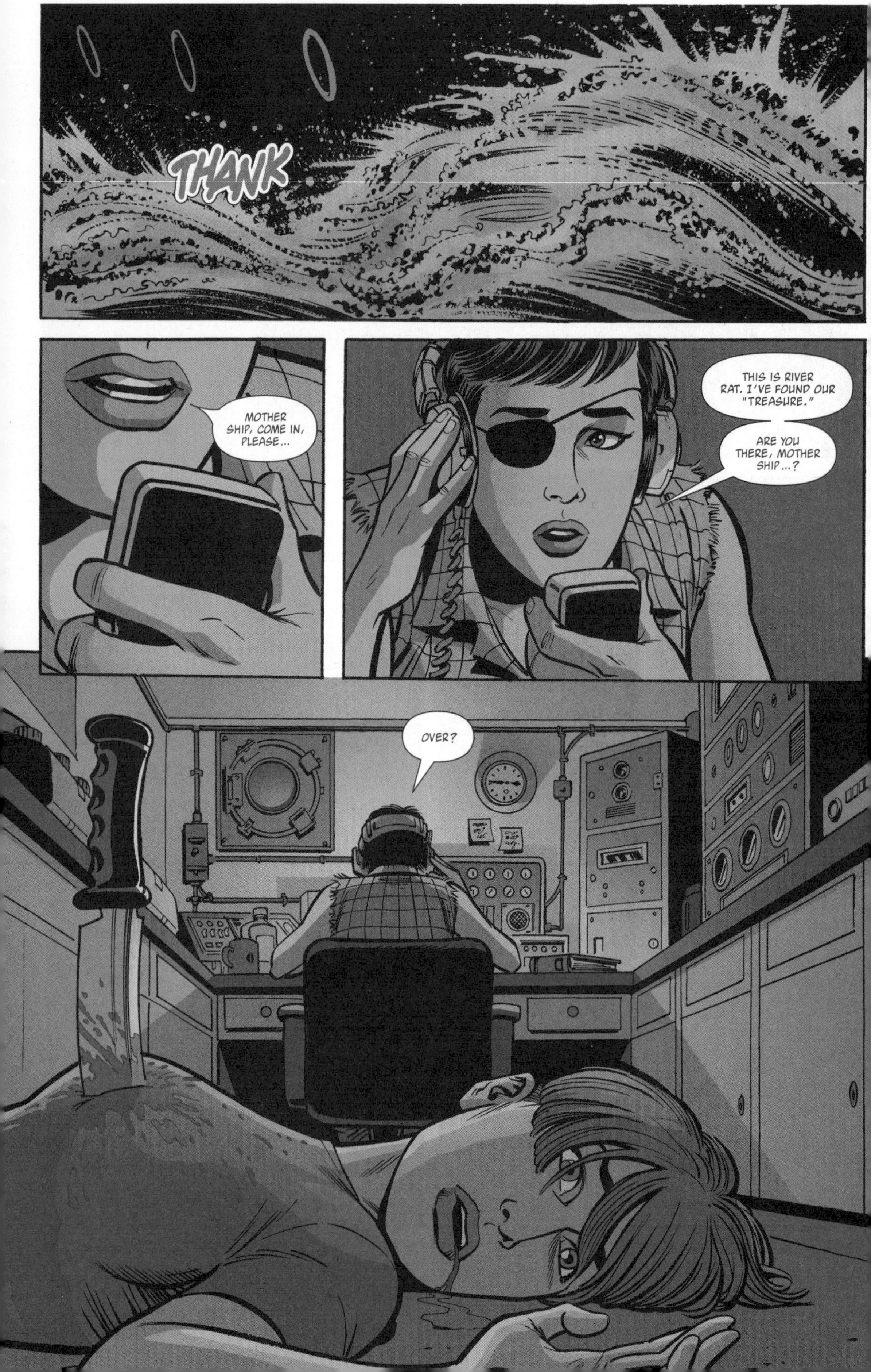
THANK
MOTHER SHIP, COME IN, PLEASE...
THIS IS RIVER RAT. I'VE FOUND OUR "TREASURE."
ARE YOU THERE, MOTHER SHIP...?
OVER?

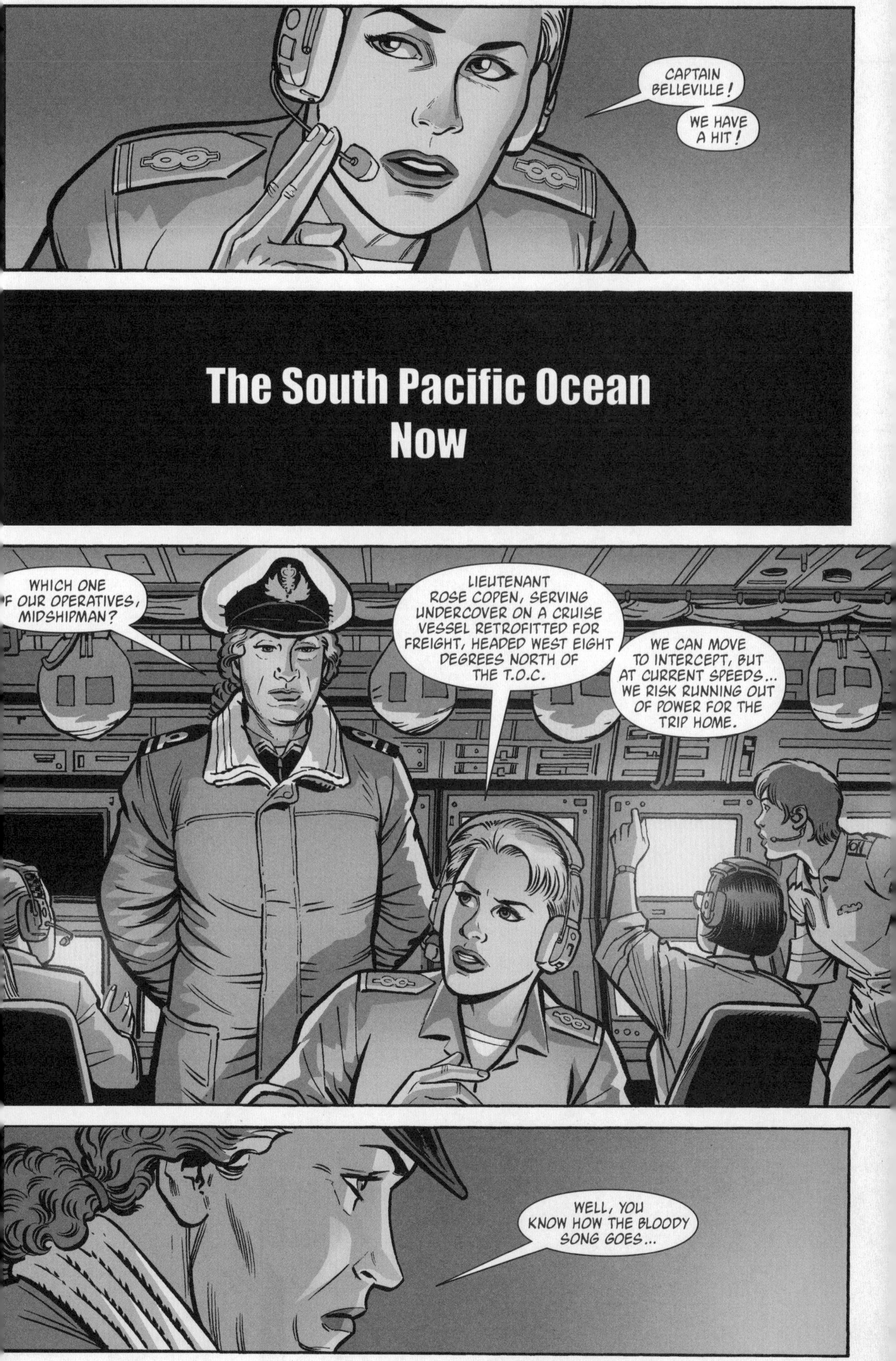
CAPTAIN BELLEVILLE!
WE HAVE A HIT!
The South Pacific Ocean
Now
WHICH ONE F OUR OPERATIVES, MIDSHIPMAN?
LIEUTENANT ROSE COPEN, SERVING UNDERCOVER ON A CRUISE VESSEL RETROFITTED FOR FREIGHT, HEADED WEST EIGHT DEGREES NORTH OF THE T.O.C.
WE CAN MOVE TO INTERCEPT, BUT AT CURRENT SPEEDS... WE RISK RUNNING OUT OF POWER FOR THE TRIP HOME.
WELL, YOU KNOW HOW THE BLOODY SONG GOES...

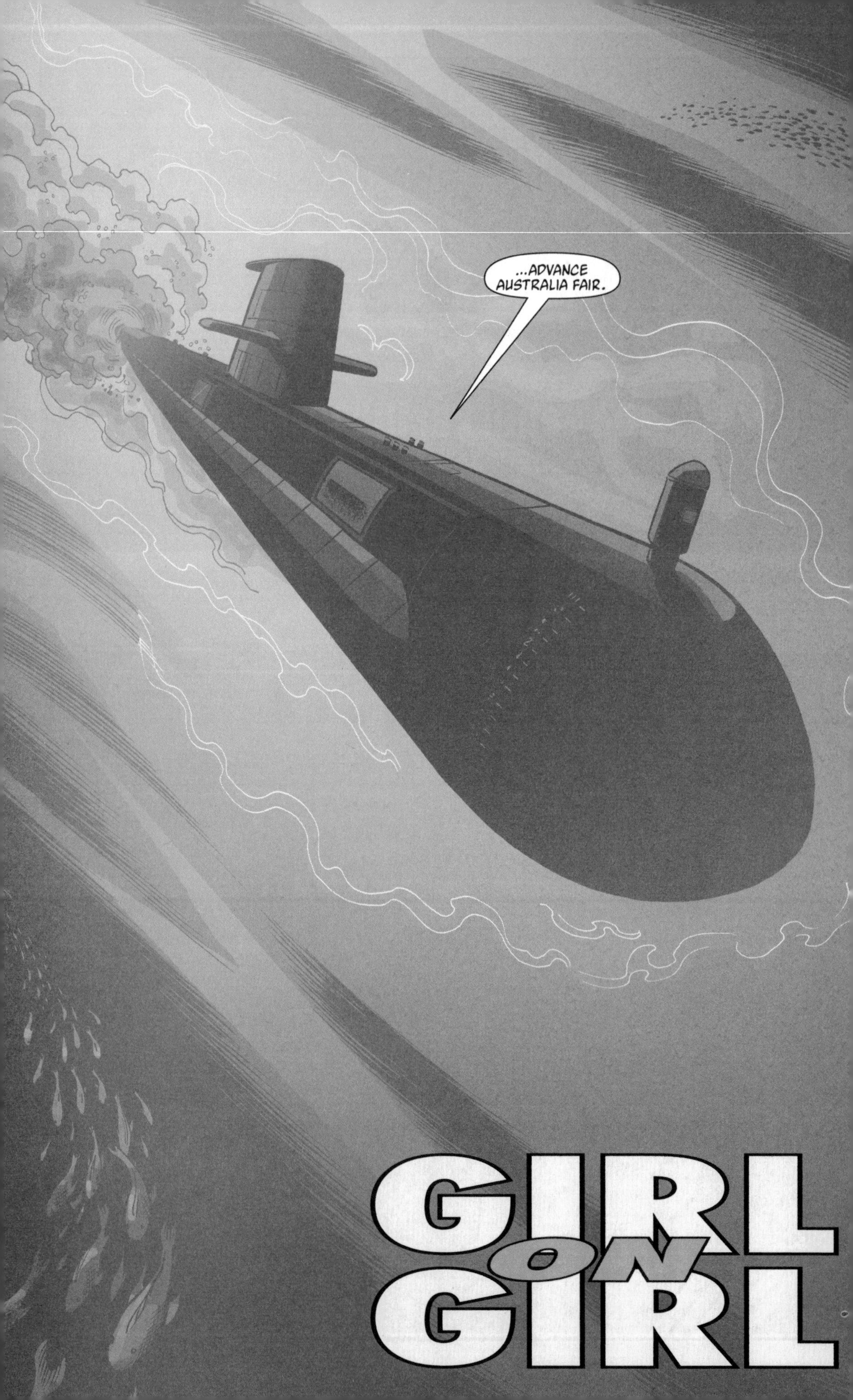
...ADVANCE AUSTRALIA FAIR.
GIRL ON GIRL

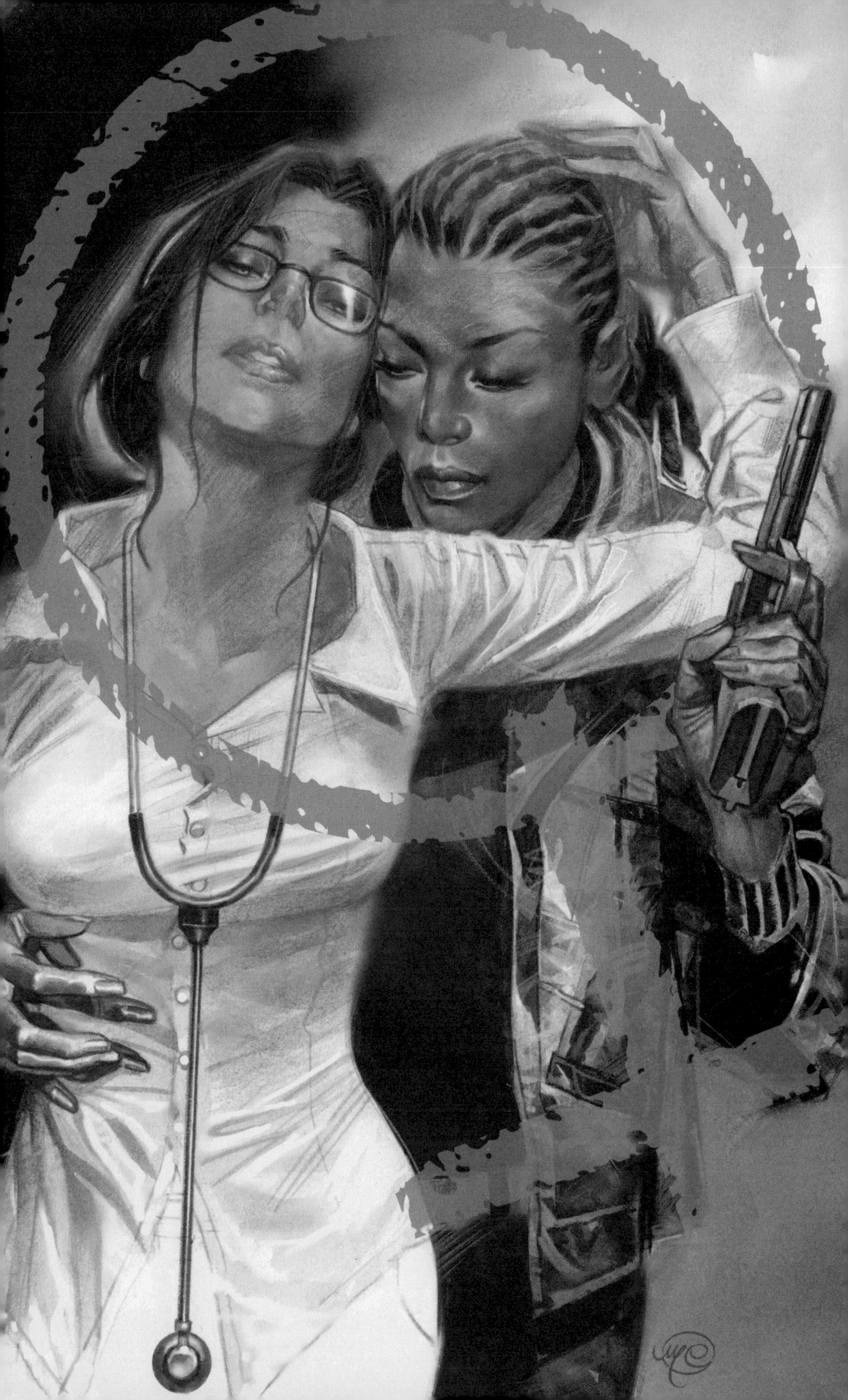

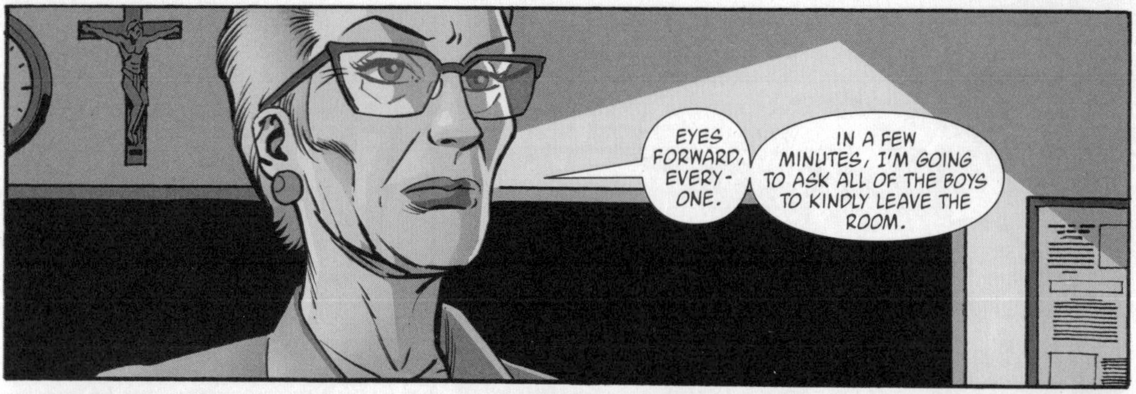
EYES FORWARD, EVERY-ONE.
IN A FEW MINUTES, I'M GOING TO ASK ALL OF THE BOYS TO KINDLY LEAVE THE ROOM.

Dallas, Texas
Fourteen Years Ago

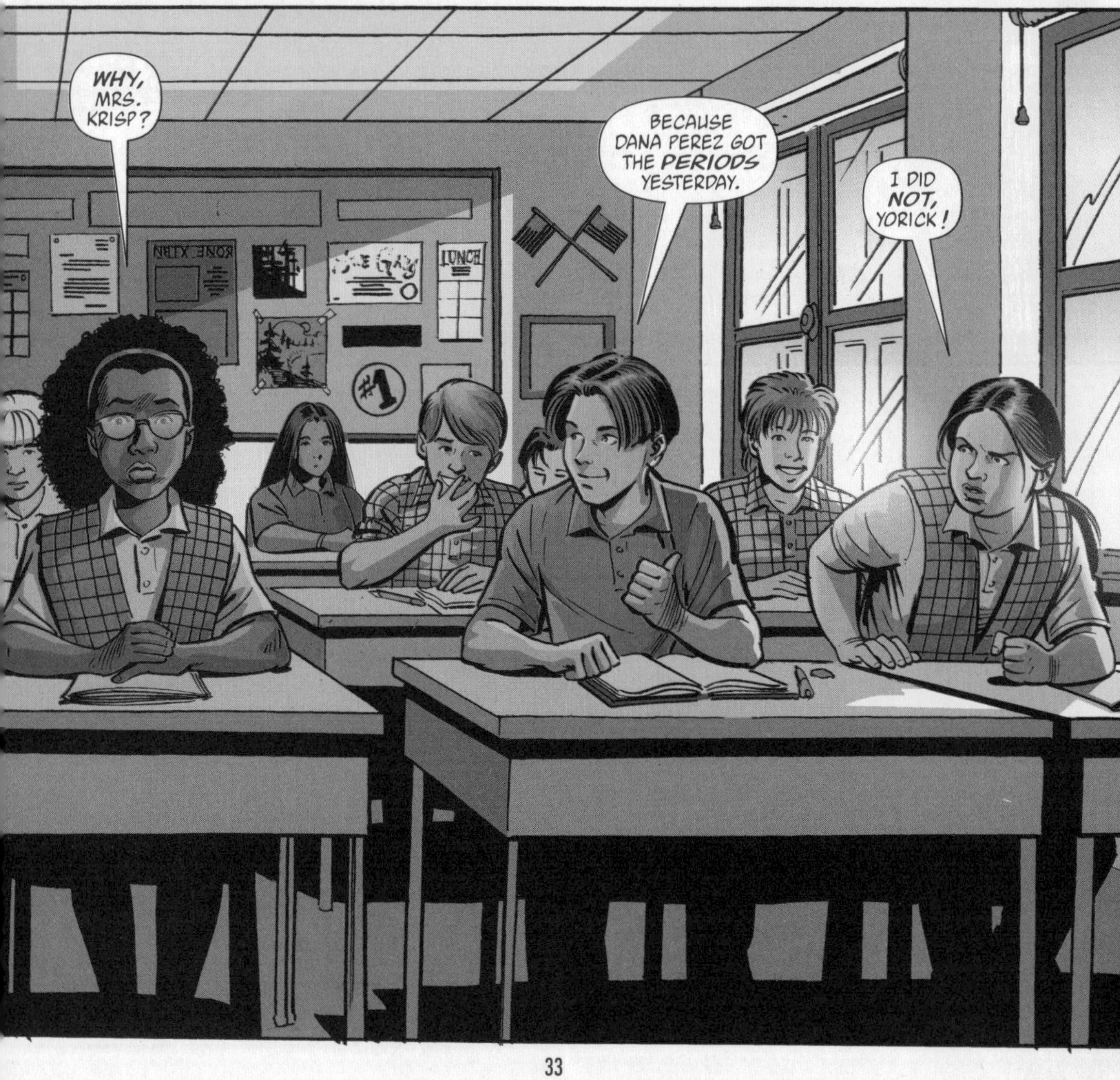
WHY, MRS. KRISP?
BECAUSE DANA PEREZ GOT THE PERIODS YESTERDAY.
I DID NOT, YORICK!

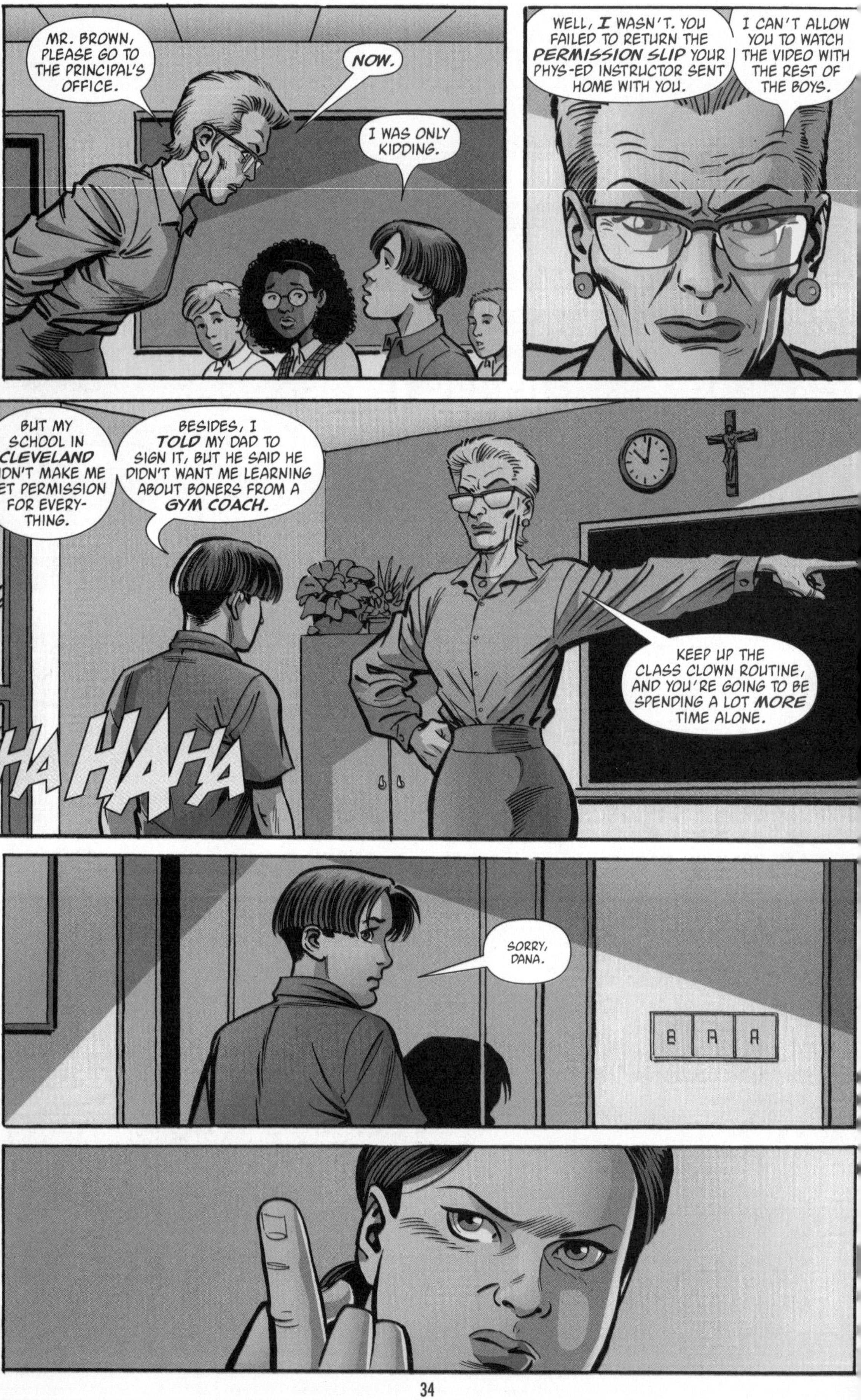

MR. BROWN, PLEASE GO TO THE PRINCIPAL'S OFFICE.
NOW.
I WAS ONLY KIDDING.
WELL, I WASN'T. YOU FAILED TO RETURN THE PERMISSION SLIP YOUR PHYS-ED INSTRUCTOR SENT HOME WITH YOU.
I CAN'T ALLOW YOU TO WATCH THE VIDEO WITH THE REST OF THE BOYS.
BUT MY SCHOOL IN CLEVELAND DIDN'T MAKE ME GET PERMISSION FOR EVERY-THING.
BESIDES, I TOLD MY DAD TO SIGN IT, BUT HE SAID HE DIDN'T WANT ME LEARNING ABOUT BONERS FROM A GYM COACH.
KEEP UP THE CLASS CLOWN ROUTINE, AND YOU'RE GOING TO BE SPENDING A LOT MORE TIME ALONE.
HAHAHAHA
SORRY, DANA.
B A A

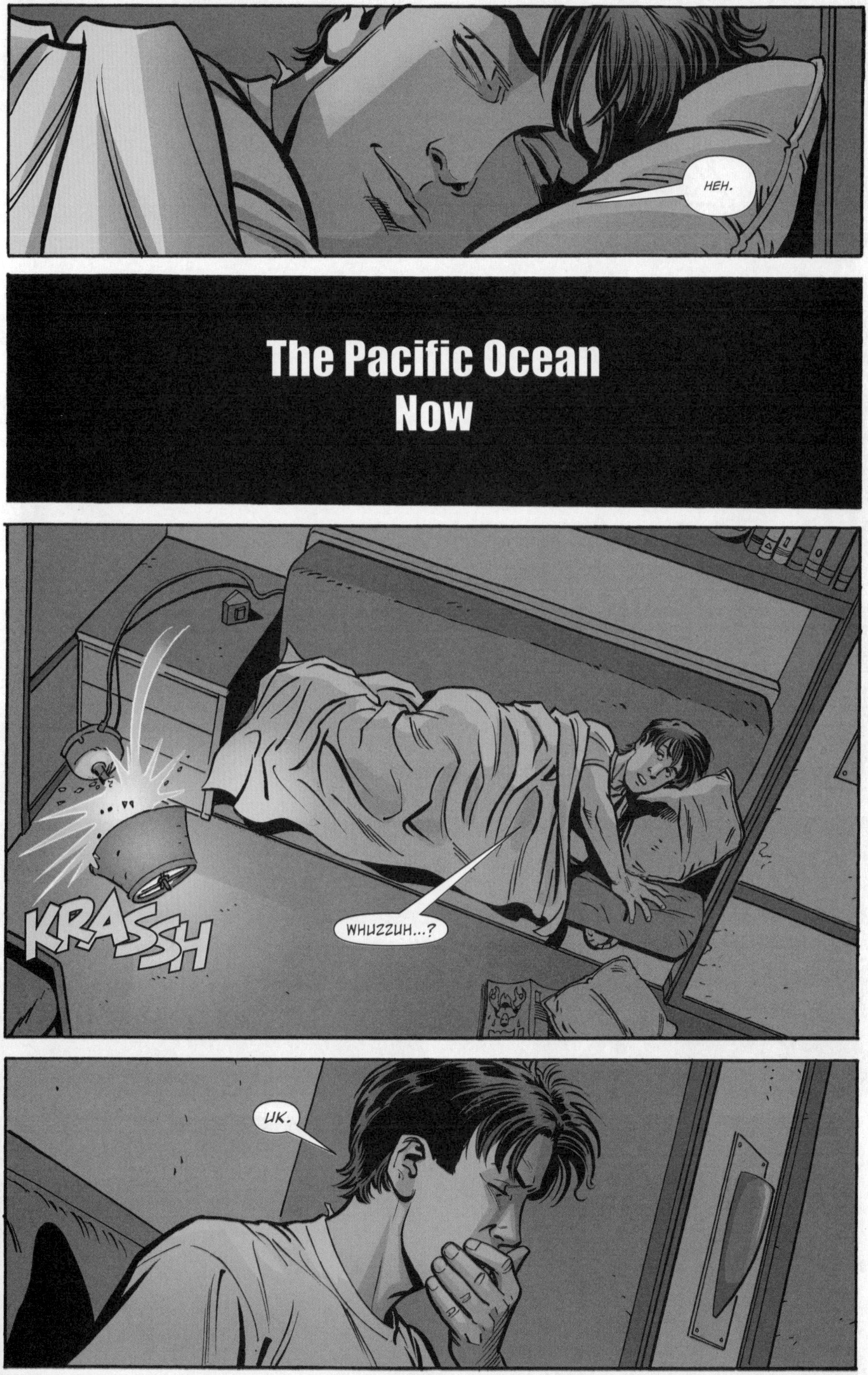
HEH.
The Pacific Ocean
Now
KRASSH
WHUZZUH...?
UK.

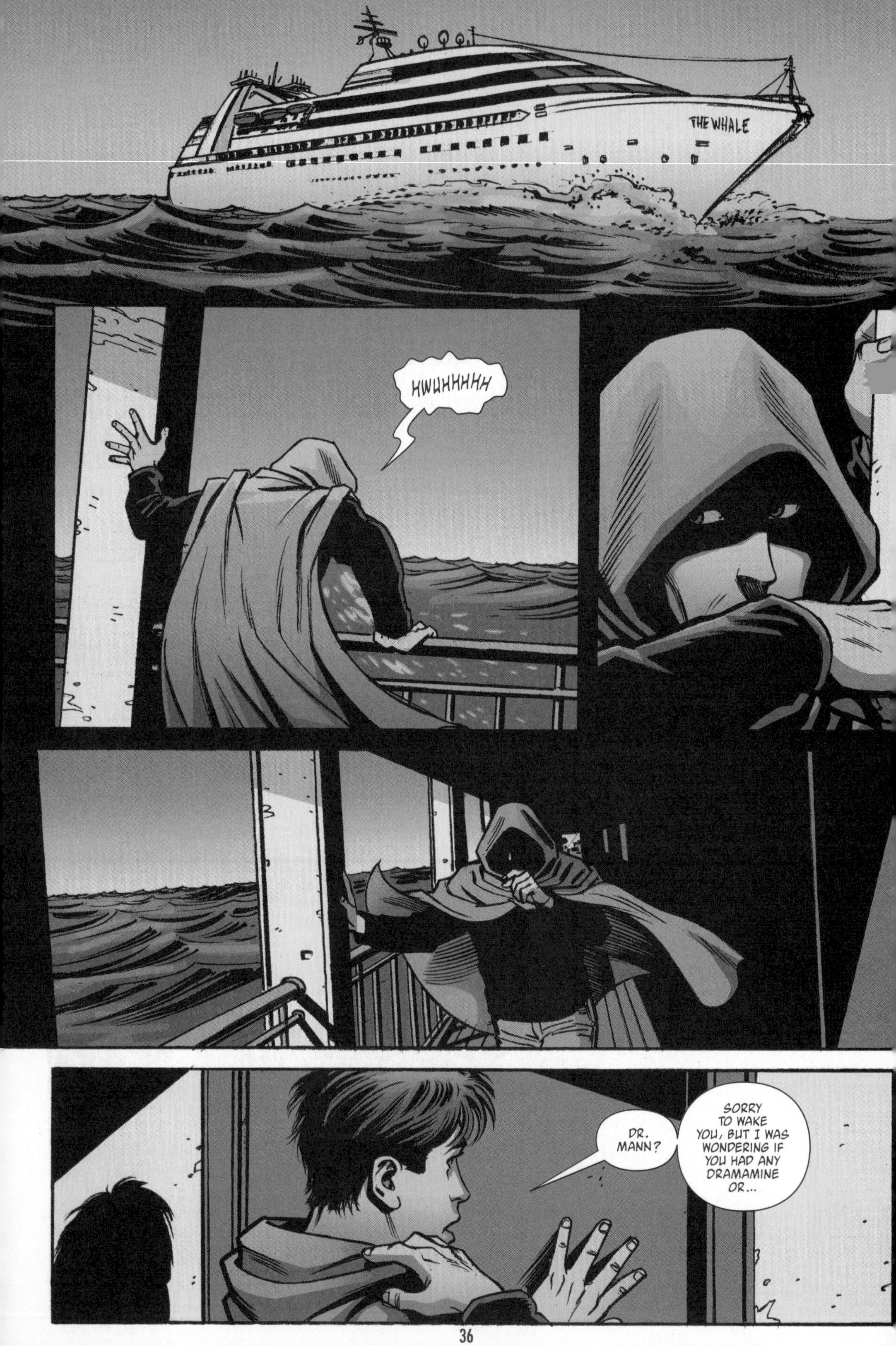
THE WHALE
HWUHHHHH
DR. MANN?
SORRY TO WAKE YOU, BUT I WAS WONDERING IF YOU HAD ANY DRAMAMINE OR...

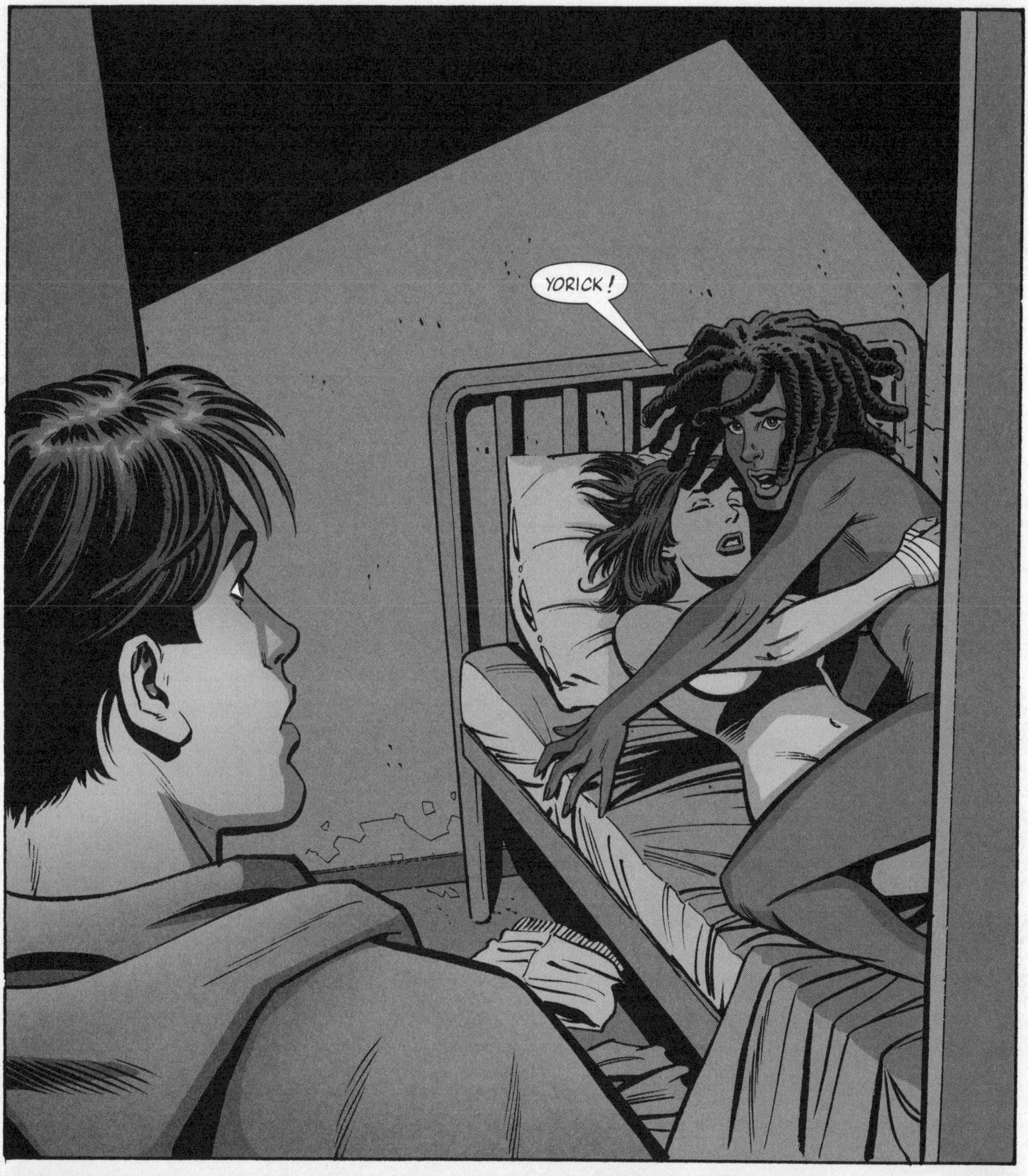
YORICK!

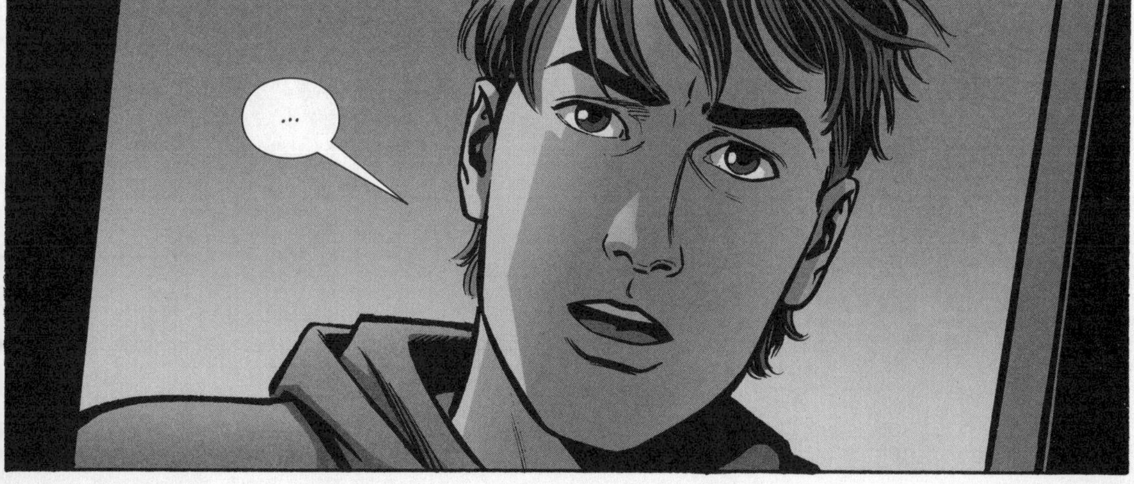
...

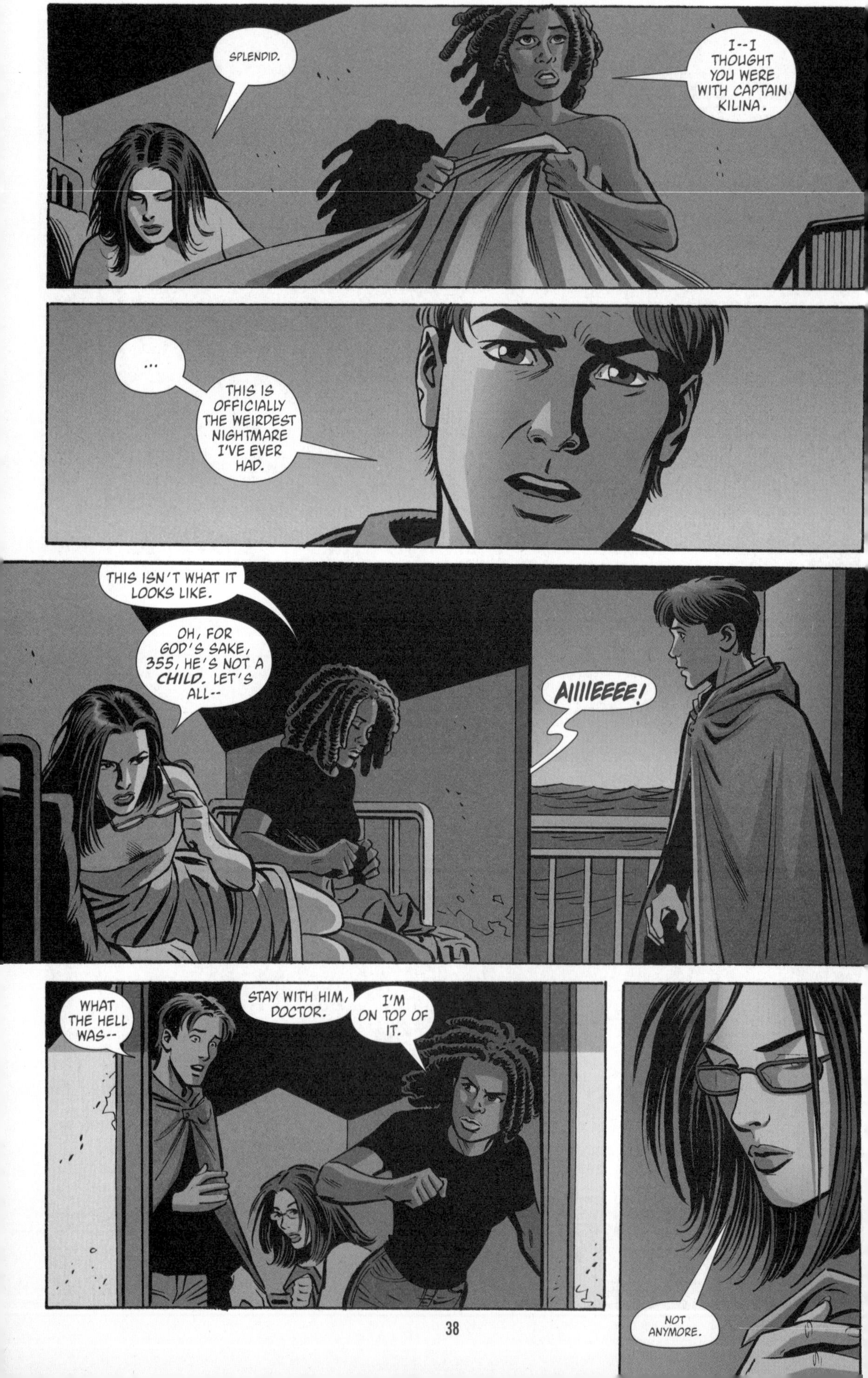
SPLENDID.
I--I THOUGHT YOU WERE WITH CAPTAIN KILINA.
...
THIS IS OFFICIALLY THE WEIRDEST NIGHTMARE I'VE EVER HAD.
THIS ISN'T WHAT IT LOOKS LIKE.
OH, FOR GOD'S SAKE, 355, HE'S NOT A CHILD. LET'S ALL--
AIIIIEEEE!
WHAT THE HELL WAS--
STAY WITH HIM, DOCTOR.
I'M ON TOP OF IT.
NOT ANYMORE.

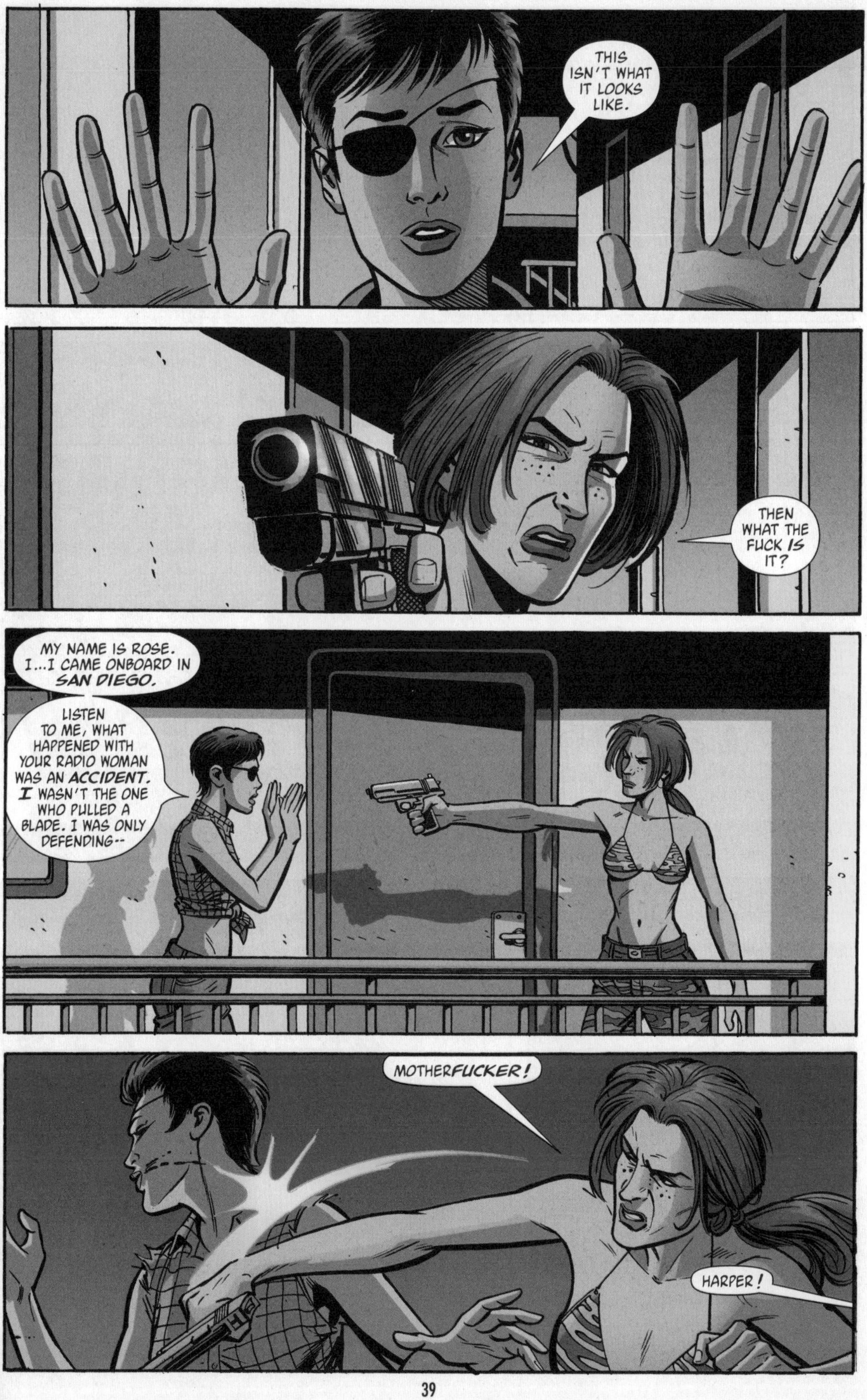
THIS ISN'T WHAT IT LOOKS LIKE.
THEN WHAT THE FUCK *IS* IT?
MY NAME IS ROSE. I...I CAME ONBOARD IN *SAN DIEGO.*
LISTEN TO ME, WHAT HAPPENED WITH YOUR RADIO WOMAN WAS AN *ACCIDENT*. *I* WASN'T THE ONE WHO PULLED A BLADE. I WAS ONLY DEFENDING--
MOTHER*FUCKER!*
HARPER!

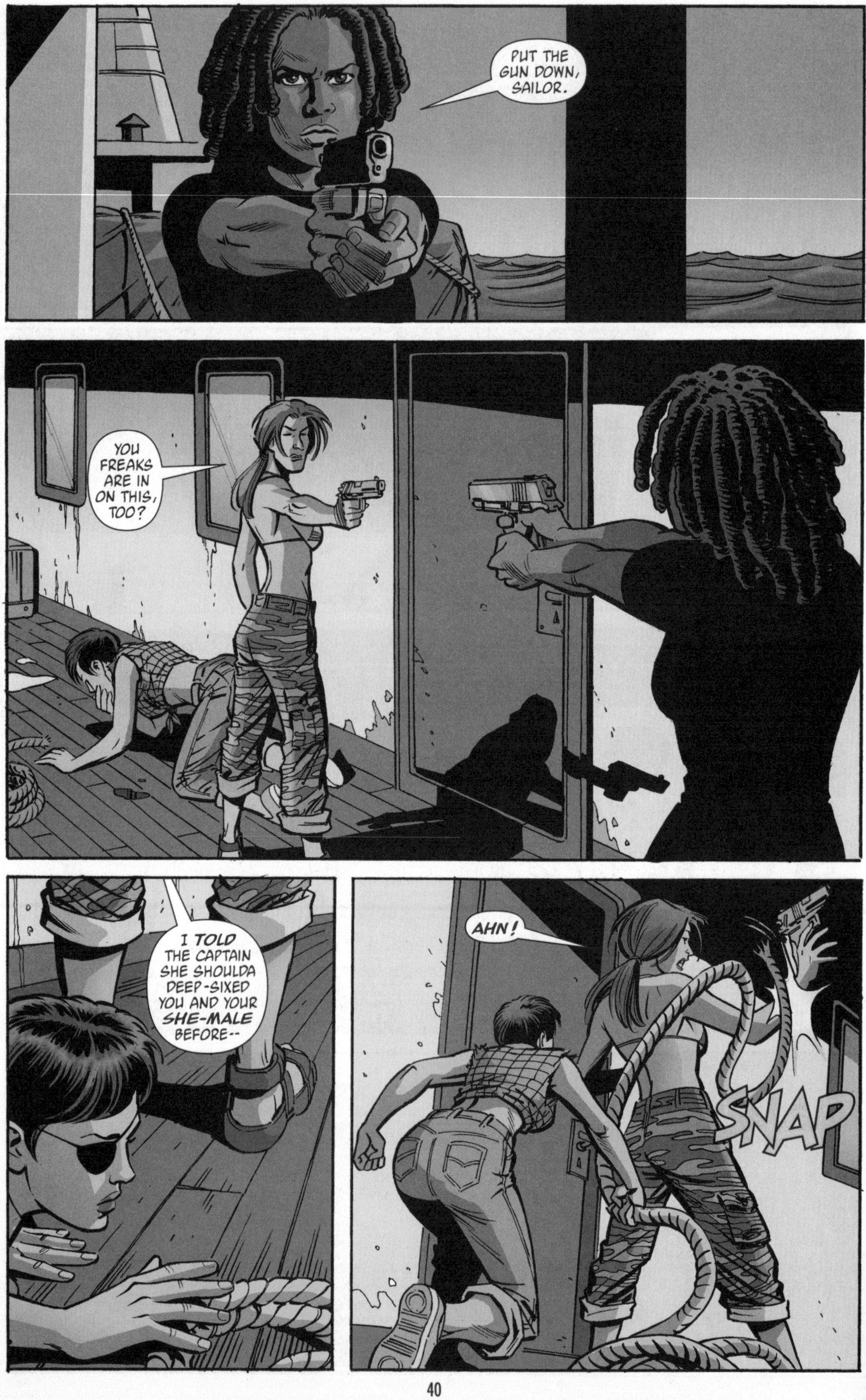
PUT THE GUN DOWN, SAILOR.
YOU FREAKS ARE IN ON THIS, TOO?
I TOLD THE CAPTAIN SHE SHOULDA DEEP-SIXED YOU AND YOUR SHE-MALE BEFORE--
AHN!
SNAP

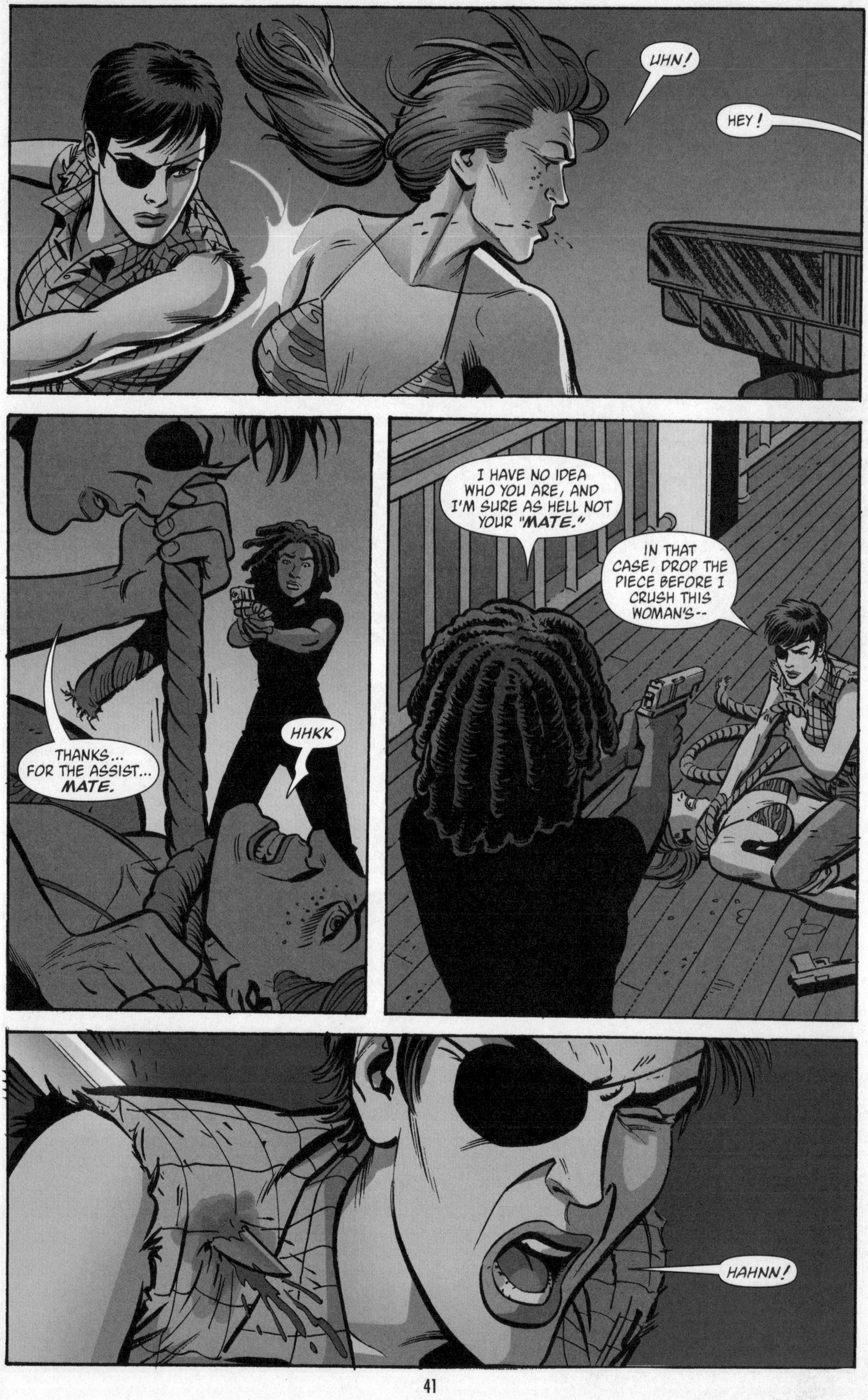
UHN!
HEY!
THANKS... FOR THE ASSIST... MATE.
HHKK
I HAVE NO IDEA WHO YOU ARE, AND I'M SURE AS HELL NOT YOUR "MATE."
IN THAT CASE, DROP THE PIECE BEFORE I CRUSH THIS WOMAN'S--
HAHNN!

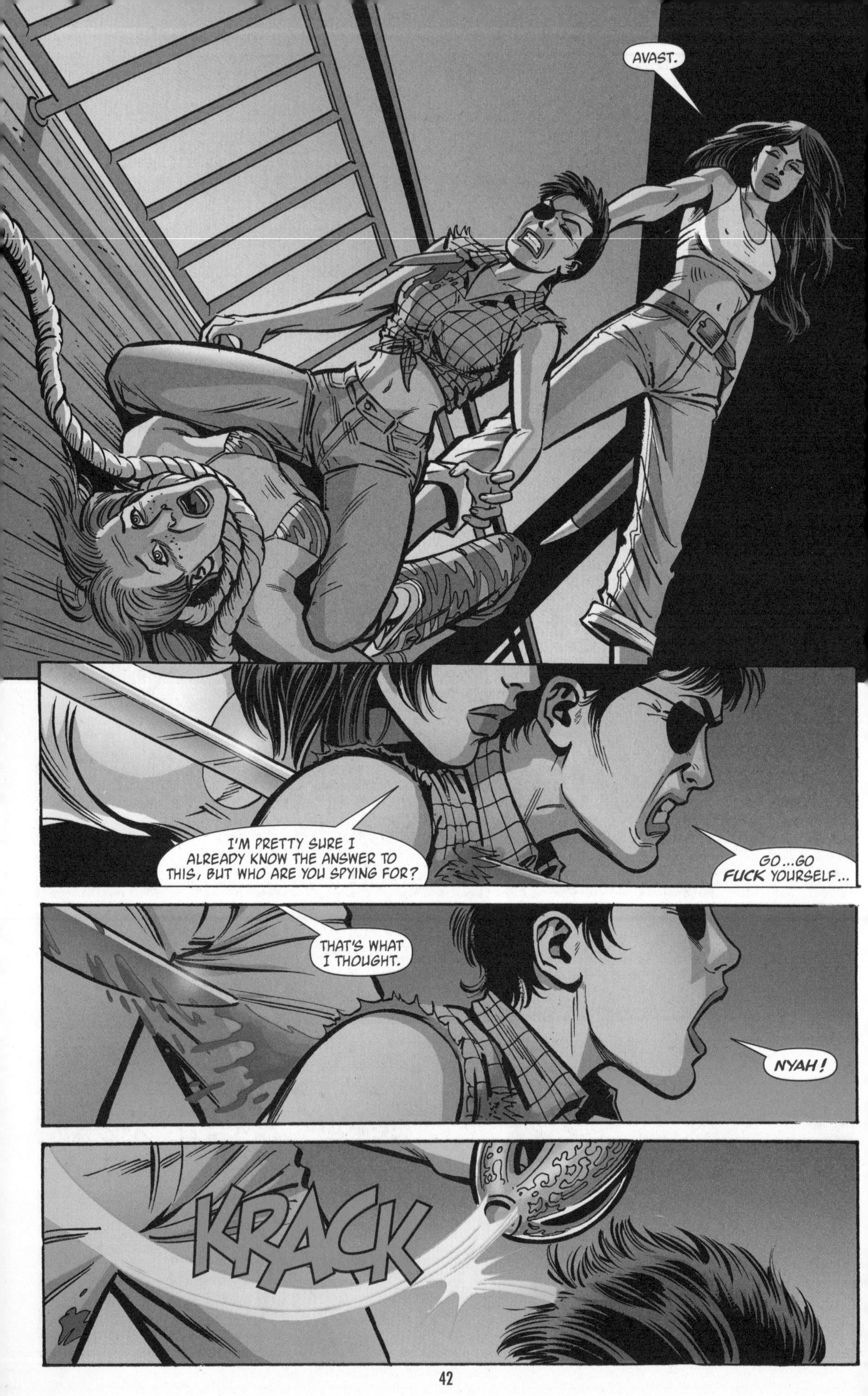
AVAST.
I'M PRETTY SURE I ALREADY KNOW THE ANSWER TO THIS, BUT WHO ARE YOU SPYING FOR?
GO...GO FUCK YOURSELF...
THAT'S WHAT I THOUGHT.
NYAH!
KRACK

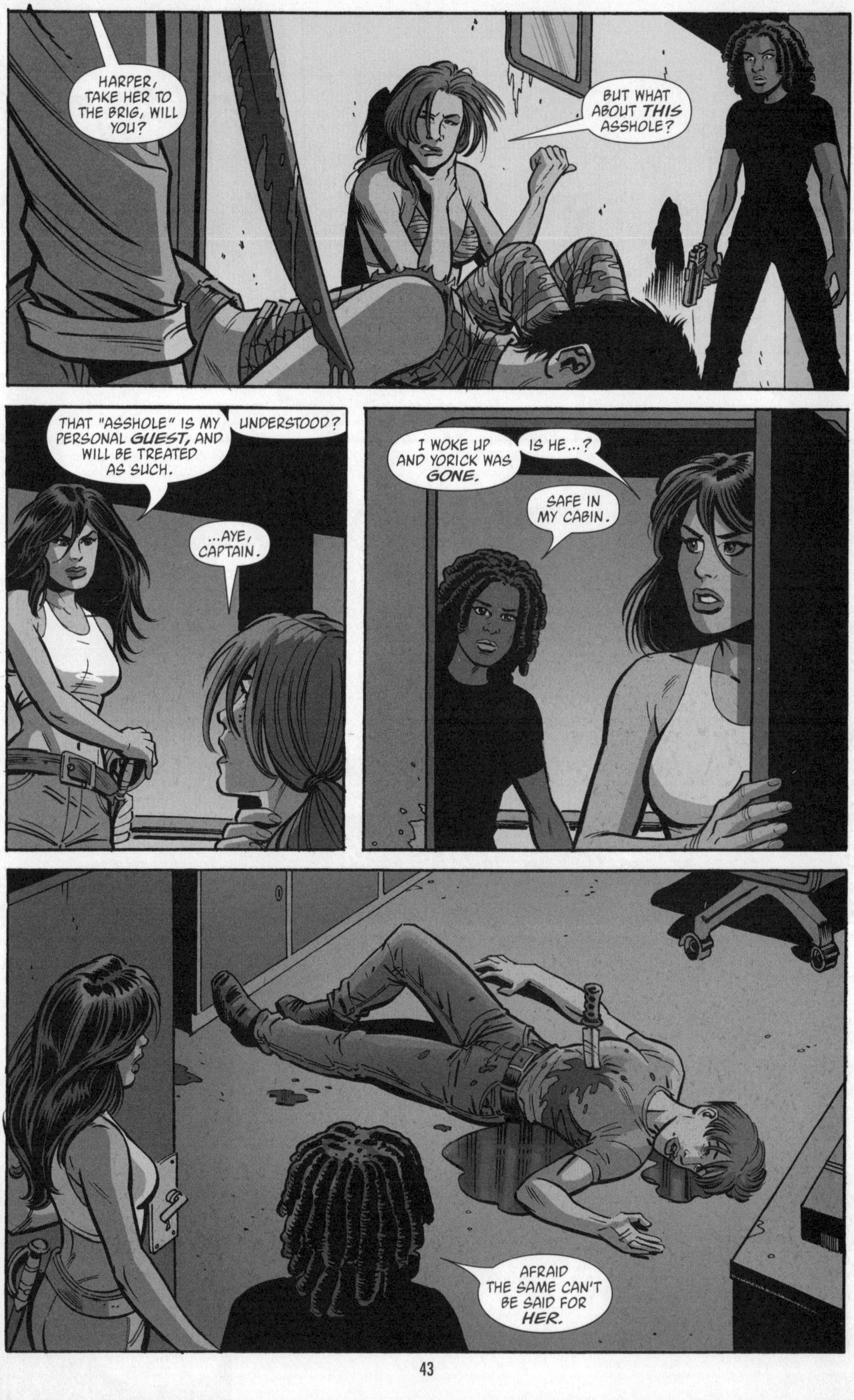
HARPER, TAKE HER TO THE BRIG, WILL YOU?
BUT WHAT ABOUT THIS ASSHOLE?
THAT "ASSHOLE" IS MY PERSONAL GUEST, AND WILL BE TREATED AS SUCH.
UNDERSTOOD?
...AYE, CAPTAIN.
I WOKE UP AND YORICK WAS GONE.
IS HE...?
SAFE IN MY CABIN.
AFRAID THE SAME CAN'T BE SAID FOR HER.

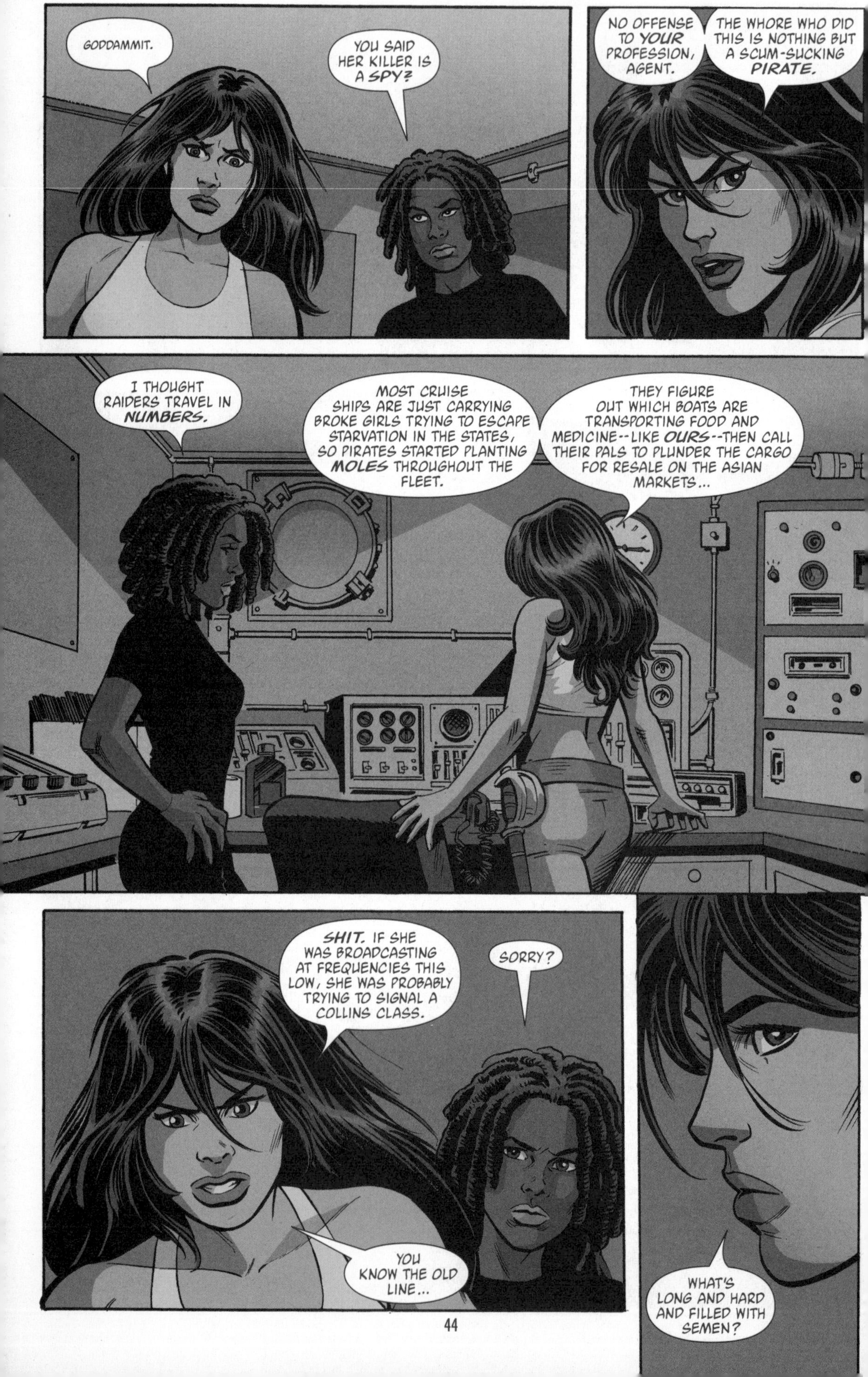
GODDAMMIT.
YOU SAID HER KILLER IS A SPY?
NO OFFENSE TO YOUR PROFESSION, AGENT.
THE WHORE WHO DID THIS IS NOTHING BUT A SCUM-SUCKING PIRATE.
I THOUGHT RAIDERS TRAVEL IN NUMBERS.
MOST CRUISE SHIPS ARE JUST CARRYING BROKE GIRLS TRYING TO ESCAPE STARVATION IN THE STATES, SO PIRATES STARTED PLANTING MOLES THROUGHOUT THE FLEET.
THEY FIGURE OUT WHICH BOATS ARE TRANSPORTING FOOD AND MEDICINE--LIKE OURS--THEN CALL THEIR PALS TO PLUNDER THE CARGO FOR RESALE ON THE ASIAN MARKETS...
SHIT. IF SHE WAS BROADCASTING AT FREQUENCIES THIS LOW, SHE WAS PROBABLY TRYING TO SIGNAL A COLLINS CLASS.
SORRY?
YOU KNOW THE OLD LINE...
WHAT'S LONG AND HARD AND FILLED WITH SEMEN?

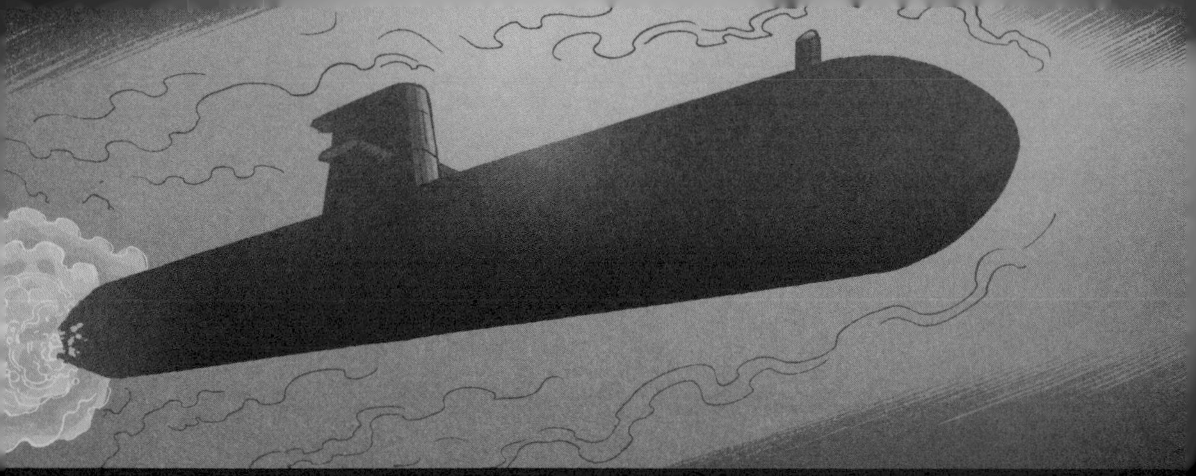

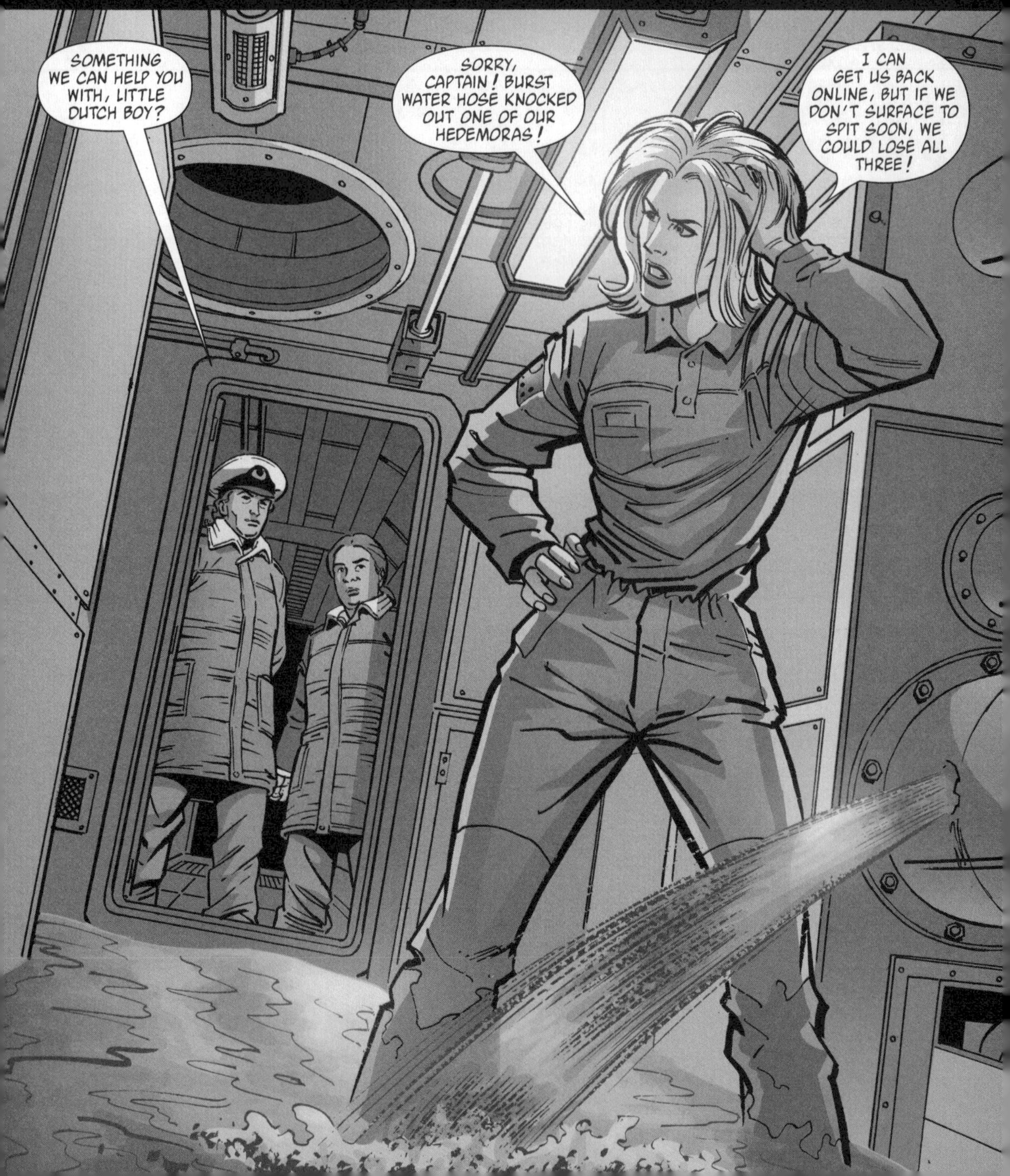

SOMETHING WE CAN HELP YOU WITH, LITTLE DUTCH BOY?
SORRY, CAPTAIN! BURST WATER HOSE KNOCKED OUT ONE OF OUR HEDEMORAS!
I CAN GET US BACK ONLINE, BUT IF WE DON'T SURFACE TO SPIT SOON, WE COULD LOSE ALL THREE!

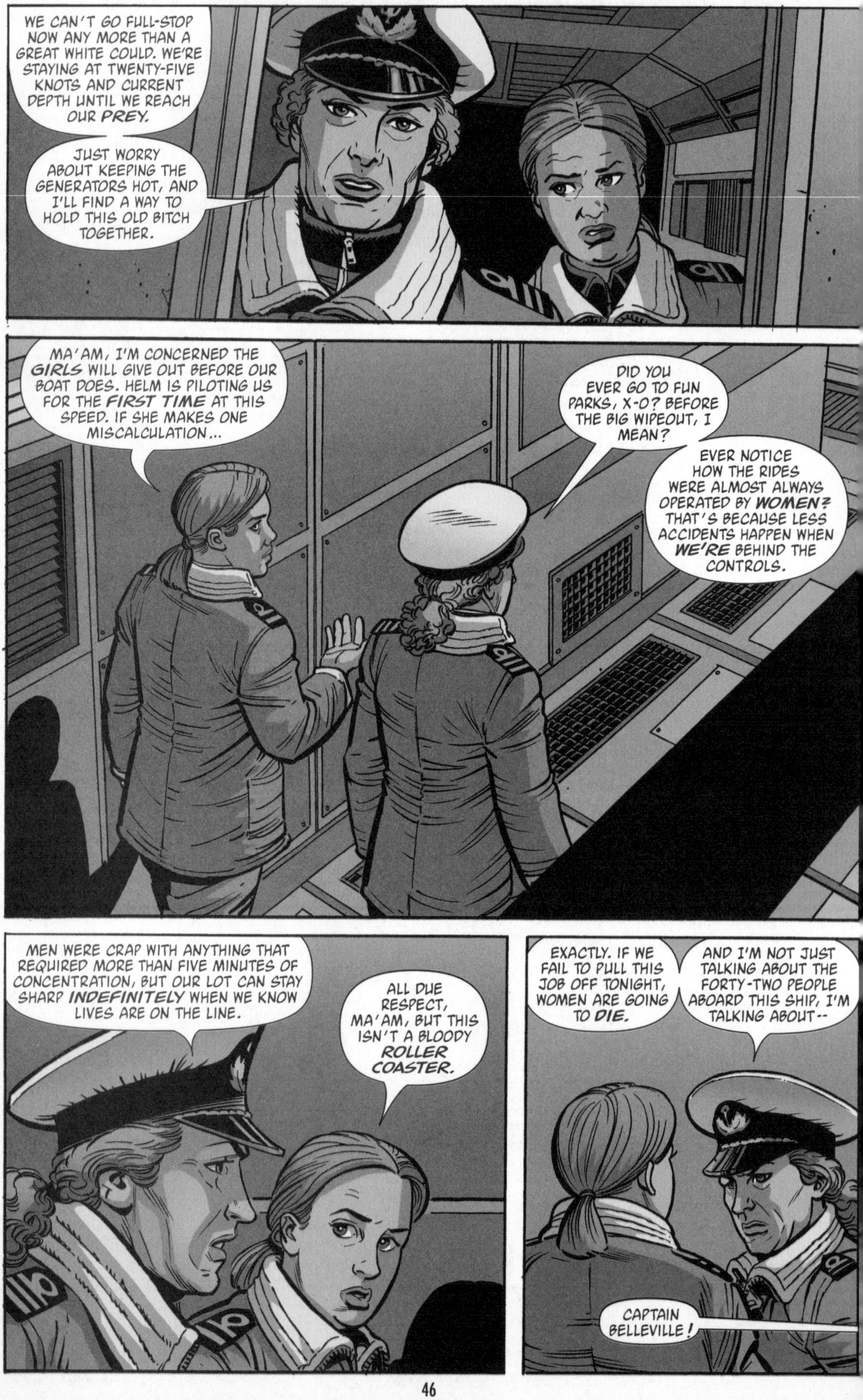
WE CAN'T GO FULL-STOP NOW ANY MORE THAN A GREAT WHITE COULD. WE'RE STAYING AT TWENTY-FIVE KNOTS AND CURRENT DEPTH UNTIL WE REACH OUR PREY.
JUST WORRY ABOUT KEEPING THE GENERATORS HOT, AND I'LL FIND A WAY TO HOLD THIS OLD BITCH TOGETHER.
MA'AM, I'M CONCERNED THE GIRLS WILL GIVE OUT BEFORE OUR BOAT DOES. HELM IS PILOTING US FOR THE FIRST TIME AT THIS SPEED. IF SHE MAKES ONE MISCALCULATION...
DID YOU EVER GO TO FUN PARKS, X-O? BEFORE THE BIG WIPEOUT, I MEAN?
EVER NOTICE HOW THE RIDES WERE ALMOST ALWAYS OPERATED BY WOMEN? THAT'S BECAUSE LESS ACCIDENTS HAPPEN WHEN WE'RE BEHIND THE CONTROLS.
MEN WERE CRAP WITH ANYTHING THAT REQUIRED MORE THAN FIVE MINUTES OF CONCENTRATION, BUT OUR LOT CAN STAY SHARP INDEFINITELY WHEN WE KNOW LIVES ARE ON THE LINE.
ALL DUE RESPECT, MA'AM, BUT THIS ISN'T A BLOODY ROLLER COASTER.
EXACTLY. IF WE FAIL TO PULL THIS JOB OFF TONIGHT, WOMEN ARE GOING TO DIE.
AND I'M NOT JUST TALKING ABOUT THE FORTY-TWO PEOPLE ABOARD THIS SHIP, I'M TALKING ABOUT--
CAPTAIN BELLEVILLE!

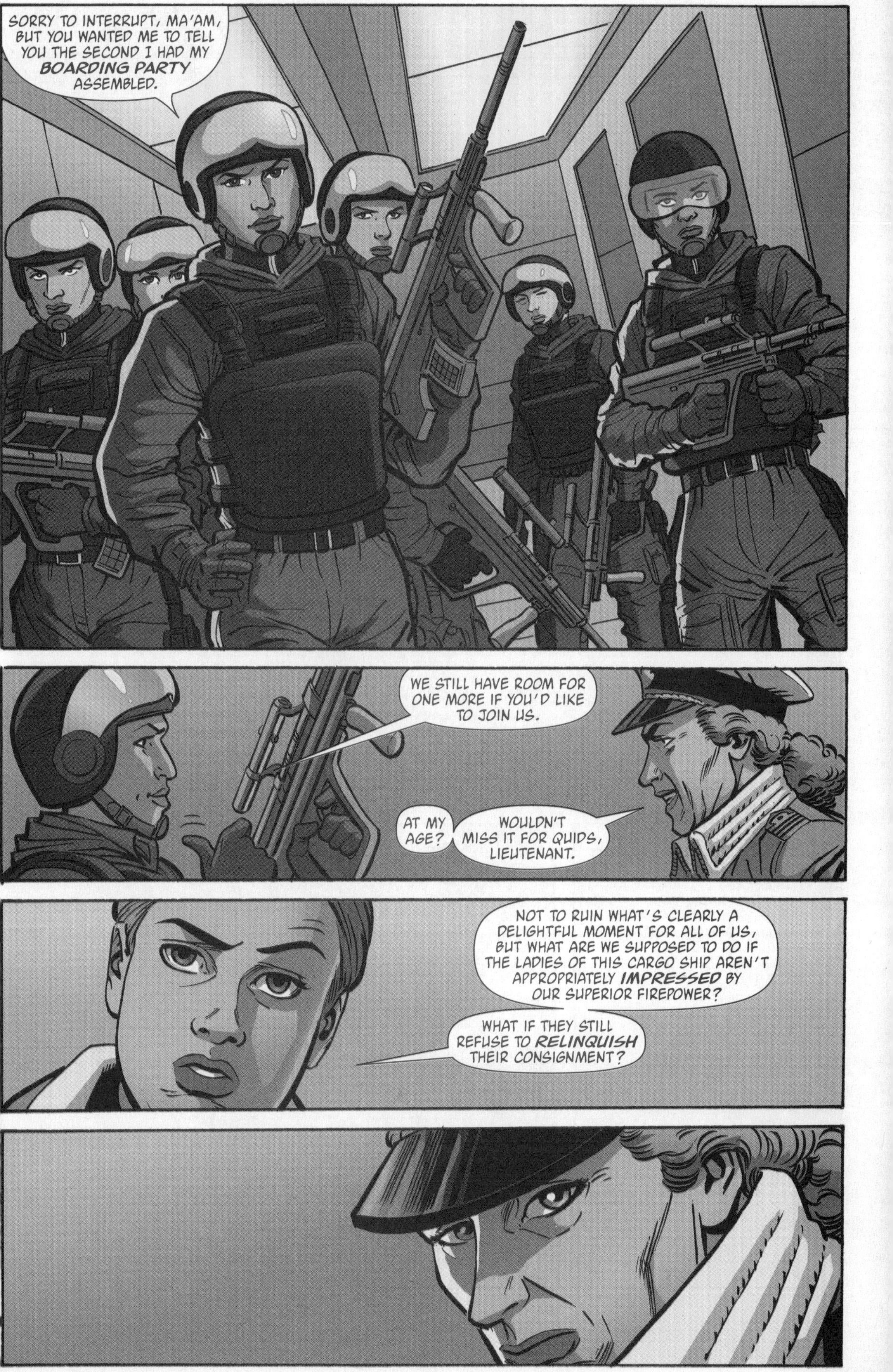
SORRY TO INTERRUPT, MA'AM, BUT YOU WANTED ME TO TELL YOU THE SECOND I HAD MY **BOARDING PARTY** ASSEMBLED.
WE STILL HAVE ROOM FOR ONE MORE IF YOU'D LIKE TO JOIN US.
AT MY AGE?
WOULDN'T MISS IT FOR QUIDS, LIEUTENANT.
NOT TO RUIN WHAT'S CLEARLY A DELIGHTFUL MOMENT FOR ALL OF US, BUT WHAT ARE WE SUPPOSED TO DO IF THE LADIES OF THIS CARGO SHIP AREN'T APPROPRIATELY **IMPRESSED** BY OUR SUPERIOR FIREPOWER?
WHAT IF THEY STILL REFUSE TO **RELINQUISH** THEIR CONSIGNMENT?

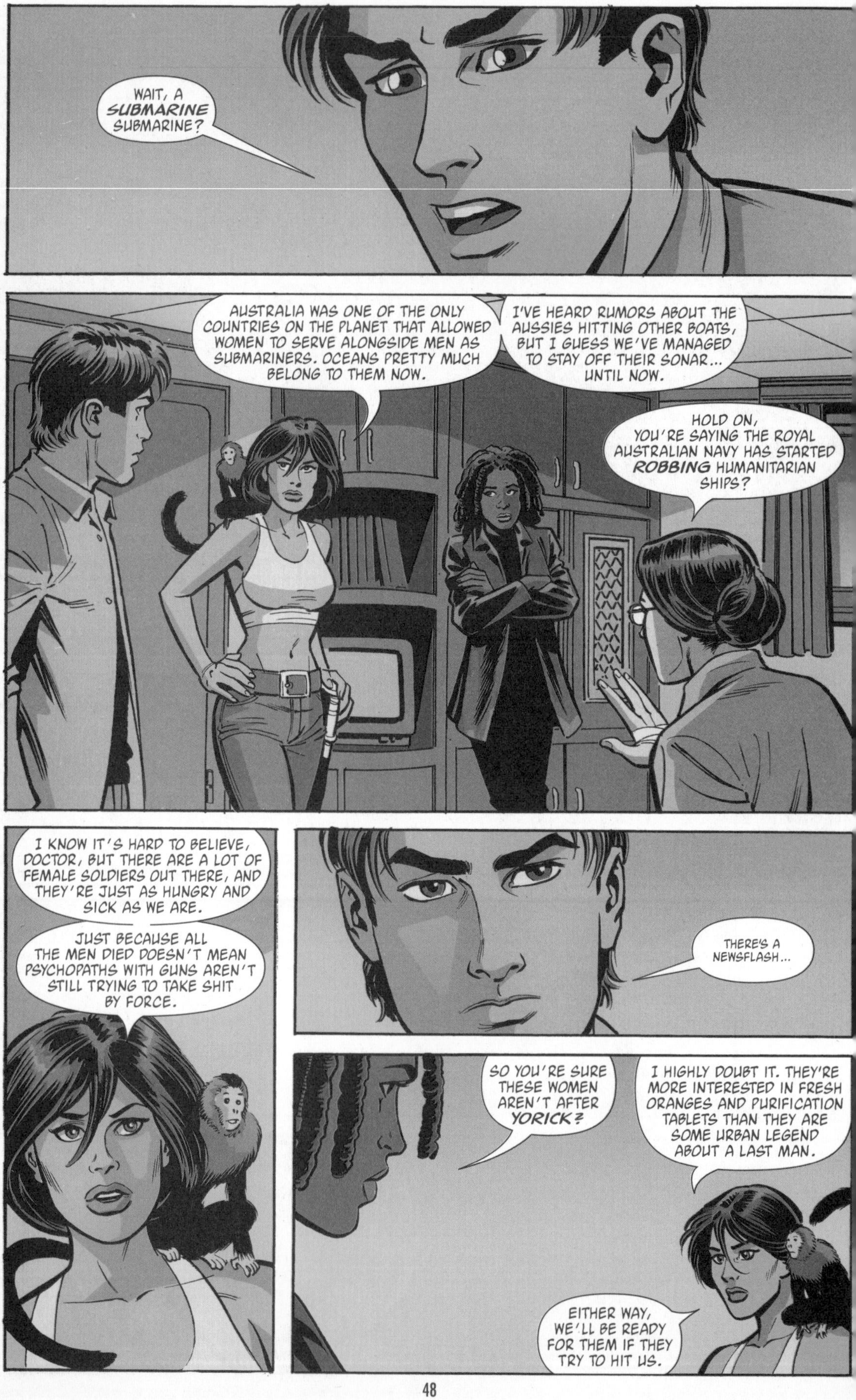
WAIT, A SUBMARINE SUBMARINE?
AUSTRALIA WAS ONE OF THE ONLY COUNTRIES ON THE PLANET THAT ALLOWED WOMEN TO SERVE ALONGSIDE MEN AS SUBMARINERS. OCEANS PRETTY MUCH BELONG TO THEM NOW.
I'VE HEARD RUMORS ABOUT THE AUSSIES HITTING OTHER BOATS, BUT I GUESS WE'VE MANAGED TO STAY OFF THEIR SONAR... UNTIL NOW.
HOLD ON, YOU'RE SAYING THE ROYAL AUSTRALIAN NAVY HAS STARTED ROBBING HUMANITARIAN SHIPS?
I KNOW IT'S HARD TO BELIEVE, DOCTOR, BUT THERE ARE A LOT OF FEMALE SOLDIERS OUT THERE, AND THEY'RE JUST AS HUNGRY AND SICK AS WE ARE.
JUST BECAUSE ALL THE MEN DIED DOESN'T MEAN PSYCHOPATHS WITH GUNS AREN'T STILL TRYING TO TAKE SHIT BY FORCE.
THERE'S A NEWSFLASH...
SO YOU'RE SURE THESE WOMEN AREN'T AFTER YORICK?
I HIGHLY DOUBT IT. THEY'RE MORE INTERESTED IN FRESH ORANGES AND PURIFICATION TABLETS THAN THEY ARE SOME URBAN LEGEND ABOUT A LAST MAN.
EITHER WAY, WE'LL BE READY FOR THEM IF THEY TRY TO HIT US.

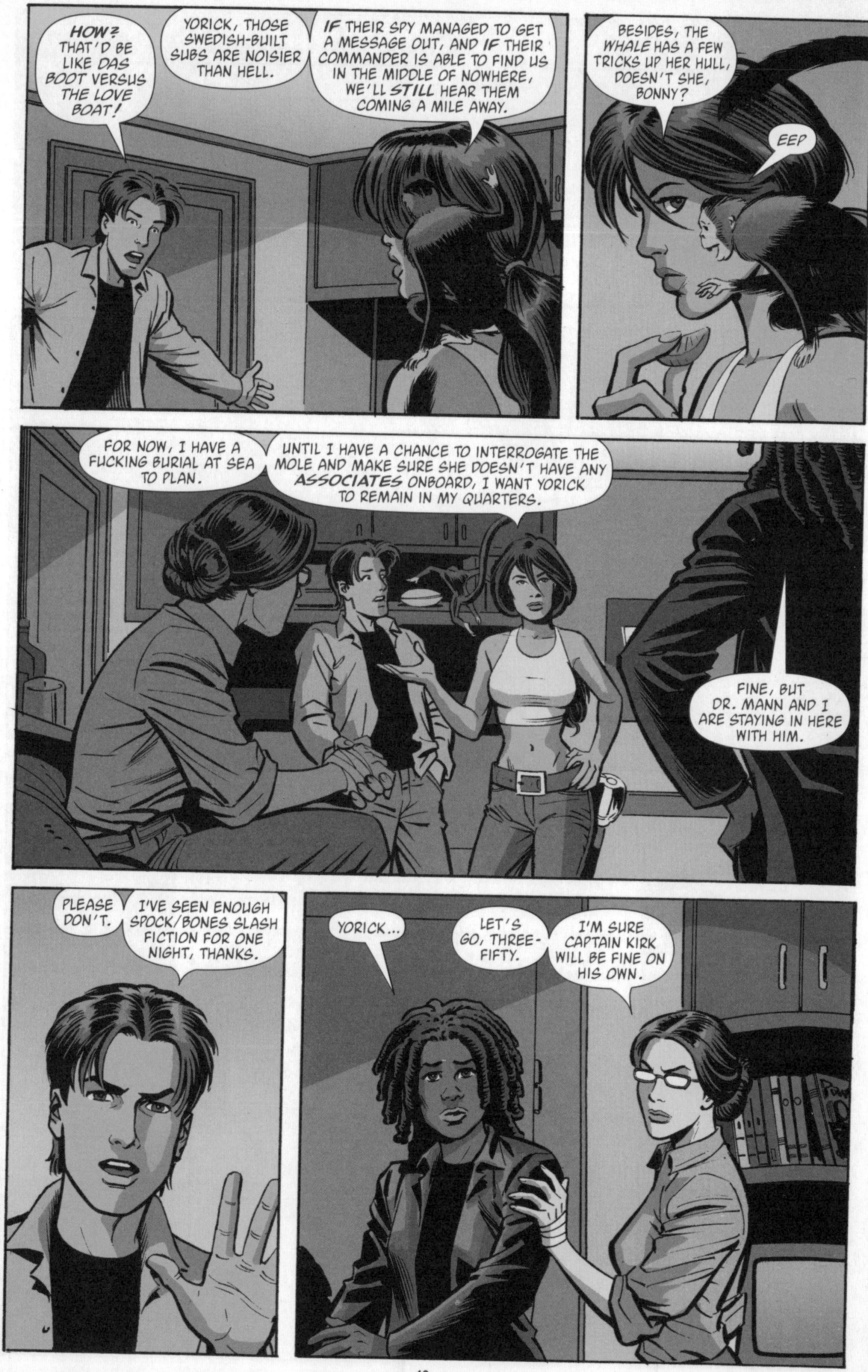
HOW? THAT'D BE LIKE DAS BOOT VERSUS THE LOVE BOAT!
YORICK, THOSE SWEDISH-BUILT SUBS ARE NOISIER THAN HELL.
IF THEIR SPY MANAGED TO GET A MESSAGE OUT, AND IF THEIR COMMANDER IS ABLE TO FIND US IN THE MIDDLE OF NOWHERE, WE'LL STILL HEAR THEM COMING A MILE AWAY.
BESIDES, THE WHALE HAS A FEW TRICKS UP HER HULL, DOESN'T SHE, BONNY?
EEP
FOR NOW, I HAVE A FUCKING BURIAL AT SEA TO PLAN.
UNTIL I HAVE A CHANCE TO INTERROGATE THE MOLE AND MAKE SURE SHE DOESN'T HAVE ANY ASSOCIATES ONBOARD, I WANT YORICK TO REMAIN IN MY QUARTERS.
FINE, BUT DR. MANN AND I ARE STAYING IN HERE WITH HIM.
PLEASE DON'T.
I'VE SEEN ENOUGH SPOCK/BONES SLASH FICTION FOR ONE NIGHT, THANKS.
YORICK...
LET'S GO, THREE-FIFTY.
I'M SURE CAPTAIN KIRK WILL BE FINE ON HIS OWN.

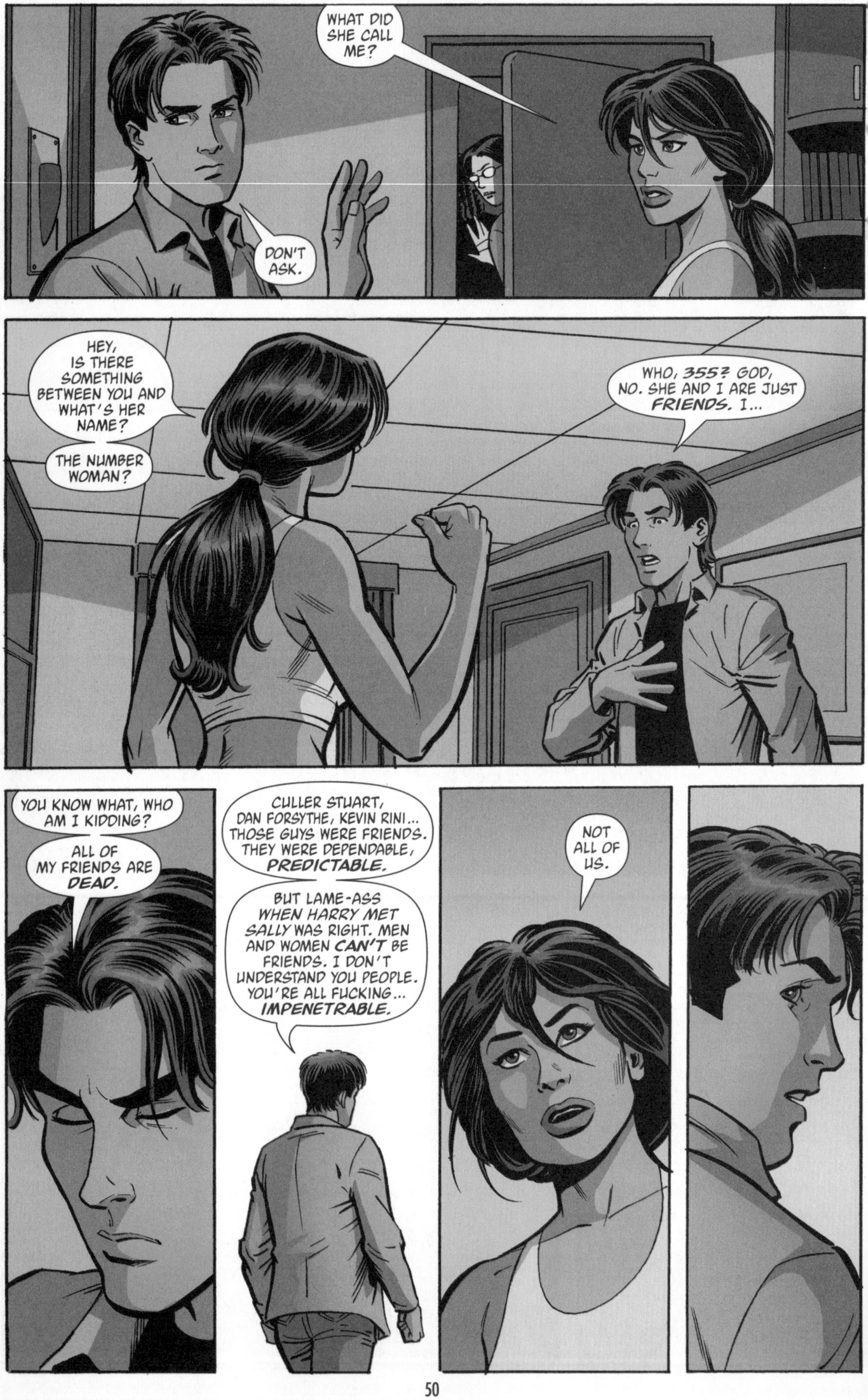
WHAT DID SHE CALL ME?
DON'T ASK.
HEY, IS THERE SOMETHING BETWEEN YOU AND WHAT'S HER NAME?
THE NUMBER WOMAN?
WHO, 355? GOD, NO. SHE AND I ARE JUST FRIENDS. I...
YOU KNOW WHAT, WHO AM I KIDDING?
ALL OF MY FRIENDS ARE DEAD.
CULLER STUART, DAN FORSYTHE, KEVIN RINI... THOSE GUYS WERE FRIENDS. THEY WERE DEPENDABLE, PREDICTABLE.
BUT LAME-ASS WHEN HARRY MET SALLY WAS RIGHT. MEN AND WOMEN CAN'T BE FRIENDS. I DON'T UNDERSTAND YOU PEOPLE. YOU'RE ALL FUCKING... IMPENETRABLE.
NOT ALL OF US.

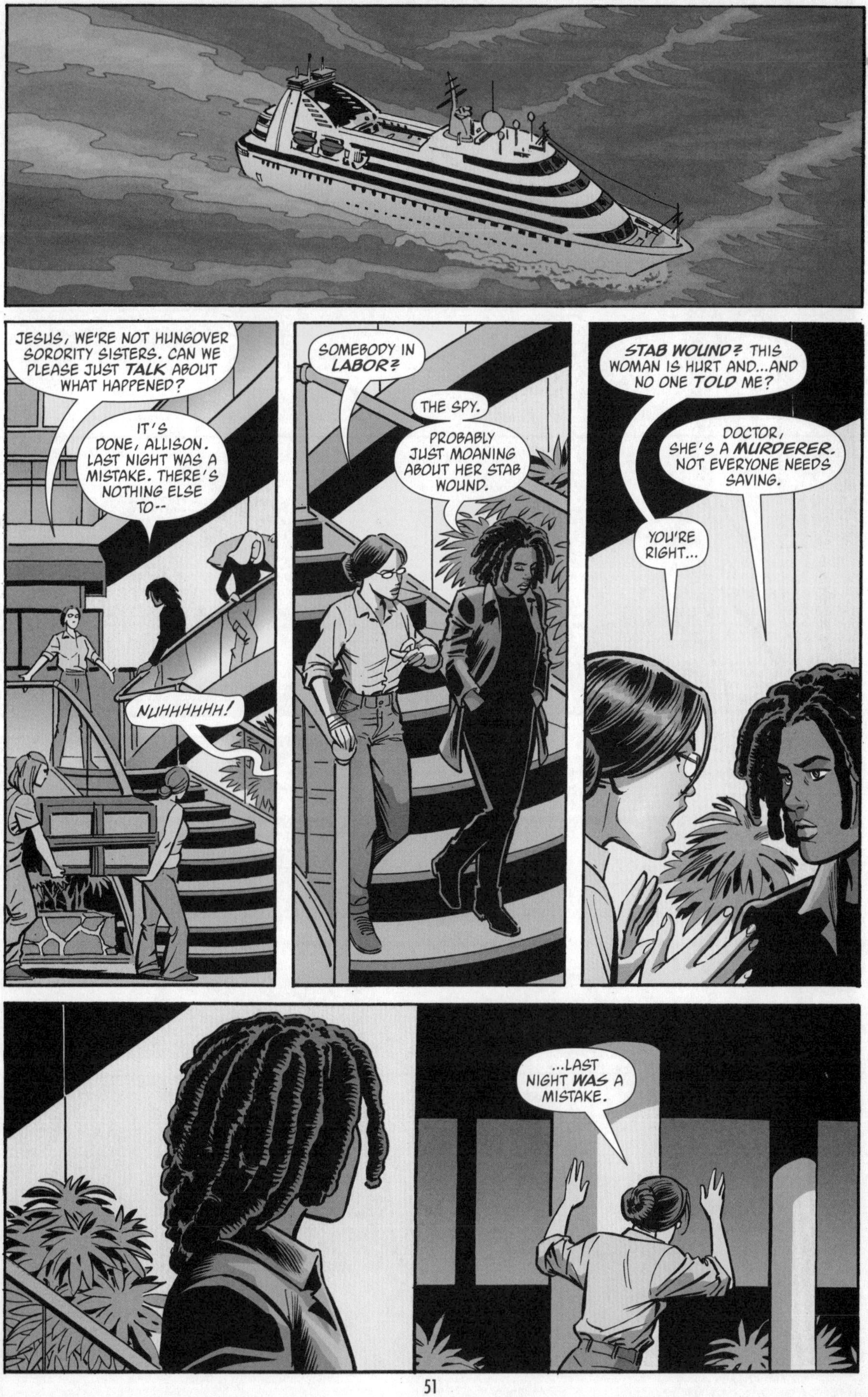
JESUS, WE'RE NOT HUNGOVER SORORITY SISTERS. CAN WE PLEASE JUST TALK ABOUT WHAT HAPPENED?
IT'S DONE, ALLISON. LAST NIGHT WAS A MISTAKE. THERE'S NOTHING ELSE TO--
NUHHHHHH!
SOMEBODY IN LABOR?
THE SPY.
PROBABLY JUST MOANING ABOUT HER STAB WOUND.
STAB WOUND? THIS WOMAN IS HURT AND...AND NO ONE TOLD ME?
DOCTOR, SHE'S A MURDERER. NOT EVERYONE NEEDS SAVING.
YOU'RE RIGHT...
...LAST NIGHT WAS A MISTAKE.

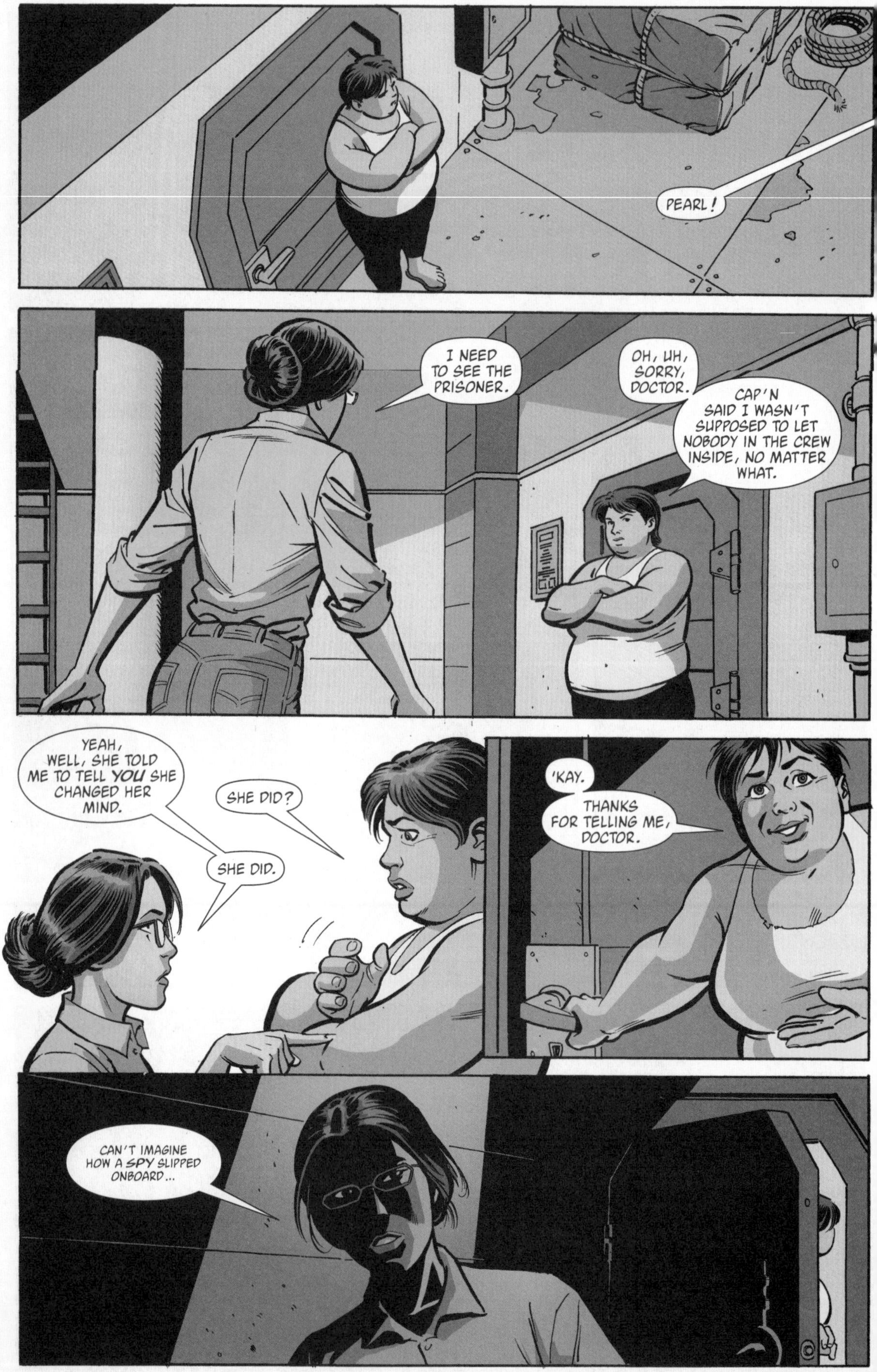
PEARL!
I NEED TO SEE THE PRISONER.
OH, UH, SORRY, DOCTOR.
CAP'N SAID I WASN'T SUPPOSED TO LET NOBODY IN THE CREW INSIDE, NO MATTER WHAT.
YEAH, WELL, SHE TOLD ME TO TELL *YOU* SHE CHANGED HER MIND.
SHE DID?
SHE DID.
'KAY.
THANKS FOR TELLING ME, DOCTOR.
CAN'T IMAGINE HOW A *SPY* SLIPPED ONBOARD...

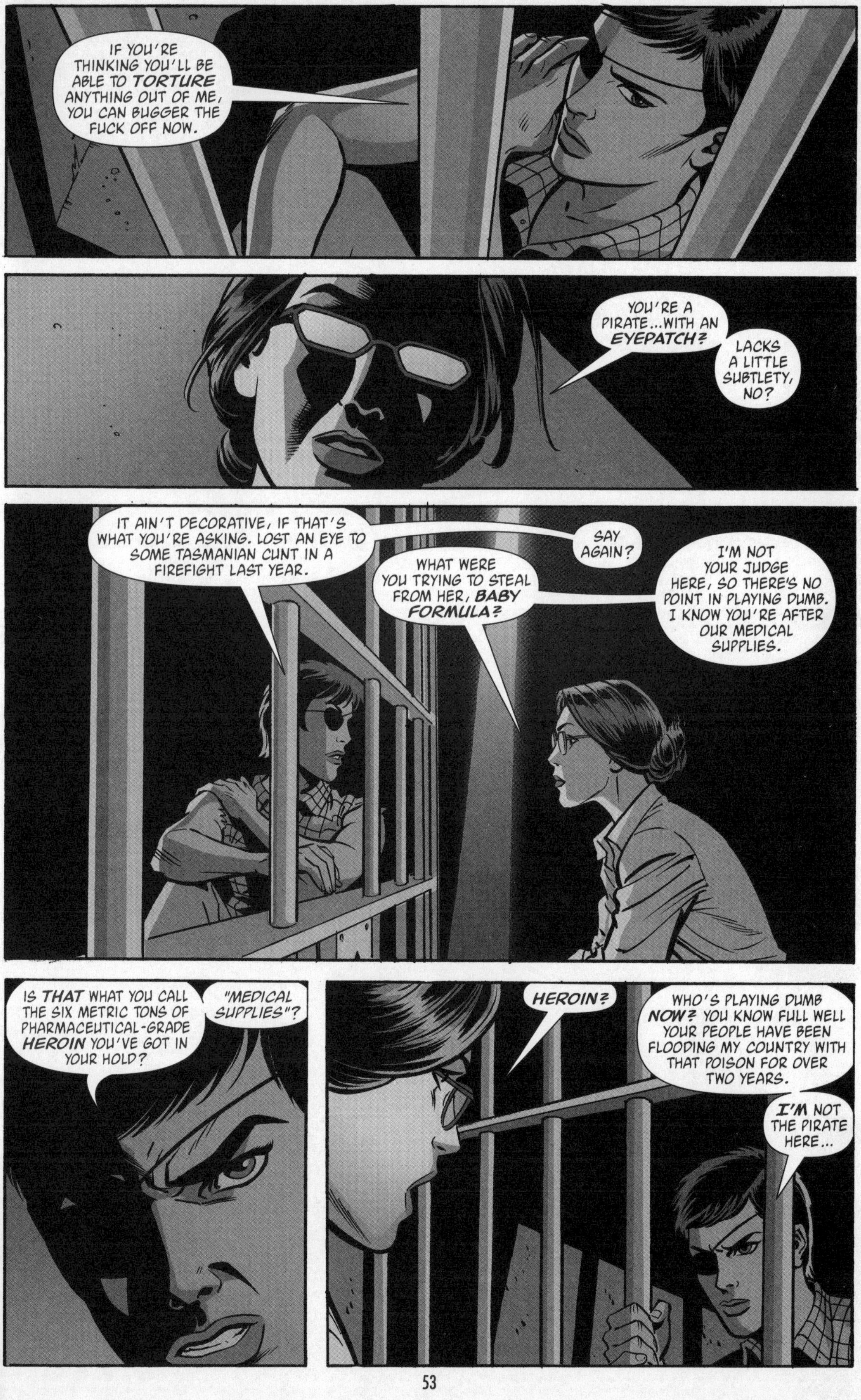
IF YOU'RE THINKING YOU'LL BE ABLE TO TORTURE ANYTHING OUT OF ME, YOU CAN BUGGER THE FUCK OFF NOW.
YOU'RE A PIRATE...WITH AN EYEPATCH?
LACKS A LITTLE SUBTLETY, NO?
IT AIN'T DECORATIVE, IF THAT'S WHAT YOU'RE ASKING. LOST AN EYE TO SOME TASMANIAN CUNT IN A FIREFIGHT LAST YEAR.
WHAT WERE YOU TRYING TO STEAL FROM HER, BABY FORMULA?
SAY AGAIN?
I'M NOT YOUR JUDGE HERE, SO THERE'S NO POINT IN PLAYING DUMB. I KNOW YOU'RE AFTER OUR MEDICAL SUPPLIES.
IS THAT WHAT YOU CALL THE SIX METRIC TONS OF PHARMACEUTICAL-GRADE HEROIN YOU'VE GOT IN YOUR HOLD?
"MEDICAL SUPPLIES"?
HEROIN?
WHO'S PLAYING DUMB NOW? YOU KNOW FULL WELL YOUR PEOPLE HAVE BEEN FLOODING MY COUNTRY WITH THAT POISON FOR OVER TWO YEARS.
I'M NOT THE PIRATE HERE...

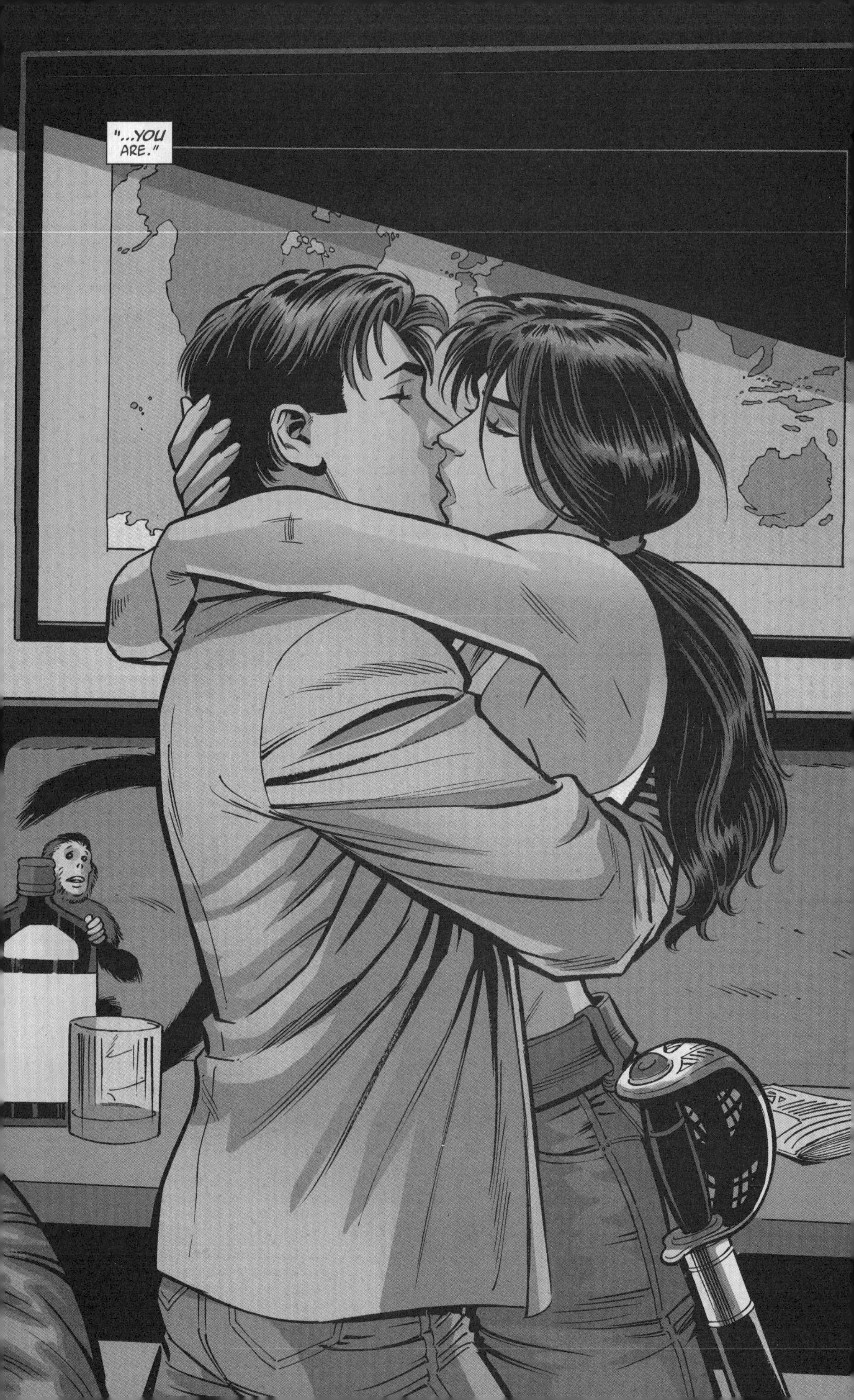
"...YOU ARE."

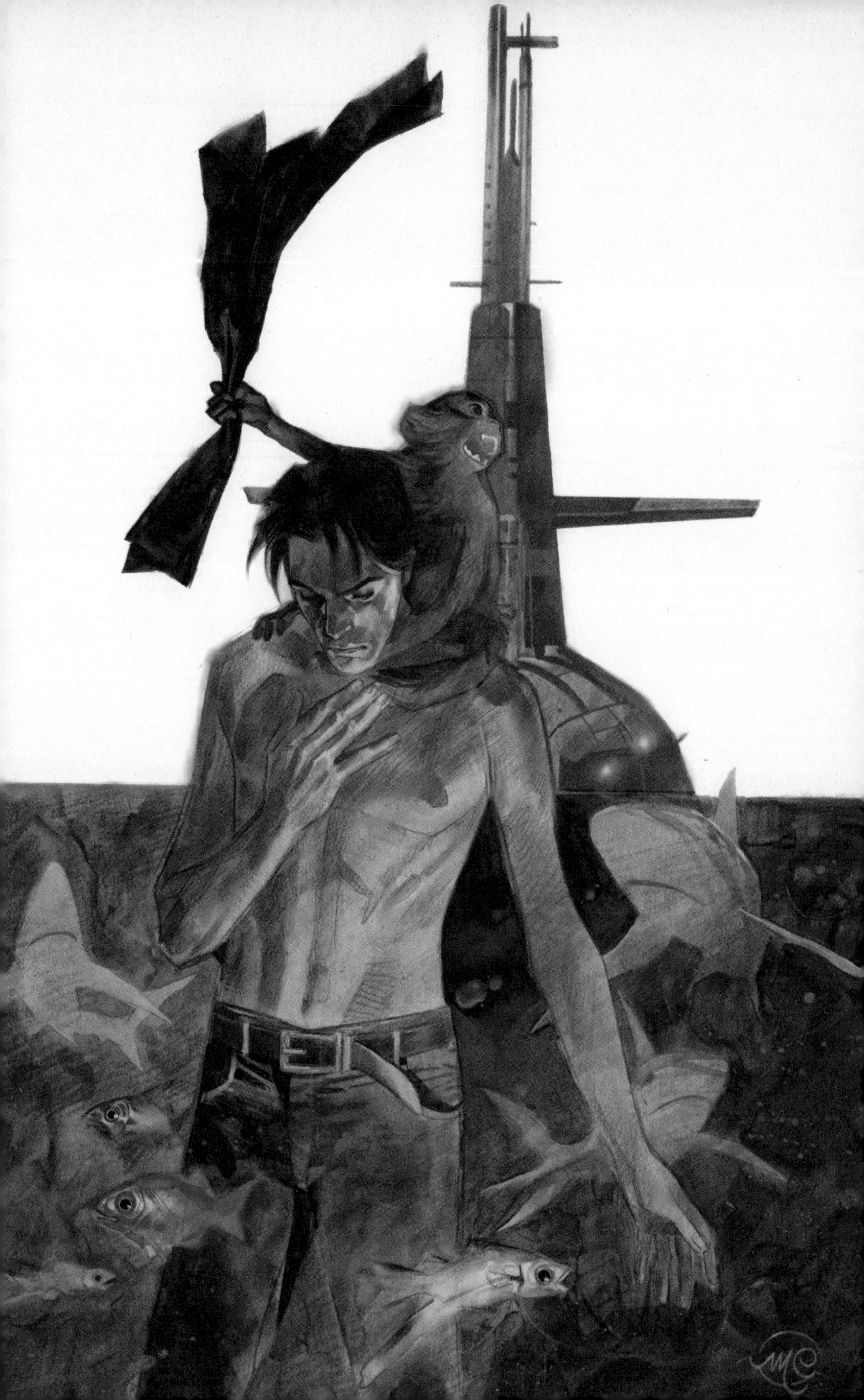

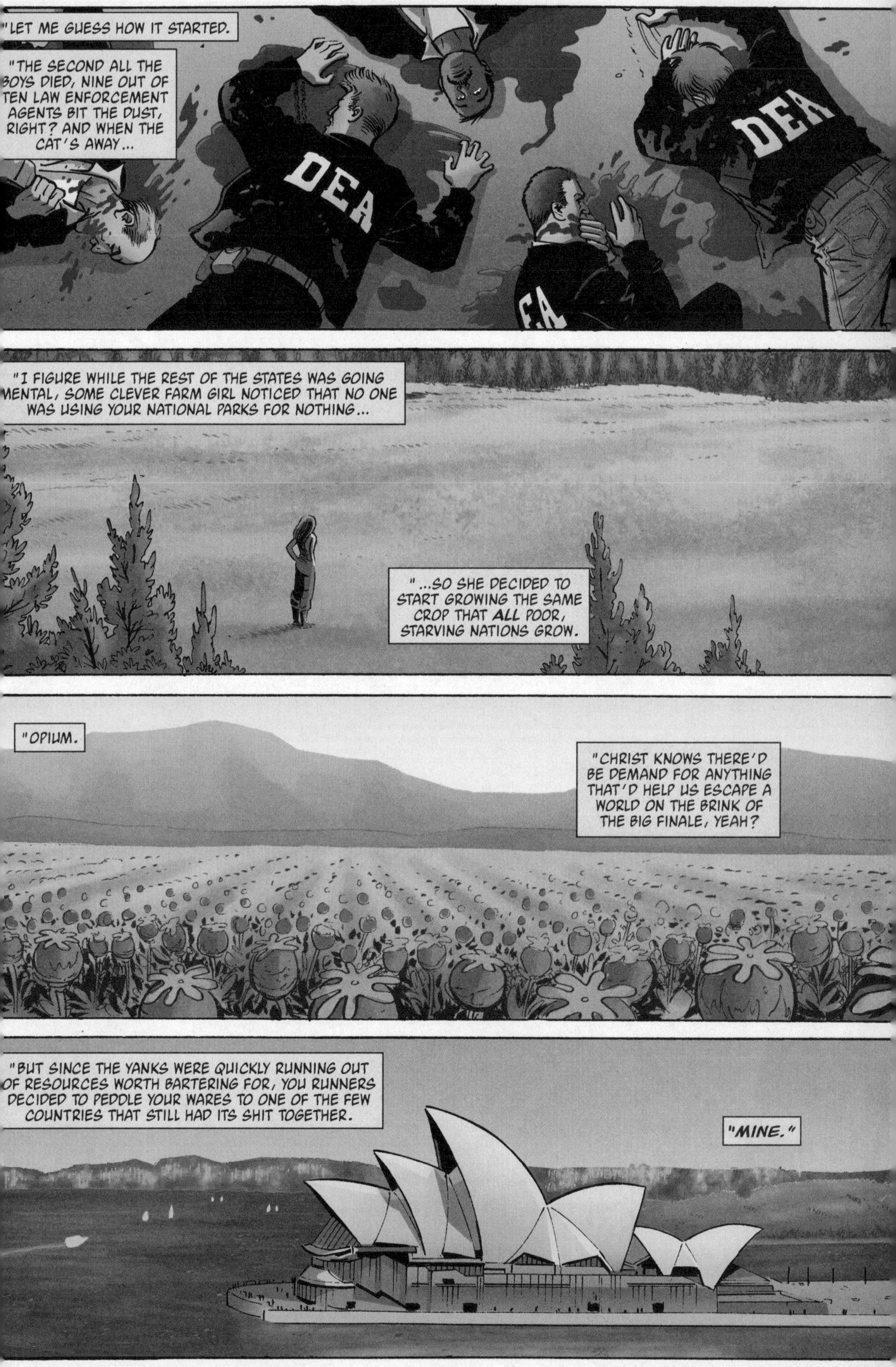
"LET ME GUESS HOW IT STARTED.
"THE SECOND ALL THE BOYS DIED, NINE OUT OF TEN LAW ENFORCEMENT AGENTS BIT THE DUST, RIGHT? AND WHEN THE CAT'S AWAY...
DEA
DEA
DEA
"I FIGURE WHILE THE REST OF THE STATES WAS GOING MENTAL, SOME CLEVER FARM GIRL NOTICED THAT NO ONE WAS USING YOUR NATIONAL PARKS FOR NOTHING...
"...SO SHE DECIDED TO START GROWING THE SAME CROP THAT **ALL** POOR, STARVING NATIONS GROW.
"OPIUM.
"CHRIST KNOWS THERE'D BE DEMAND FOR ANYTHING THAT'D HELP US ESCAPE A WORLD ON THE BRINK OF THE BIG FINALE, YEAH?
"BUT SINCE THE YANKS WERE QUICKLY RUNNING OUT OF RESOURCES WORTH BARTERING FOR, YOU RUNNERS DECIDED TO PEDDLE YOUR WARES TO ONE OF THE FEW COUNTRIES THAT STILL HAD ITS SHIT TOGETHER.
"*MINE.*"

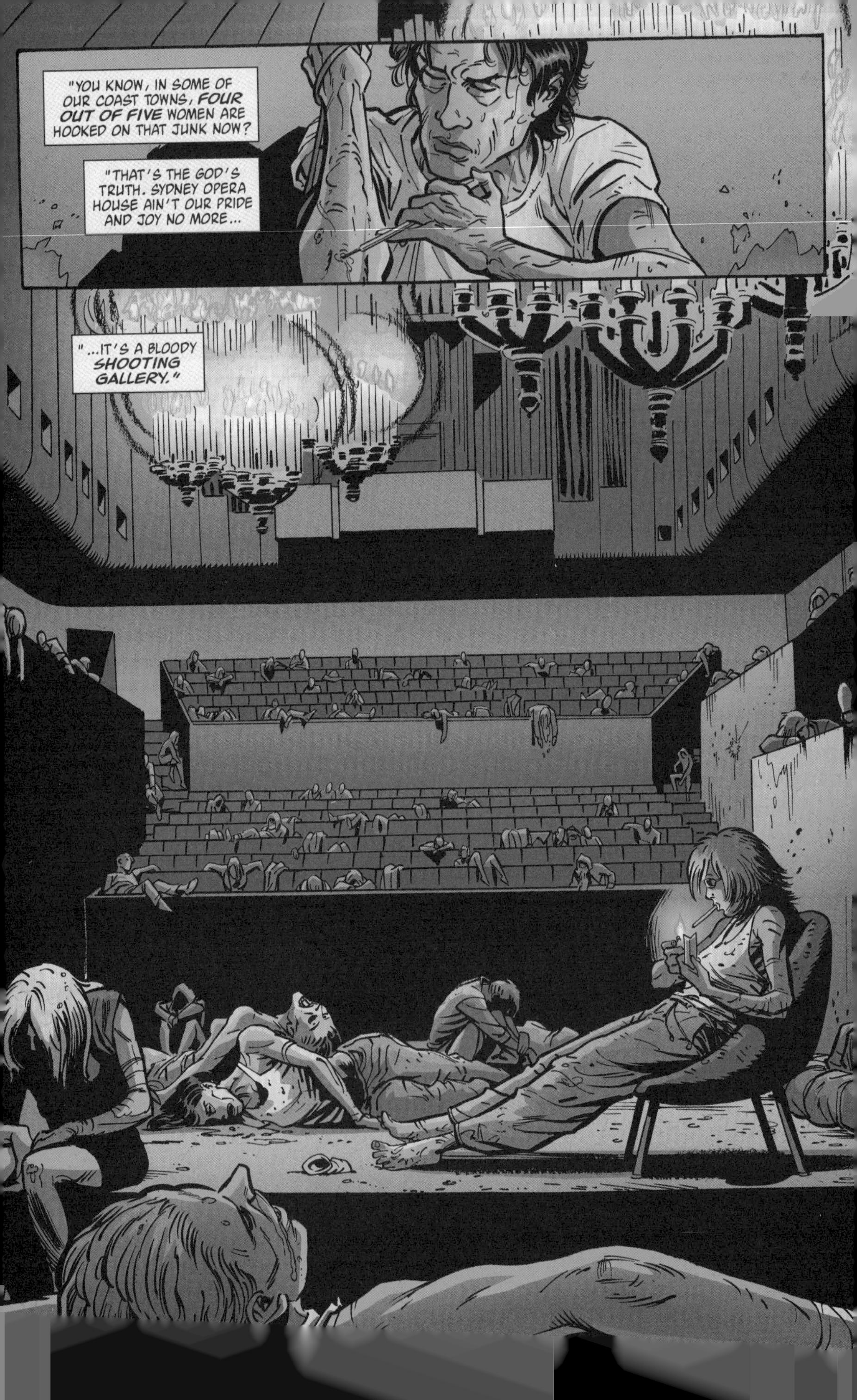
"YOU KNOW, IN SOME OF OUR COAST TOWNS, FOUR OUT OF FIVE WOMEN ARE HOOKED ON THAT JUNK NOW?
"THAT'S THE GOD'S TRUTH. SYDNEY OPERA HOUSE AIN'T OUR PRIDE AND JOY NO MORE...
"...IT'S A BLOODY SHOOTING GALLERY."

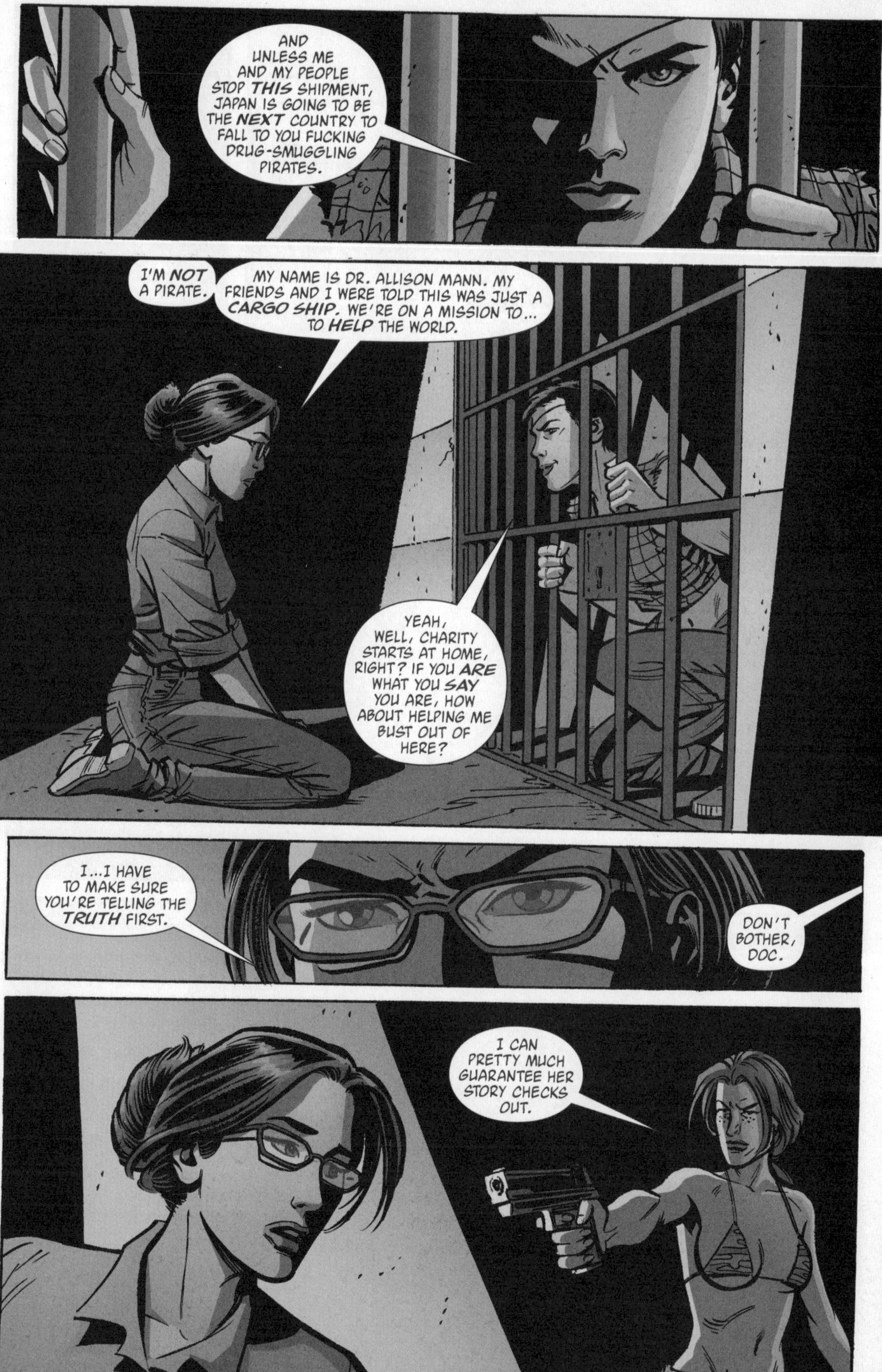
AND UNLESS ME AND MY PEOPLE STOP THIS SHIPMENT, JAPAN IS GOING TO BE THE NEXT COUNTRY TO FALL TO YOU FUCKING DRUG-SMUGGLING PIRATES.
I'M NOT A PIRATE.
MY NAME IS DR. ALLISON MANN. MY FRIENDS AND I WERE TOLD THIS WAS JUST A CARGO SHIP. WE'RE ON A MISSION TO... TO HELP THE WORLD.
YEAH, WELL, CHARITY STARTS AT HOME, RIGHT? IF YOU ARE WHAT YOU SAY YOU ARE, HOW ABOUT HELPING ME BUST OUT OF HERE?
I...I HAVE TO MAKE SURE YOU'RE TELLING THE TRUTH FIRST.
DON'T BOTHER, DOC.
I CAN PRETTY MUCH GUARANTEE HER STORY CHECKS OUT.

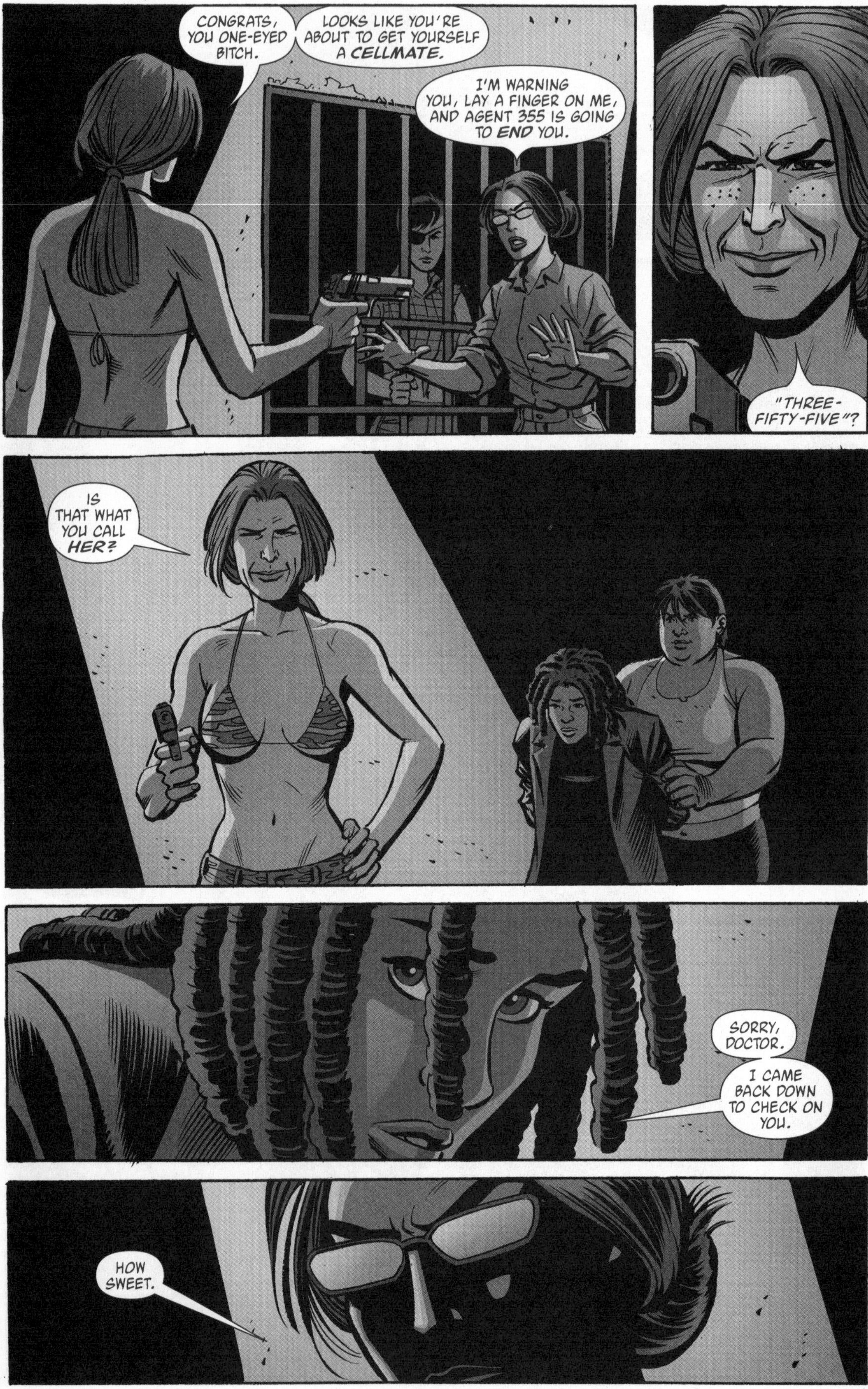
CONGRATS, YOU ONE-EYED BITCH.
LOOKS LIKE YOU'RE ABOUT TO GET YOURSELF A CELLMATE.
I'M WARNING YOU, LAY A FINGER ON ME, AND AGENT 355 IS GOING TO END YOU.
"THREE-FIFTY-FIVE"?
IS THAT WHAT YOU CALL HER?
SORRY, DOCTOR.
I CAME BACK DOWN TO CHECK ON YOU.
HOW SWEET.

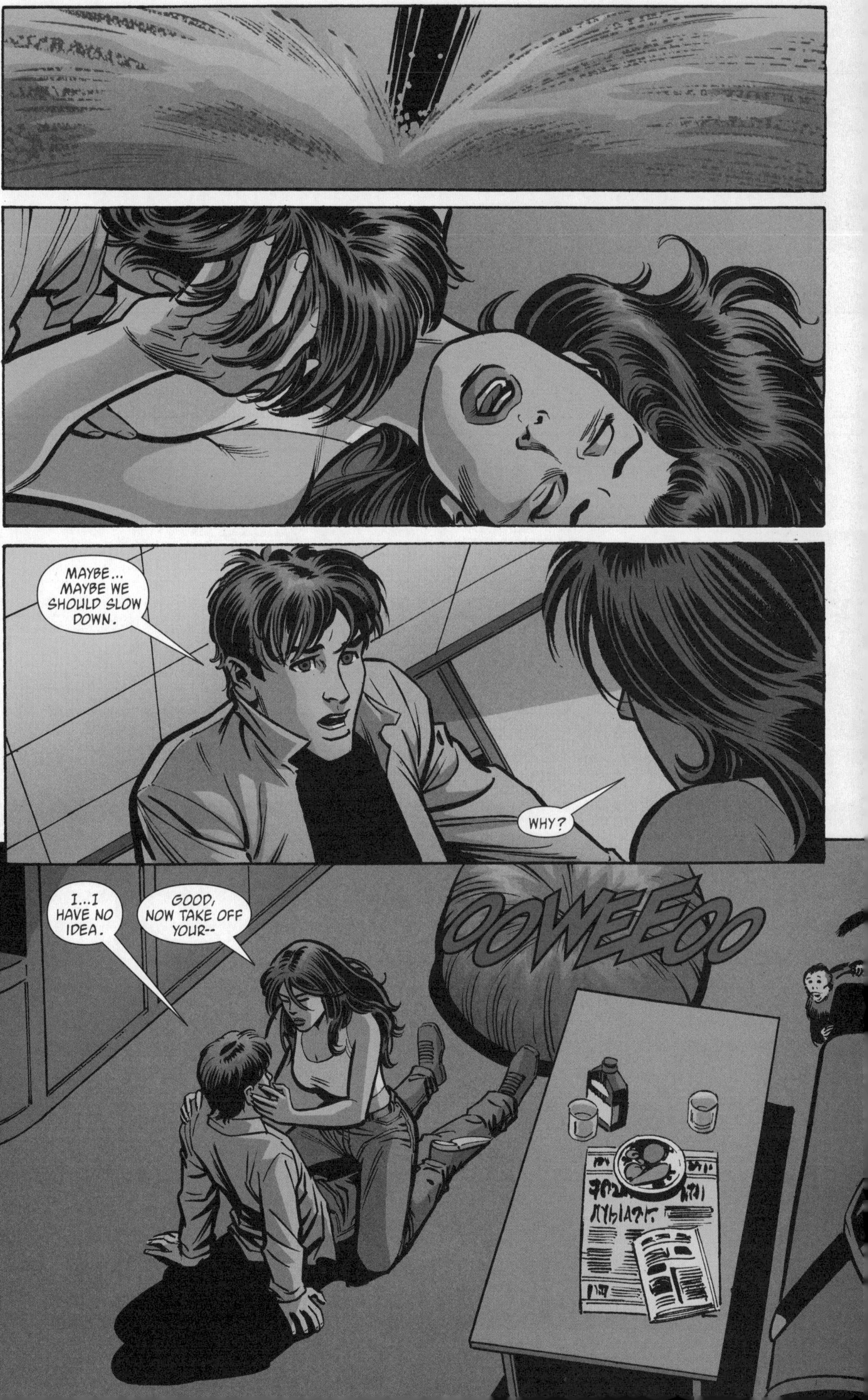
MAYBE... MAYBE WE SHOULD SLOW DOWN.
WHY?
I...I HAVE NO IDEA.
GOOD, NOW TAKE OFF YOUR--
OOWEEOO

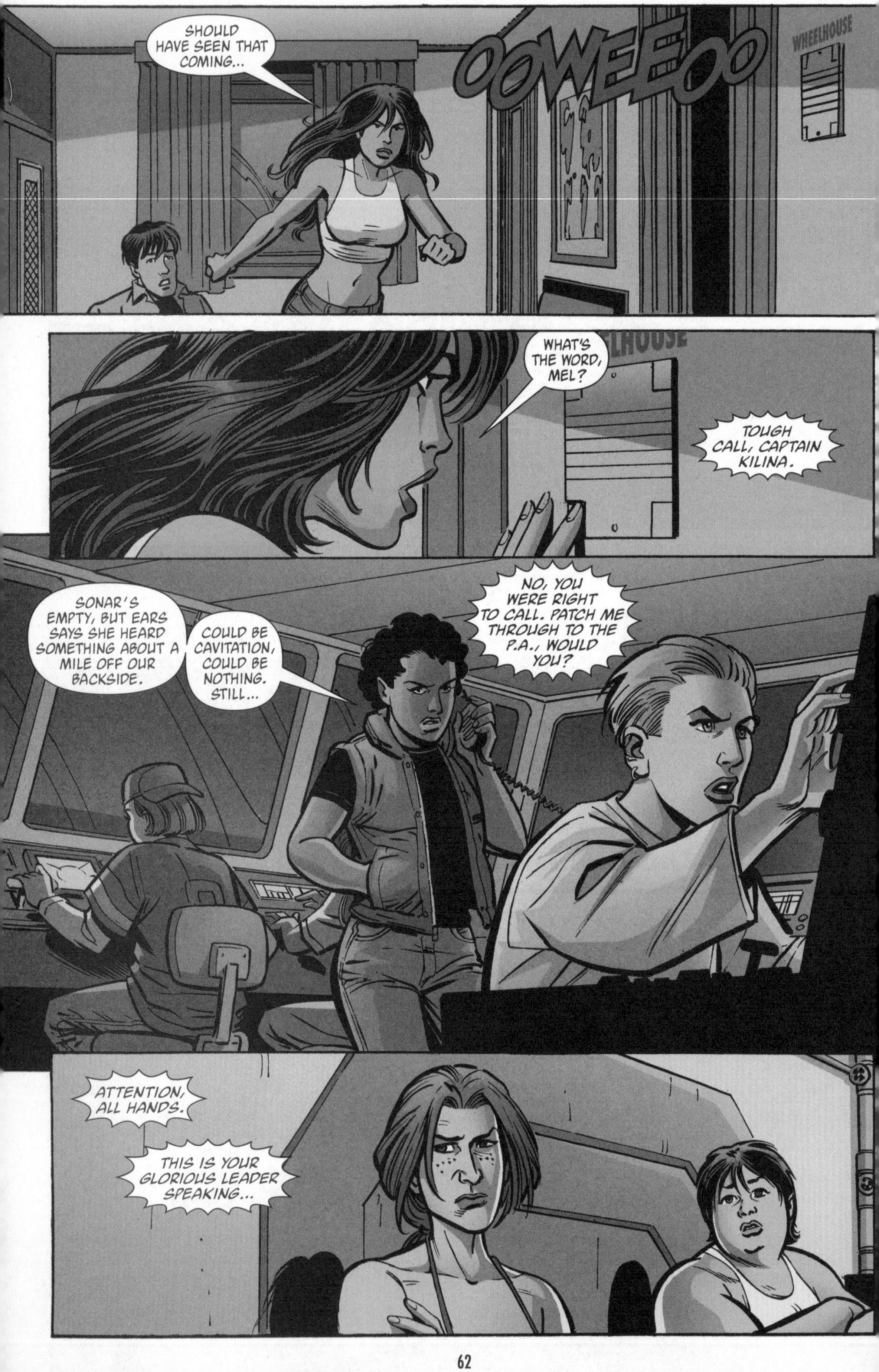
SHOULD HAVE SEEN THAT COMING...
OOWEEOO
WHEELHOUSE
WHAT'S THE WORD, MEL?
TOUGH CALL, CAPTAIN KILINA.
SONAR'S EMPTY, BUT EARS SAYS SHE HEARD SOMETHING ABOUT A MILE OFF OUR BACKSIDE.
COULD BE CAVITATION, COULD BE NOTHING. STILL...
NO, YOU WERE RIGHT TO CALL. PATCH ME THROUGH TO THE P.A., WOULD YOU?
ATTENTION, ALL HANDS.
THIS IS YOUR GLORIOUS LEADER SPEAKING...

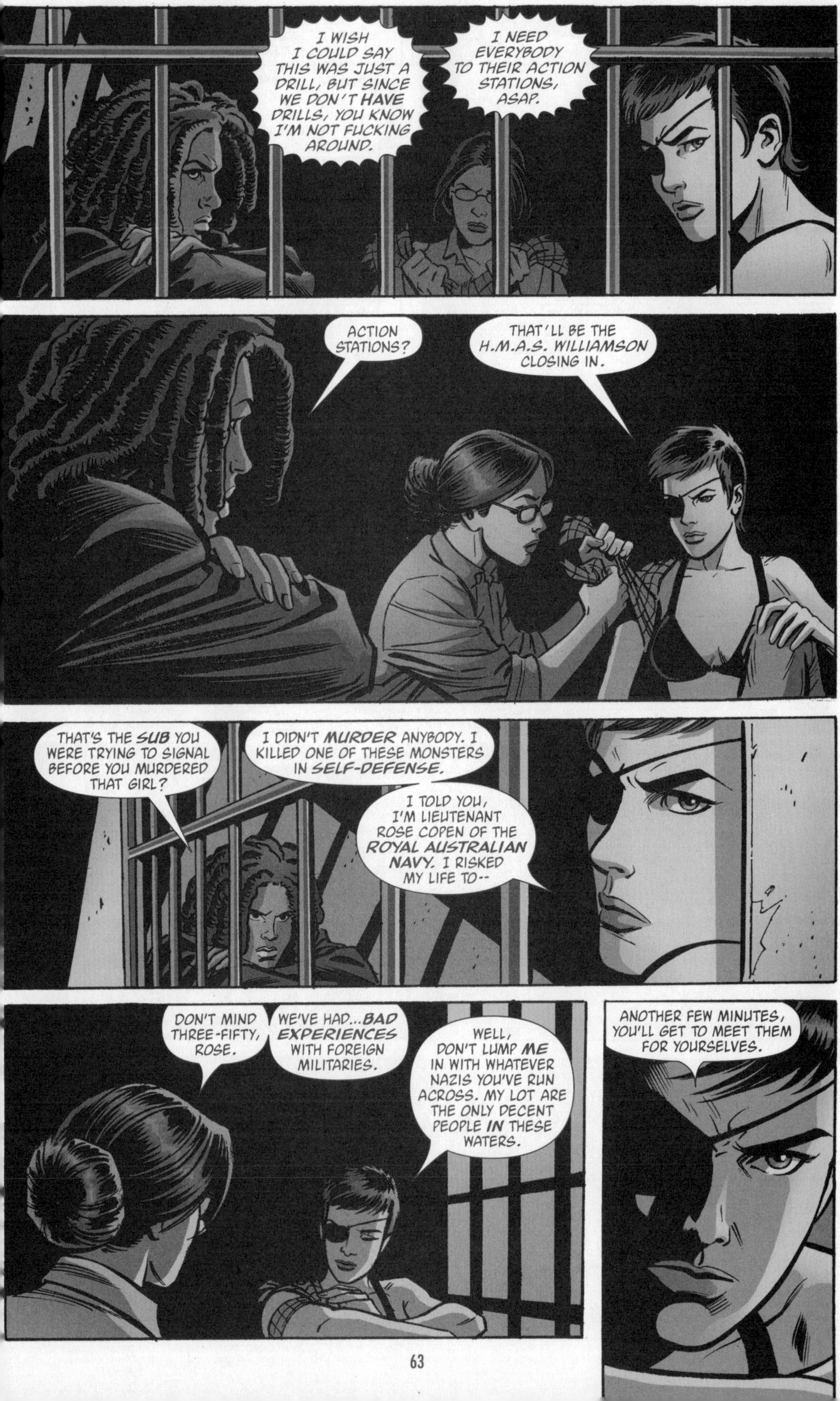
I WISH I COULD SAY THIS WAS JUST A DRILL, BUT SINCE WE DON'T HAVE DRILLS, YOU KNOW I'M NOT FUCKING AROUND.
I NEED EVERYBODY TO THEIR ACTION STATIONS, ASAP.
ACTION STATIONS?
THAT'LL BE THE H.M.A.S. WILLIAMSON CLOSING IN.
THAT'S THE SUB YOU WERE TRYING TO SIGNAL BEFORE YOU MURDERED THAT GIRL?
I DIDN'T MURDER ANYBODY. I KILLED ONE OF THESE MONSTERS IN SELF-DEFENSE.
I TOLD YOU, I'M LIEUTENANT ROSE COPEN OF THE ROYAL AUSTRALIAN NAVY. I RISKED MY LIFE TO--
DON'T MIND THREE-FIFTY, ROSE.
WE'VE HAD...BAD EXPERIENCES WITH FOREIGN MILITARIES.
WELL, DON'T LUMP ME IN WITH WHATEVER NAZIS YOU'VE RUN ACROSS. MY LOT ARE THE ONLY DECENT PEOPLE IN THESE WATERS.
ANOTHER FEW MINUTES, YOU'LL GET TO MEET THEM FOR YOURSELVES.

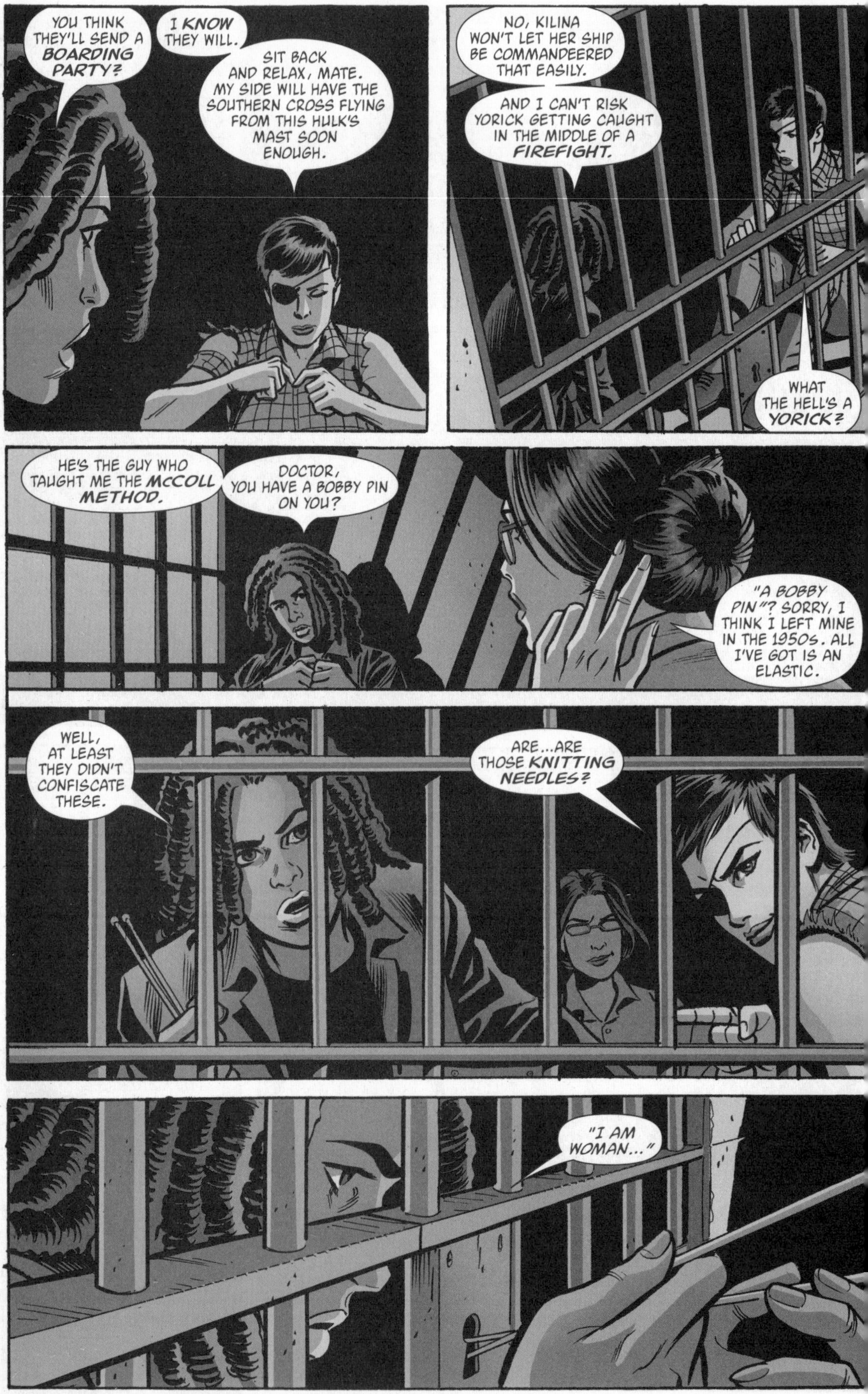
YOU THINK THEY'LL SEND A BOARDING PARTY?
I KNOW THEY WILL.
SIT BACK AND RELAX, MATE. MY SIDE WILL HAVE THE SOUTHERN CROSS FLYING FROM THIS HULK'S MAST SOON ENOUGH.
NO, KILINA WON'T LET HER SHIP BE COMMANDEERED THAT EASILY.
AND I CAN'T RISK YORICK GETTING CAUGHT IN THE MIDDLE OF A FIREFIGHT.
WHAT THE HELL'S A YORICK?
HE'S THE GUY WHO TAUGHT ME THE McCOLL METHOD.
DOCTOR, YOU HAVE A BOBBY PIN ON YOU?
"A BOBBY PIN"? SORRY, I THINK I LEFT MINE IN THE 1950s. ALL I'VE GOT IS AN ELASTIC.
WELL, AT LEAST THEY DIDN'T CONFISCATE THESE.
ARE...ARE THOSE KNITTING NEEDLES?
"I AM WOMAN..."

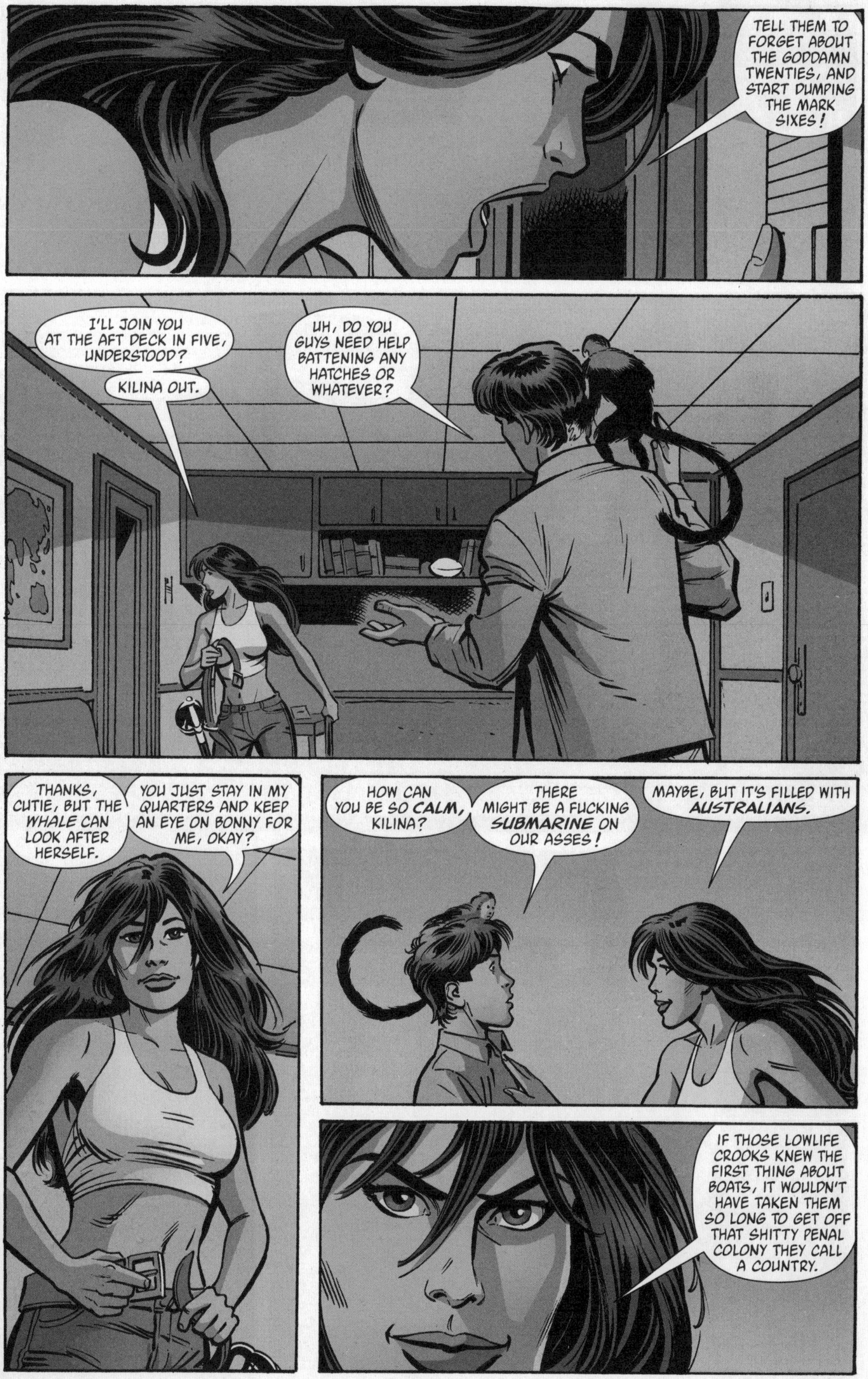

TELL THEM TO FORGET ABOUT THE GODDAMN TWENTIES, AND START DUMPING THE MARK SIXES!
I'LL JOIN YOU AT THE AFT DECK IN FIVE, UNDERSTOOD?
KILINA OUT.
UH, DO YOU GUYS NEED HELP BATTENING ANY HATCHES OR WHATEVER?
THANKS, CUTIE, BUT THE WHALE CAN LOOK AFTER HERSELF.
YOU JUST STAY IN MY QUARTERS AND KEEP AN EYE ON BONNY FOR ME, OKAY?
HOW CAN YOU BE SO CALM, KILINA?
THERE MIGHT BE A FUCKING SUBMARINE ON OUR ASSES!
MAYBE, BUT IT'S FILLED WITH AUSTRALIANS.
IF THOSE LOWLIFE CROOKS KNEW THE FIRST THING ABOUT BOATS, IT WOULDN'T HAVE TAKEN THEM SO LONG TO GET OFF THAT SHITTY PENAL COLONY THEY CALL A COUNTRY.

GO-TEAM IS PREPPED FOR STORMY WEATHER, CAPTAIN BELLEVILLE.

FINE, WE'LL RISE JUST SHY OF SURFACE, AND LET YOU GIRLS OUT INTO THE DRINK.

IF THE COAST IS CLEAR, YOU CAN INFLATE YOUR RAFT, DOCK WITH TH' CRUISE SHIP, AND SCALE ITS HULL. REMEMBER, FIRST PRIORITY IS TAKING CONTROL OF THEIR BRIDGE, AND--

MA'AM!

THERE'S...THERE'S SOMETHING IN THE WATER. LOOKS LIKE A COUPLE OF CONTAINERS, THROWN OFF OUR TARGET'S STERN.

MAYBE THEY'RE DUMPING THEIR HEROIN SUPPLY BEFORE WE CAN BOARD...?

NO, THOSE ARE SINKING TOO FAST TO BE ORDINARY FREIGHT. THEY LOOK MORE LIKE...

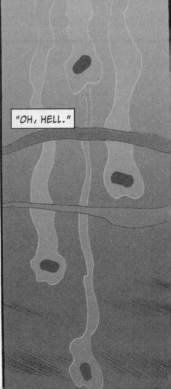

"OH, HELL."

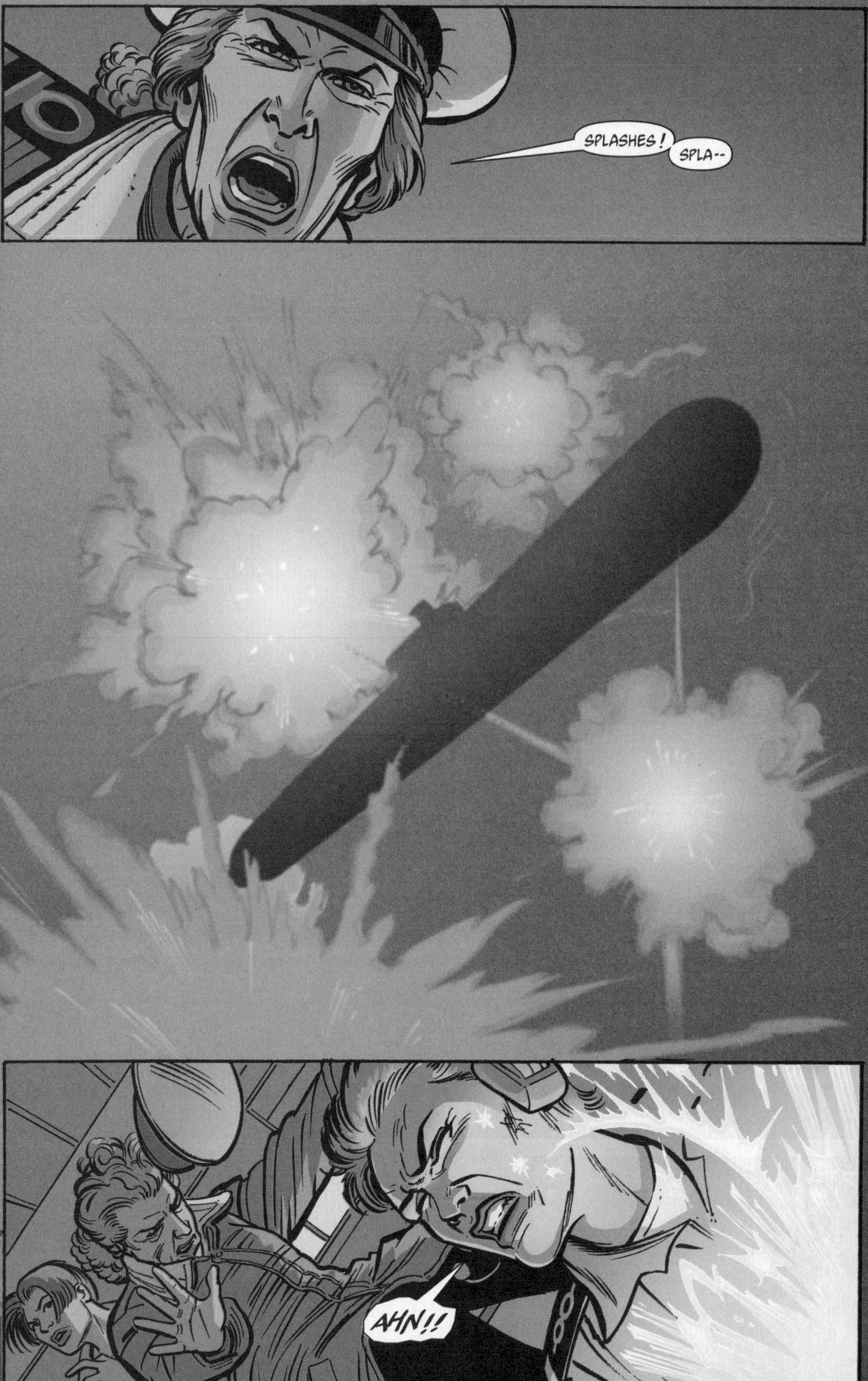
SPLASHES!
SPLA--
AHN!!

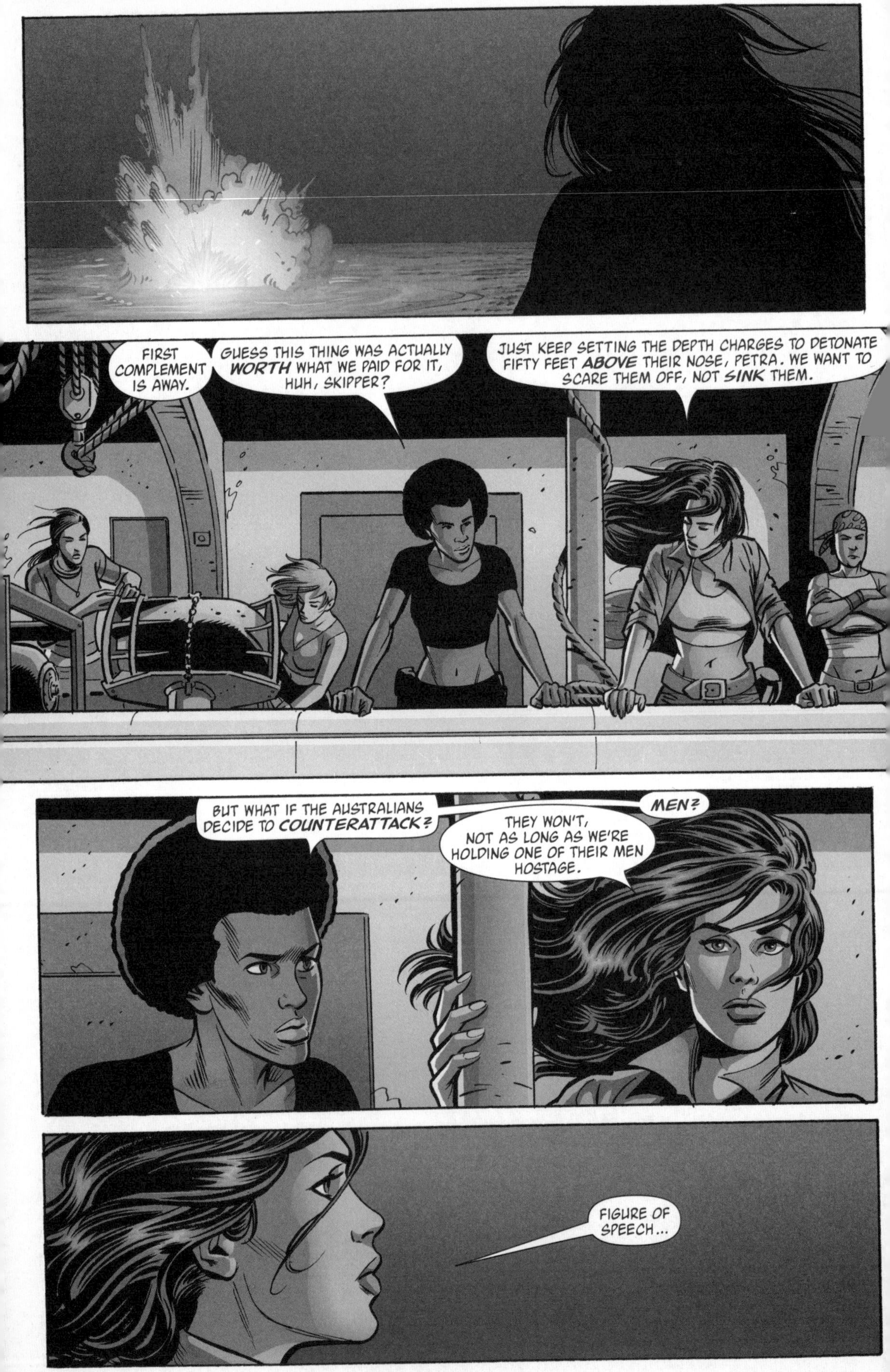
FIRST COMPLEMENT IS AWAY.
GUESS THIS THING WAS ACTUALLY WORTH WHAT WE PAID FOR IT, HUH, SKIPPER?
JUST KEEP SETTING THE DEPTH CHARGES TO DETONATE FIFTY FEET ABOVE THEIR NOSE, PETRA. WE WANT TO SCARE THEM OFF, NOT SINK THEM.
BUT WHAT IF THE AUSTRALIANS DECIDE TO COUNTERATTACK?
THEY WON'T, NOT AS LONG AS WE'RE HOLDING ONE OF THEIR MEN HOSTAGE.
MEN?
FIGURE OF SPEECH...

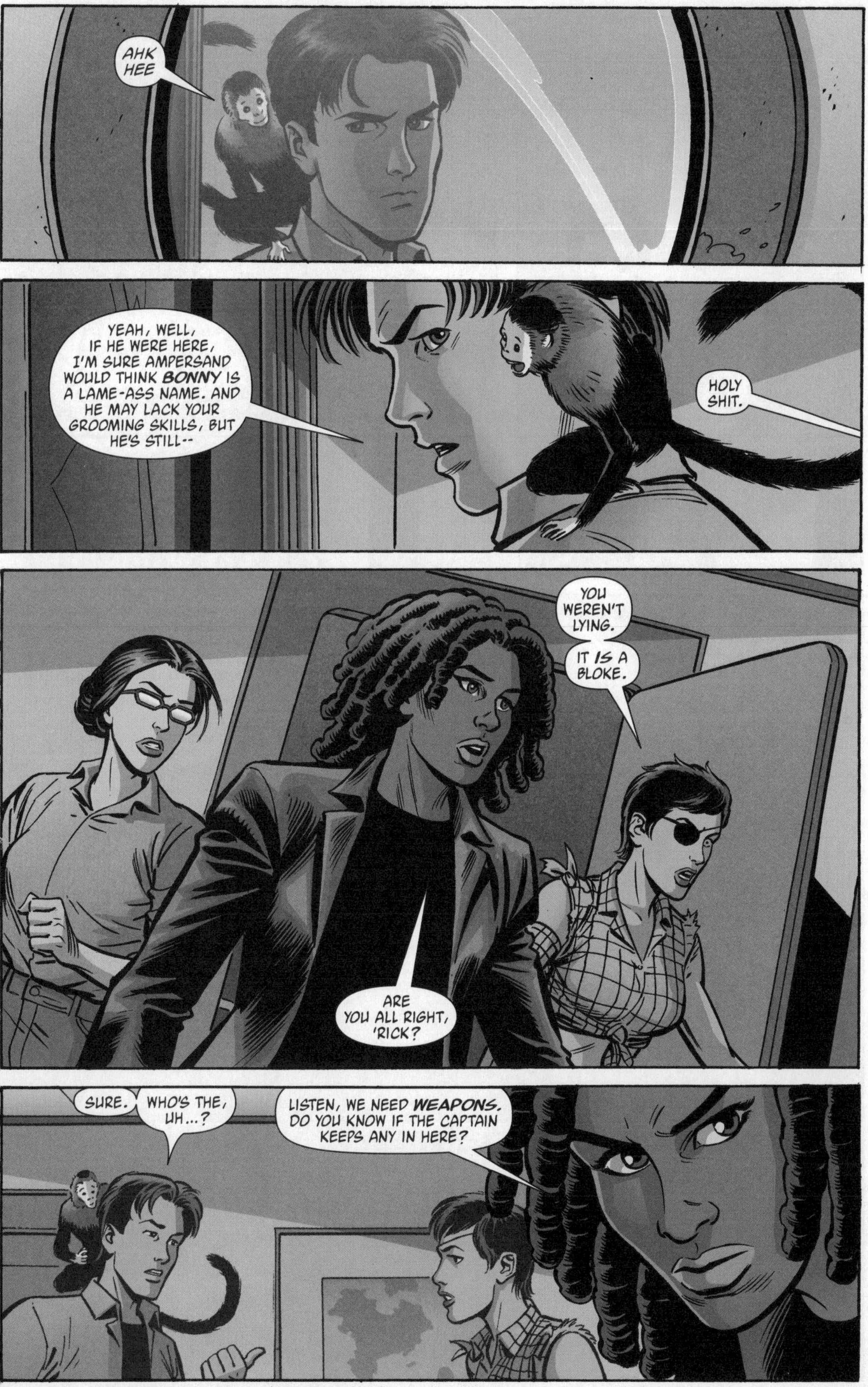
AHK HEE
YEAH, WELL, IF HE WERE HERE, I'M SURE AMPERSAND WOULD THINK BONNY IS A LAME-ASS NAME. AND HE MAY LACK YOUR GROOMING SKILLS, BUT HE'S STILL--
HOLY SHIT.
YOU WEREN'T LYING.
IT IS A BLOKE.
ARE YOU ALL RIGHT, 'RICK?
SURE.
WHO'S THE, UH...?
LISTEN, WE NEED WEAPONS. DO YOU KNOW IF THE CAPTAIN KEEPS ANY IN HERE?

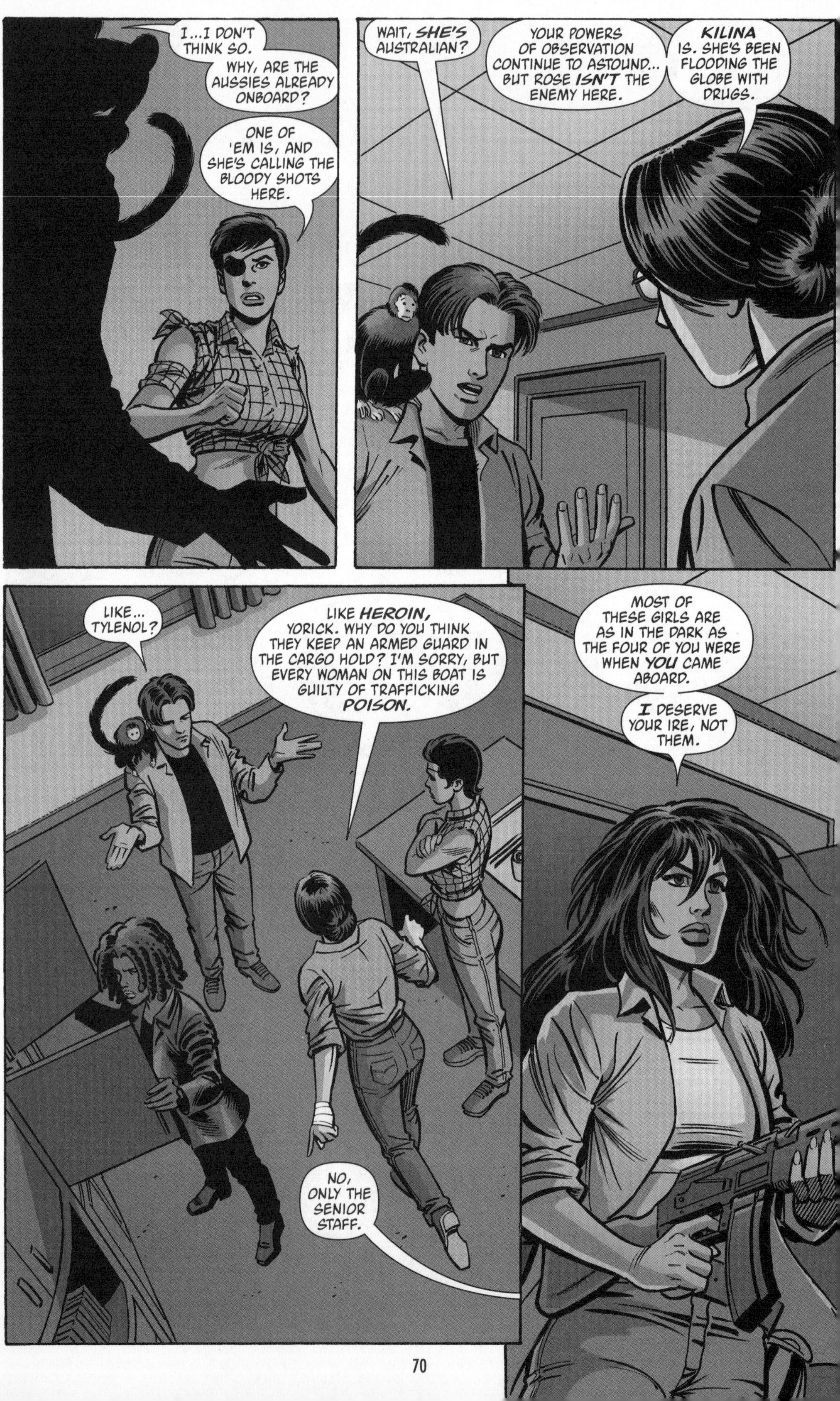
I...I DON'T THINK SO.
WHY, ARE THE AUSSIES ALREADY ONBOARD?
ONE OF 'EM IS, AND SHE'S CALLING THE BLOODY SHOTS HERE.
WAIT, SHE'S AUSTRALIAN?
YOUR POWERS OF OBSERVATION CONTINUE TO ASTOUND... BUT ROSE ISN'T THE ENEMY HERE.
KILINA IS. SHE'S BEEN FLOODING THE GLOBE WITH DRUGS.
LIKE... TYLENOL?
LIKE HEROIN, YORICK. WHY DO YOU THINK THEY KEEP AN ARMED GUARD IN THE CARGO HOLD? I'M SORRY, BUT EVERY WOMAN ON THIS BOAT IS GUILTY OF TRAFFICKING POISON.
NO, ONLY THE SENIOR STAFF.
MOST OF THESE GIRLS ARE AS IN THE DARK AS THE FOUR OF YOU WERE WHEN YOU CAME ABOARD.
I DESERVE YOUR IRE, NOT THEM.

I WENT THIRTY-ONE YEARS WITHOUT GETTING A GUN POINTED AT ME.

WHY DOES IT HAPPEN ON AN HOURLY FUCKING BASIS NOW?

WHAT THE *HELL*, KILINA? YOU TOLD ME YOU WERE TRANSPORTING *MEDICINE*.

WHICH IS EXACTLY WHAT OPIUM WAS IN THE DAYS BEFORE PROZAC AND ZOLOFT AND PAXIL...PRESCRIPTIONS THAT ALL RAN OUT *YEARS AGO*.

THIS IS THE BEST WAY TO HELP PEOPLE SUFFERING FROM DEPRESSION, DYSENTERY, *HUNGER*--

IF ANYONE'S HUNGRY, IT'S BECAUSE *YOU* TOOK ALL THEIR FOOD!

WE EXCHANGE AT REASONABLE RATES ESTABLISHED BY *YOUR* COUNTRYWOMEN. THE NAVY IS JUST UPSET THEY'RE NOT GETTING A CUT OF THE *PROFITS*.

THAT'S A *LIE*!

AM...AM I DREAMING AGAIN?

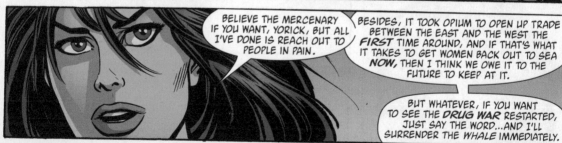

BELIEVE THE MERCENARY IF YOU WANT, YORICK, BUT ALL I'VE DONE IS REACH OUT TO PEOPLE IN PAIN.

BESIDES, IT TOOK OPIUM TO OPEN UP TRADE BETWEEN THE EAST AND THE WEST THE *FIRST* TIME AROUND, AND IF THAT'S WHAT IT TAKES TO GET WOMEN BACK OUT TO SEA *NOW*, THEN I THINK WE OWE IT TO THE FUTURE TO KEEP AT IT.

BUT WHATEVER, IF YOU WANT TO SEE THE *DRUG WAR* RESTARTED, JUST SAY THE WORD...AND I'LL SURRENDER THE *WHALE* IMMEDIATELY.

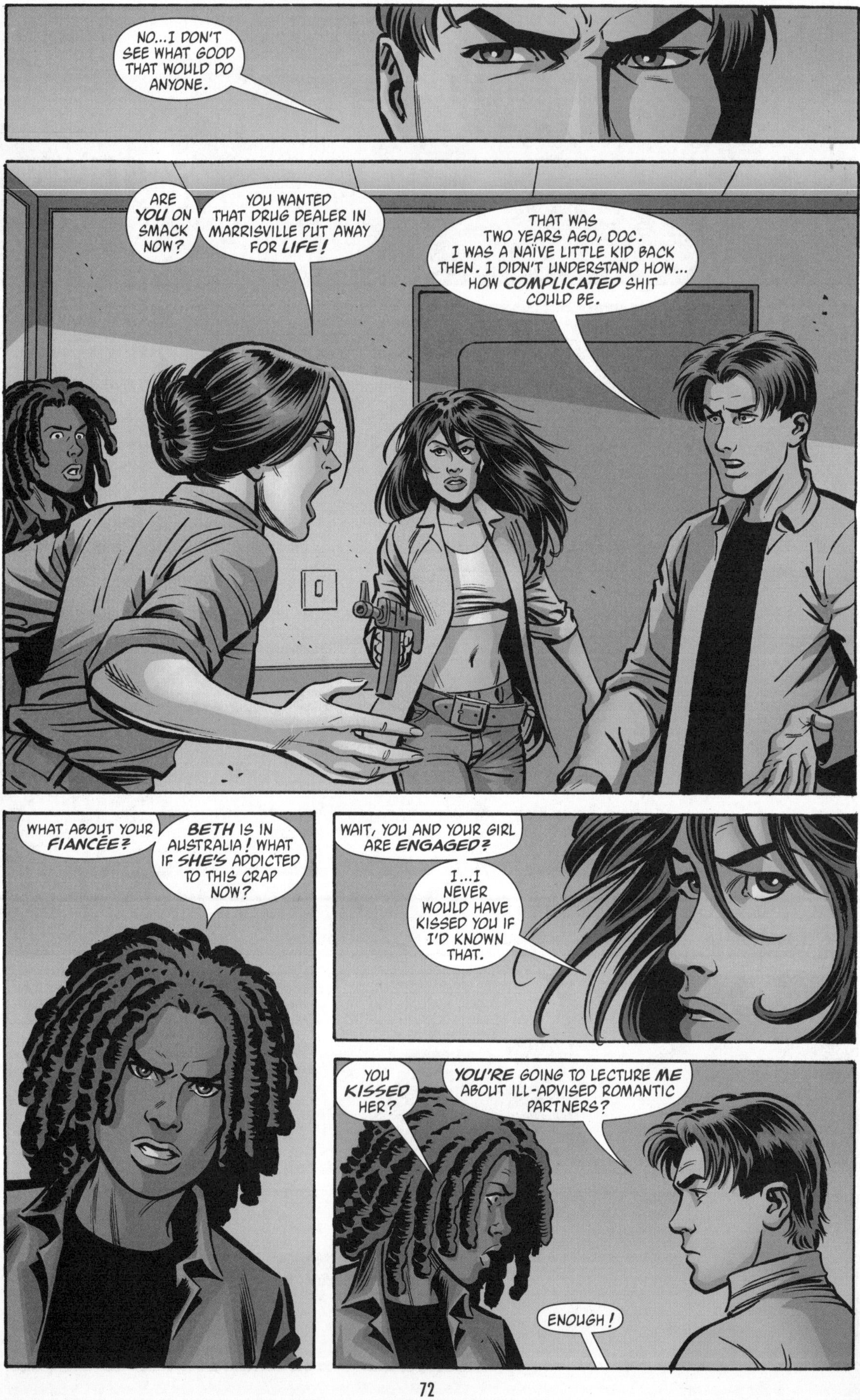
NO...I DON'T SEE WHAT GOOD THAT WOULD DO ANYONE.
ARE YOU ON SMACK NOW?
YOU WANTED THAT DRUG DEALER IN MARRISVILLE PUT AWAY FOR LIFE!
THAT WAS TWO YEARS AGO, DOC. I WAS A NAÏVE LITTLE KID BACK THEN. I DIDN'T UNDERSTAND HOW... HOW COMPLICATED SHIT COULD BE.
WHAT ABOUT YOUR FIANCÉE?
BETH IS IN AUSTRALIA! WHAT IF SHE'S ADDICTED TO THIS CRAP NOW?
WAIT, YOU AND YOUR GIRL ARE ENGAGED?
I...I NEVER WOULD HAVE KISSED YOU IF I'D KNOWN THAT.
YOU KISSED HER?
YOU'RE GOING TO LECTURE ME ABOUT ILL-ADVISED ROMANTIC PARTNERS?
ENOUGH!

YOU CAN SETTLE YOUR DOMESTIC DISPUTE AFTER WE DROP OFF OUR SHIPMENT IN *YOKOGATA*.

RIGHT NOW, I NEED THE LADIES BACK IN THE BRIG...FOR THEIR OWN SAFETY, OF COURSE.

ABSOLUTELY NOT.

YORICK, THE CYCLOPS OVER THERE *OFFED* A MEMBER OF MY CREW.

YOU'RE LUCKY I DON'T MAKE HER WALK THE *GANGPLANK* FOR--

KROOM

UHN!

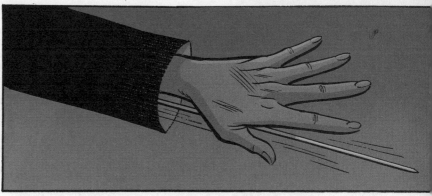

73

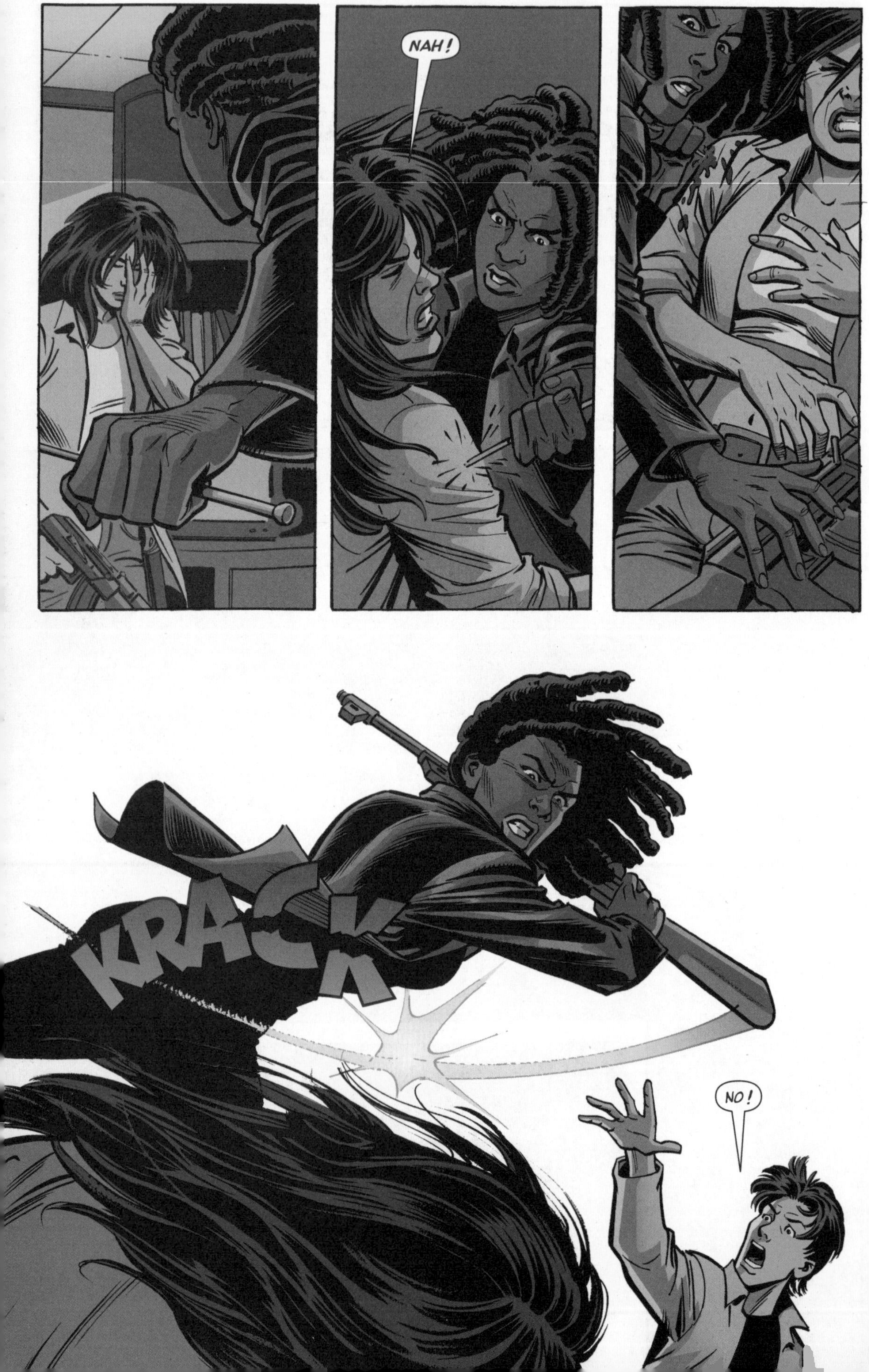
NAH!
KRACK
NO!

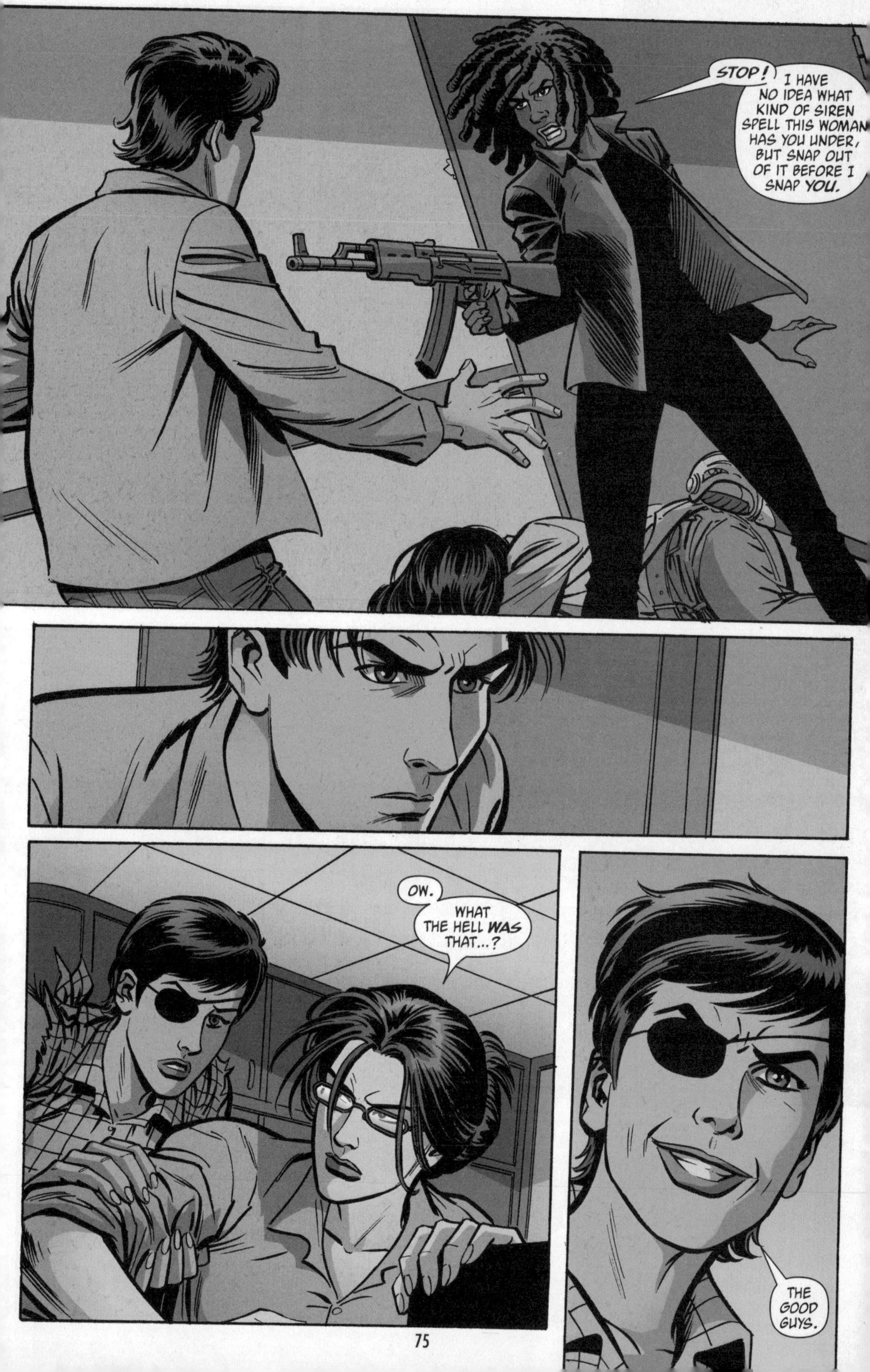
STOP! I HAVE NO IDEA WHAT KIND OF SIREN SPELL THIS WOMAN HAS YOU UNDER, BUT SNAP OUT OF IT BEFORE I SNAP YOU.
OW.
WHAT THE HELL WAS THAT...?
THE GOOD GUYS.

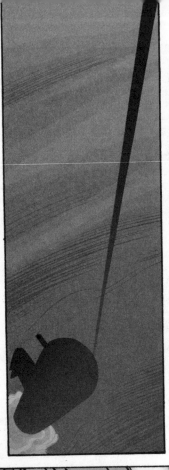

EXPLOSIVE HARP TOOK OUT THEIR STARBOARD PROPELLER SHAFT.

THEY'LL BE RUNNING IN CIRCLES IF THEY TRY TO RABBIT, MA'AM.

GOOD ENOUGH, ENSIGN.

WE'RE STILL READY TO STORM THE CASTLE AS SOON AS YOU TWO GIVE THE ORDER.

STRIKE THAT, LIEUTENANT. WE'RE HOLDING STEADY AT THIS DISTANCE.

OUR CHIEF ENGINEER IS IN CRITICAL AFTER THOSE SPLASHES. WE'RE NOT RISKING ANY MORE LIVES PLAYING *GAMES* WITH THESE WHORES.

BUT...BUT *ROSE* IS STILL ON THAT SHIP.

AND SHE KNEW THE MISSION PARAMETERS WHEN SHE VOLUNTEERED FOR UNDERCOVER.

I'M TRULY SORRY, LOVE.

READY THE MK-48S.

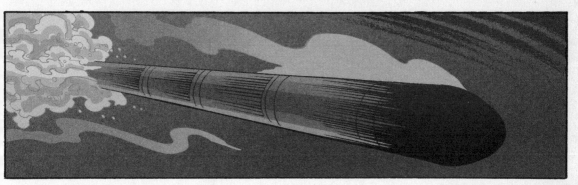

CAPTAIN, THIS IS NAVS!

TORPEDO SIGHTED OFF OUR PORT!

CAPTAIN, SHOULD WE ABANDON SHIP?

355, I--

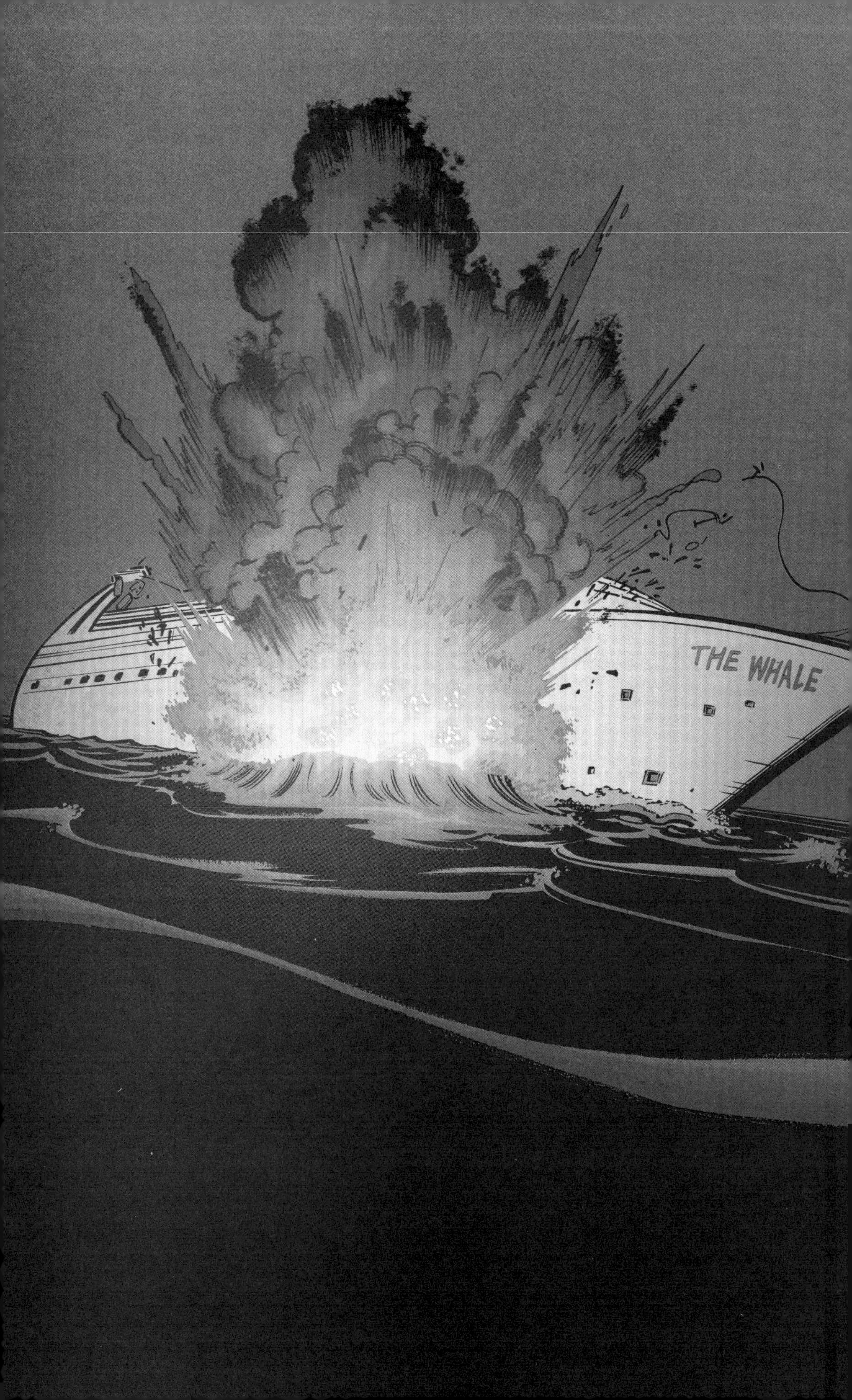
THE WHALE

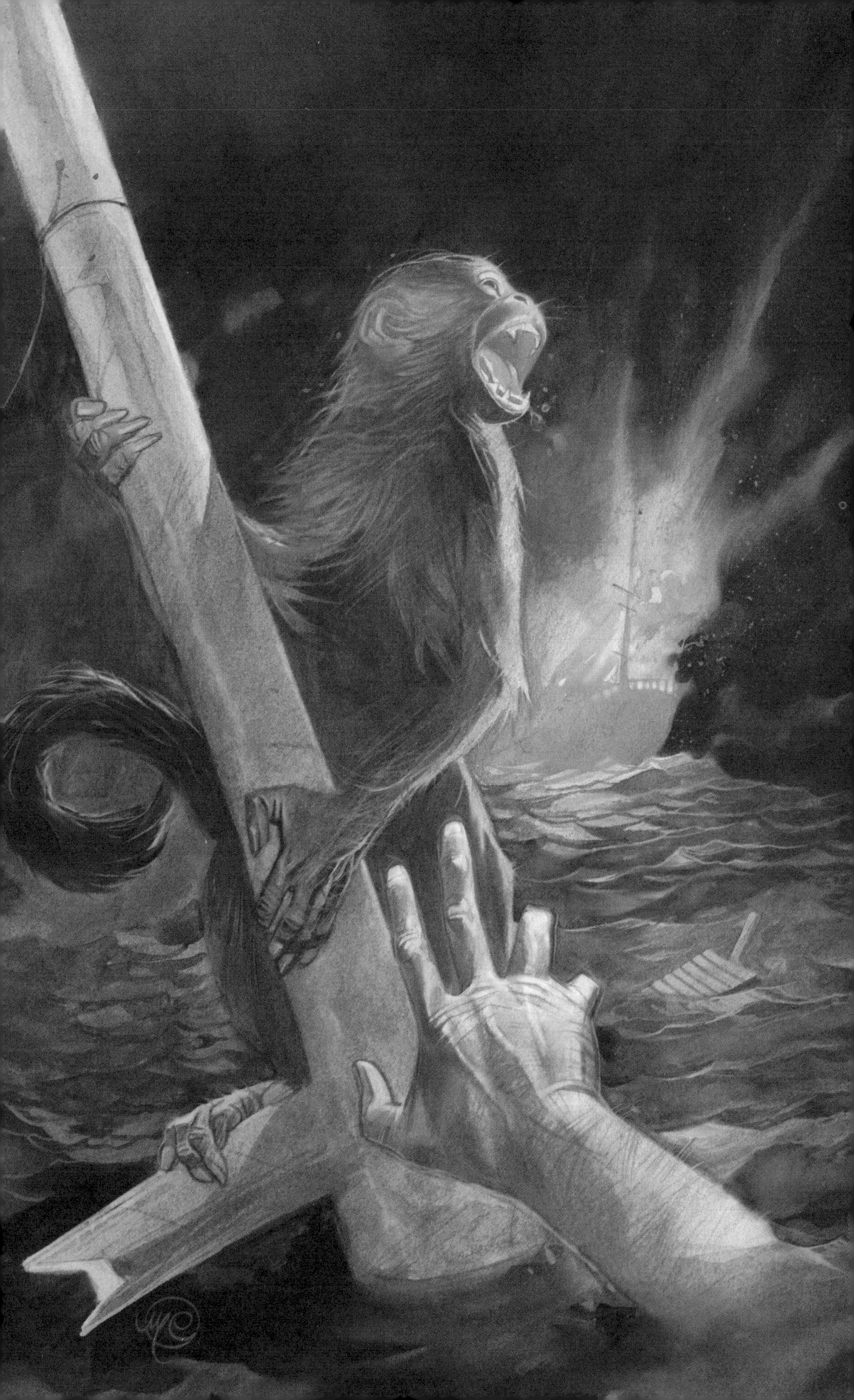

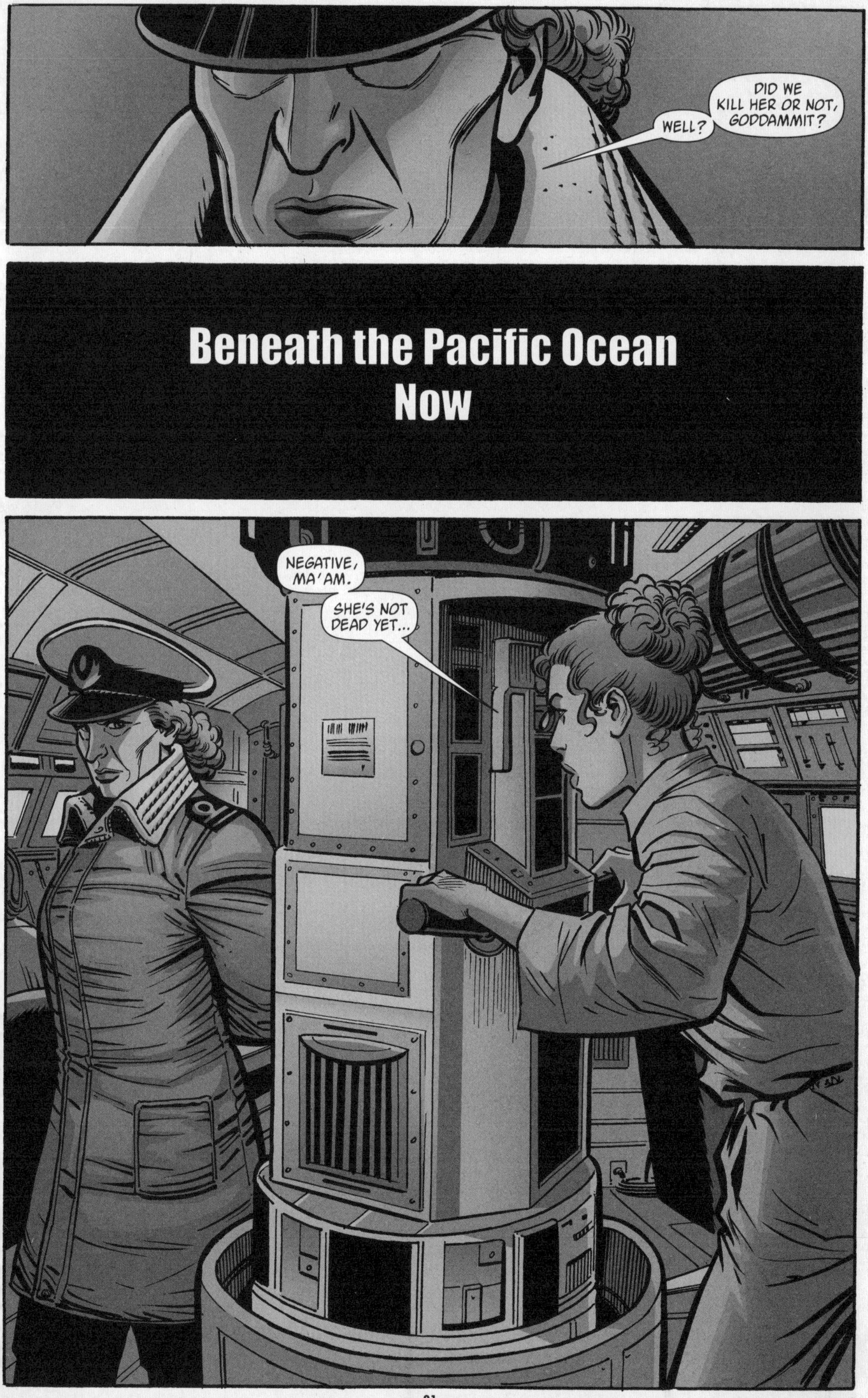
WELL?
DID WE KILL HER OR NOT, GODDAMMIT?
Beneath the Pacific Ocean
Now
NEGATIVE, MA'AM.
SHE'S NOT DEAD YET...

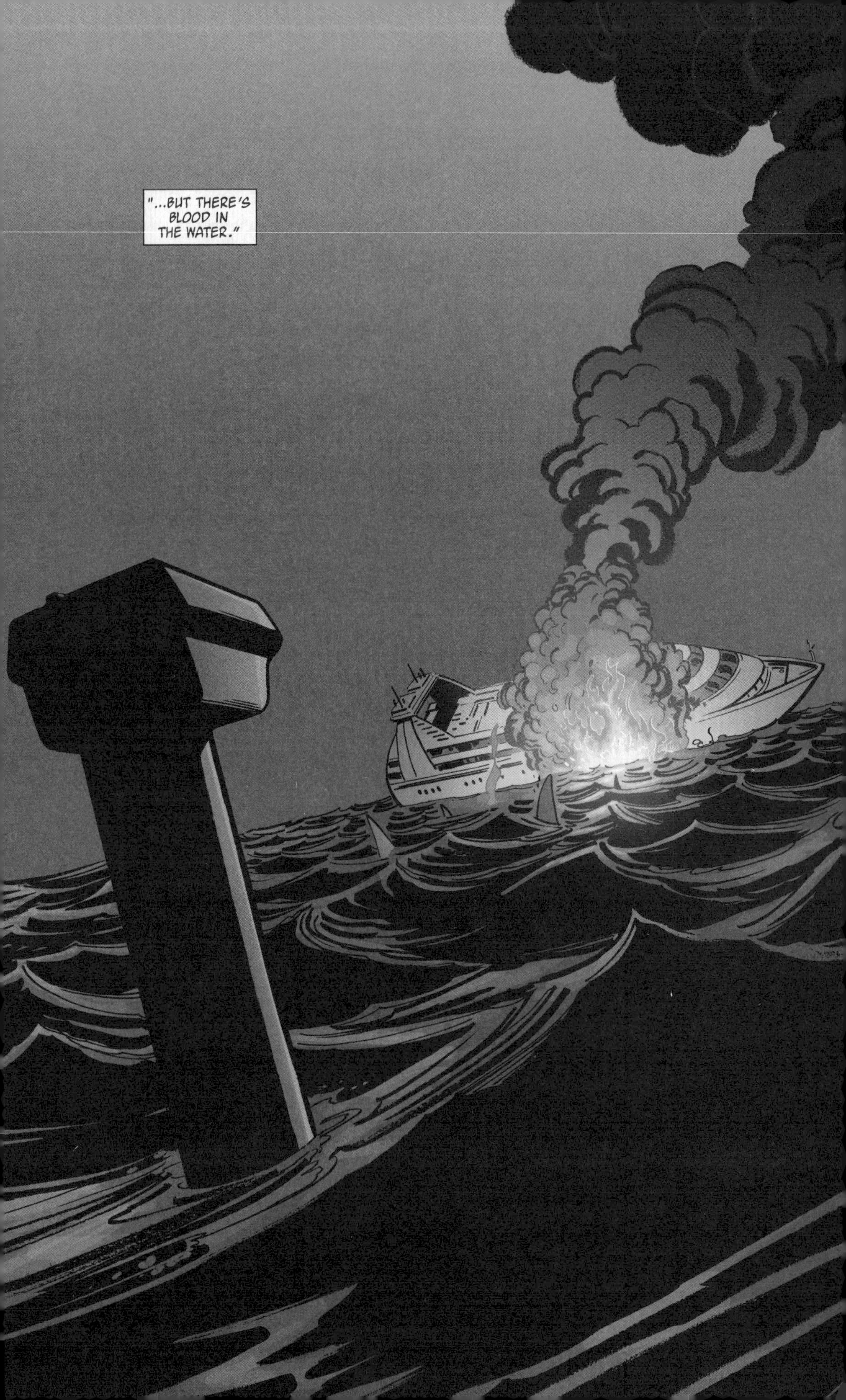
"...BUT THERE'S BLOOD IN THE WATER."

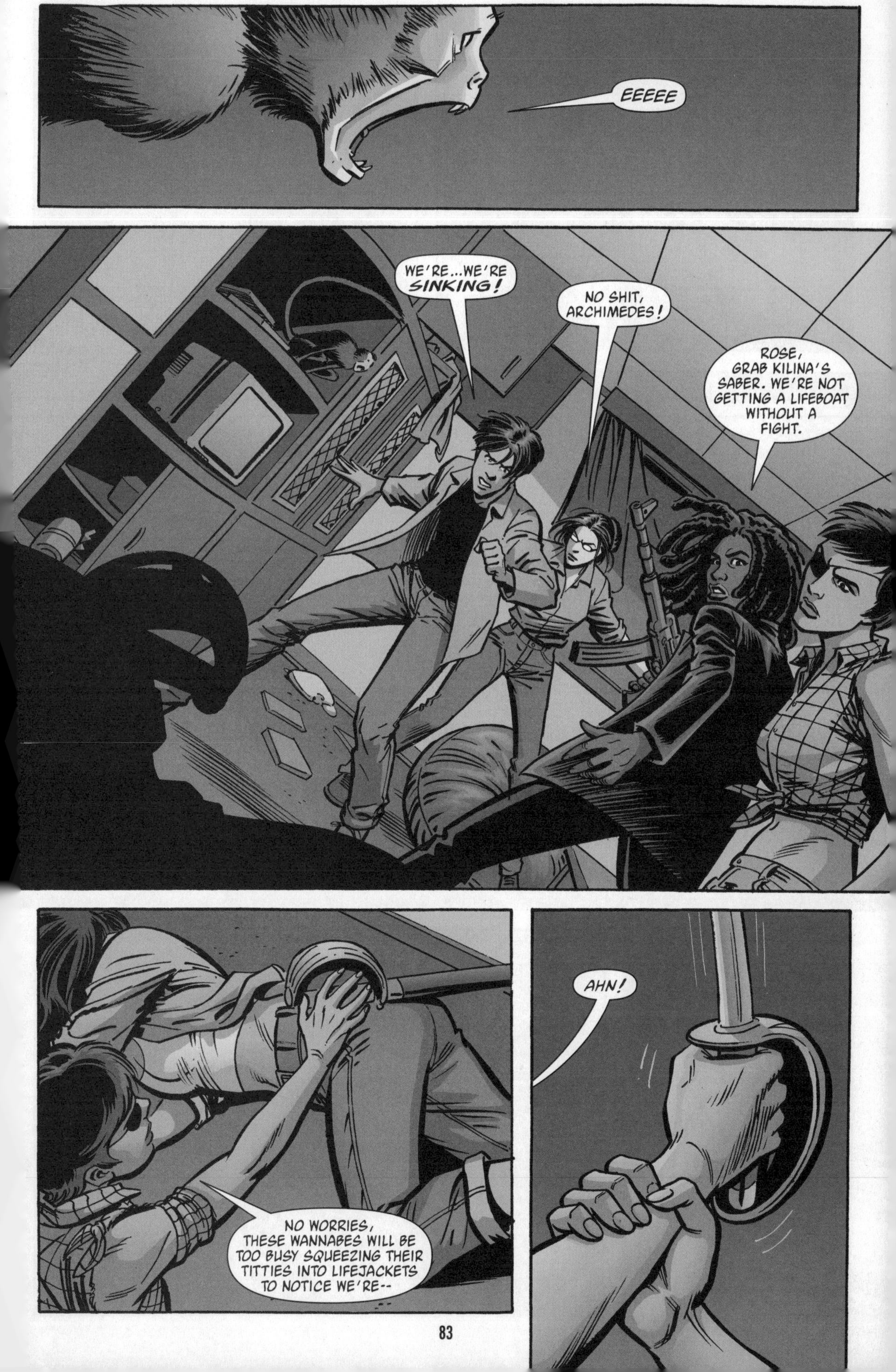
EEEEE
WE'RE...WE'RE SINKING!
NO SHIT, ARCHIMEDES!
ROSE, GRAB KILINA'S SABER. WE'RE NOT GETTING A LIFEBOAT WITHOUT A FIGHT.
NO WORRIES, THESE WANNABES WILL BE TOO BUSY SQUEEZING THEIR TITTIES INTO LIFEJACKETS TO NOTICE WE'RE--
AHN!

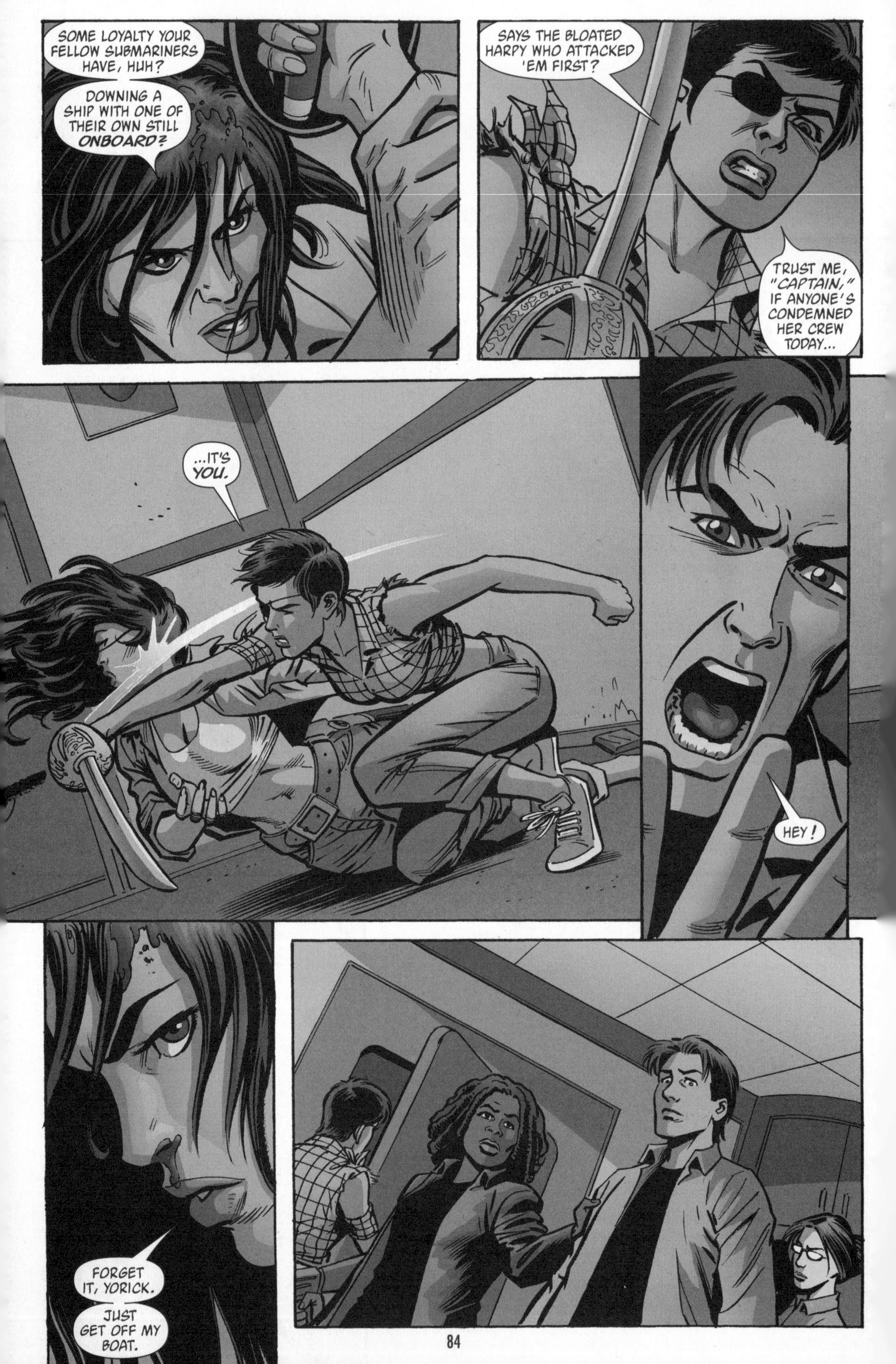
SOME LOYALTY YOUR FELLOW SUBMARINERS HAVE, HUH?
DOWNING A SHIP WITH ONE OF THEIR OWN STILL ONBOARD?
SAYS THE BLOATED HARPY WHO ATTACKED 'EM FIRST?
TRUST ME, "CAPTAIN," IF ANYONE'S CONDEMNED HER CREW TODAY...
...IT'S YOU.
HEY!
FORGET IT, YORICK.
JUST GET OFF MY BOAT.

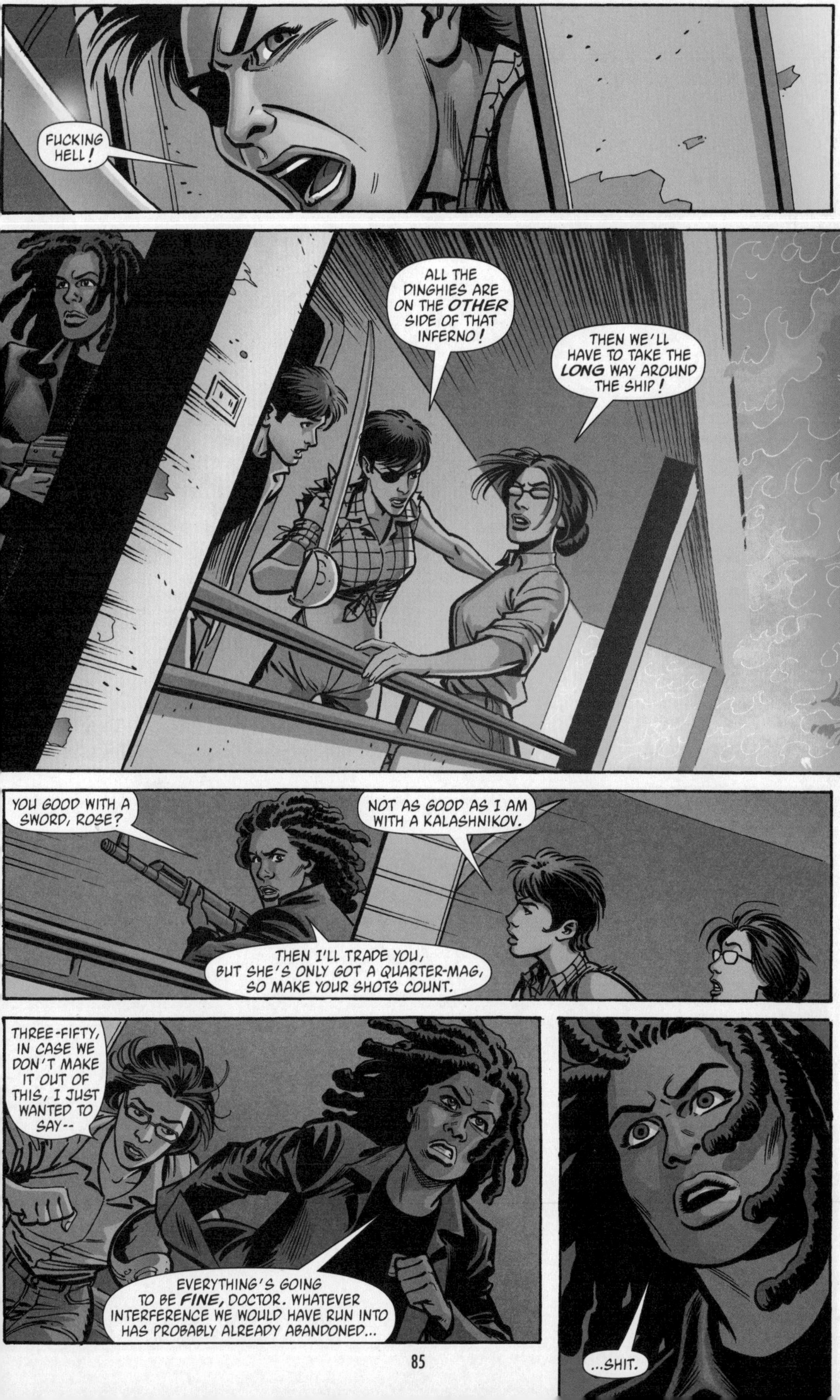
FUCKING HELL!
ALL THE DINGHIES ARE ON THE OTHER SIDE OF THAT INFERNO!
THEN WE'LL HAVE TO TAKE THE LONG WAY AROUND THE SHIP!
YOU GOOD WITH A SWORD, ROSE?
NOT AS GOOD AS I AM WITH A KALASHNIKOV.
THEN I'LL TRADE YOU, BUT SHE'S ONLY GOT A QUARTER-MAG, SO MAKE YOUR SHOTS COUNT.
THREE-FIFTY, IN CASE WE DON'T MAKE IT OUT OF THIS, I JUST WANTED TO SAY--
EVERYTHING'S GOING TO BE FINE, DOCTOR. WHATEVER INTERFERENCE WE WOULD HAVE RUN INTO HAS PROBABLY ALREADY ABANDONED...
...SHIT.

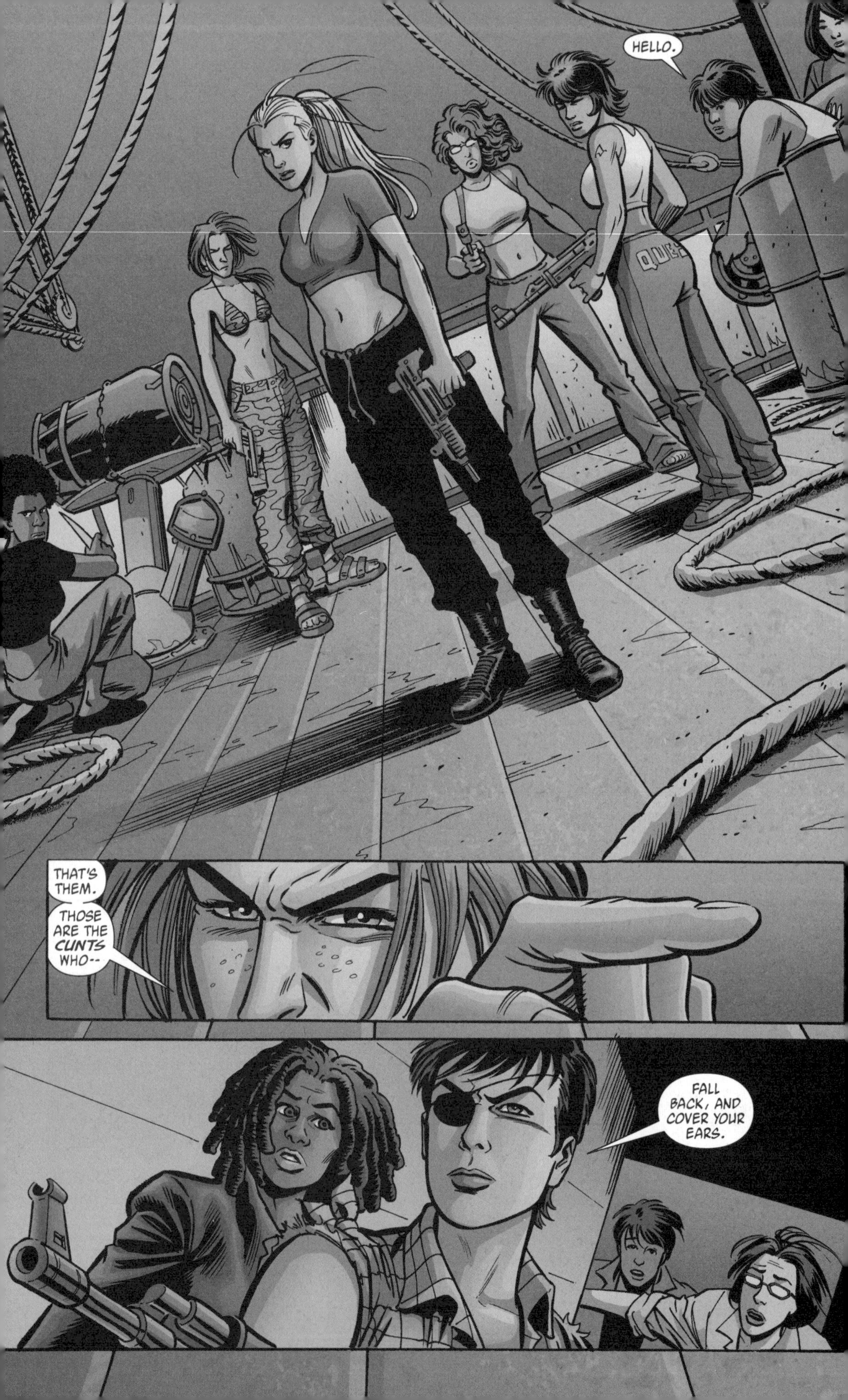
HELLO.
THAT'S THEM.
THOSE ARE THE *CUNTS* WHO--
FALL BACK, AND COVER YOUR EARS.

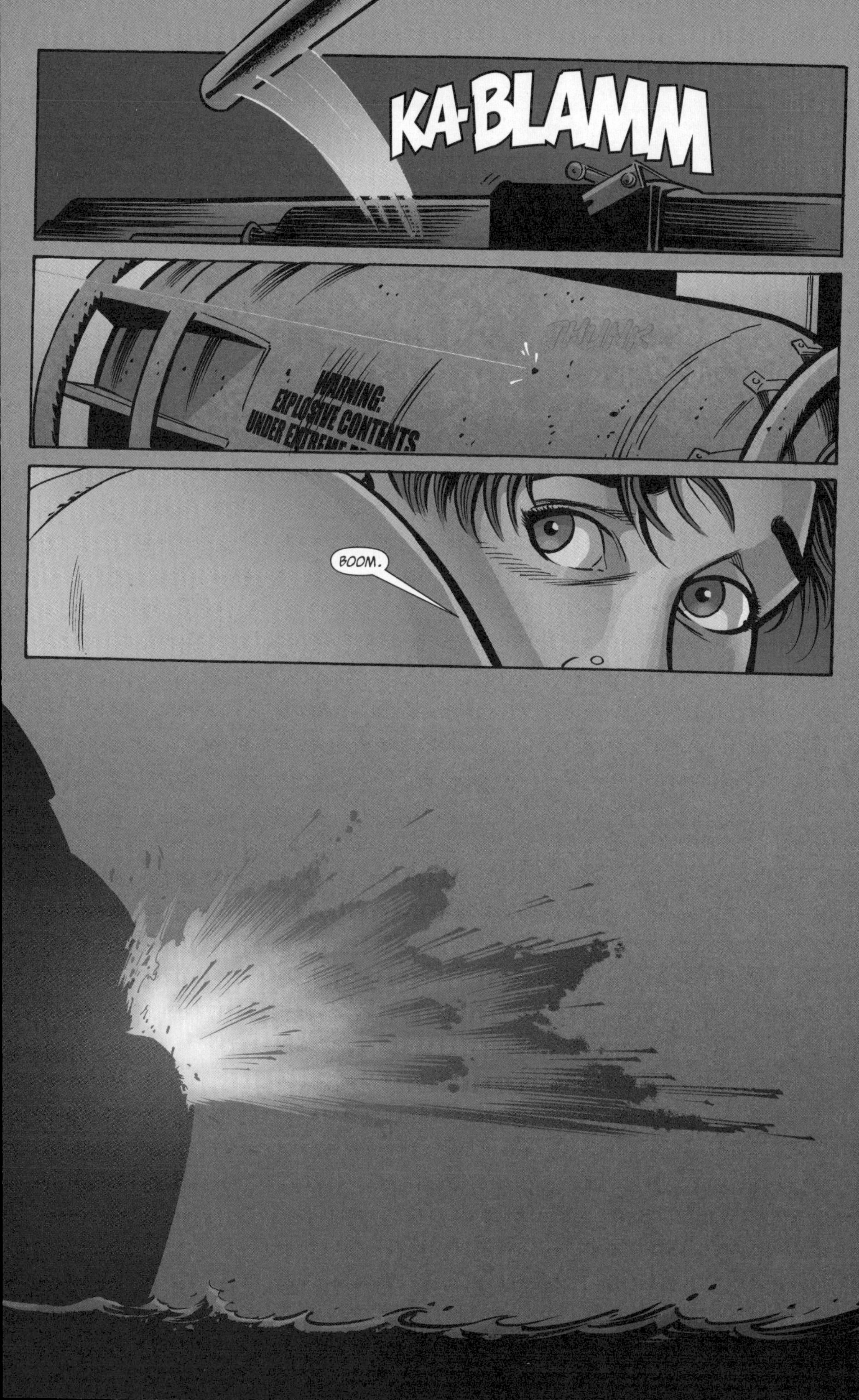
KA-BLAMM
THUNK
WARNING:
EXPLOSIVE CONTENTS
UNDER EXTREME
BOOM.

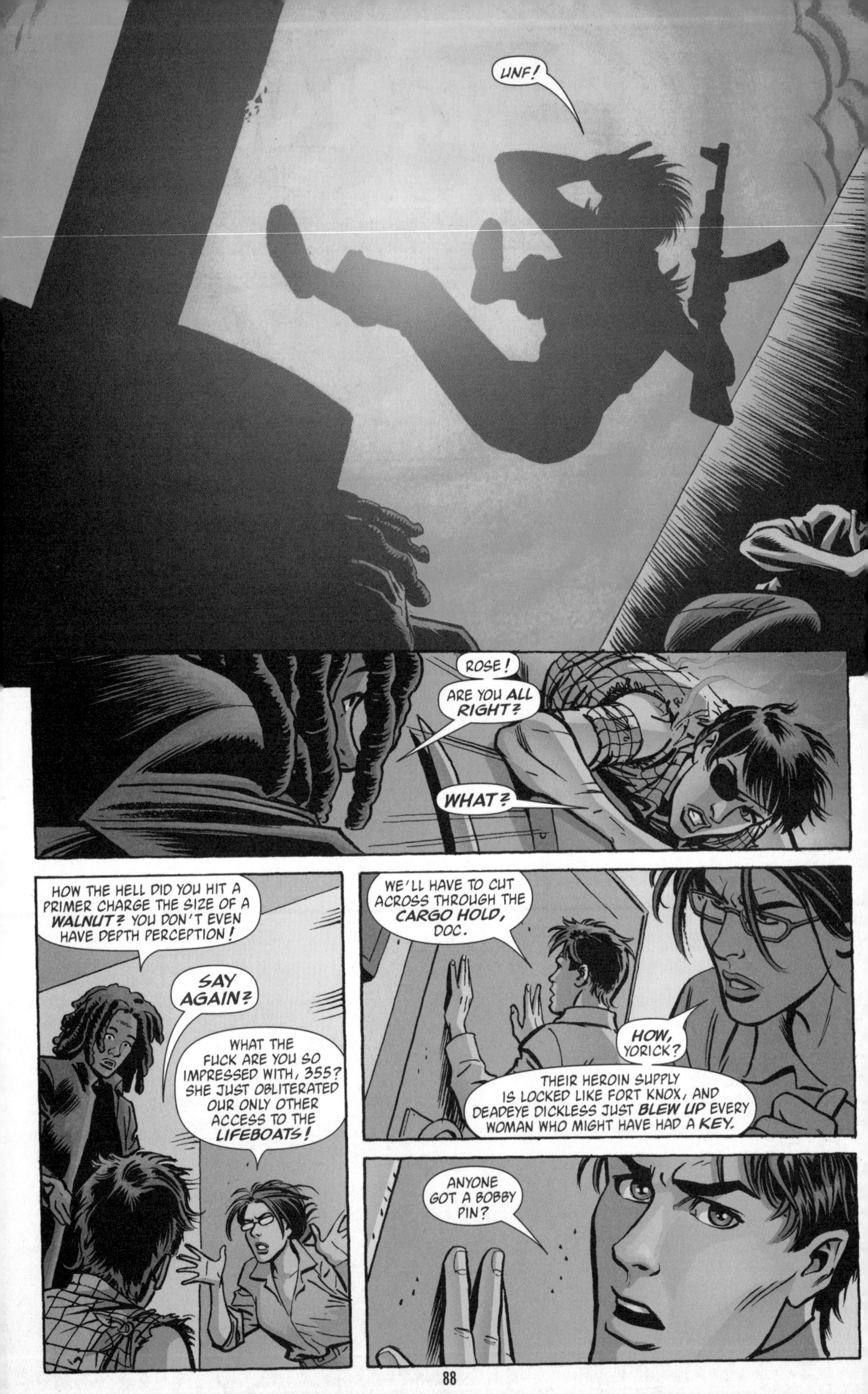
UNF!
ROSE!
ARE YOU ALL RIGHT?
WHAT?
HOW THE HELL DID YOU HIT A PRIMER CHARGE THE SIZE OF A WALNUT? YOU DON'T EVEN HAVE DEPTH PERCEPTION!
SAY AGAIN?
WHAT THE FUCK ARE YOU SO IMPRESSED WITH, 355? SHE JUST OBLITERATED OUR ONLY OTHER ACCESS TO THE LIFEBOATS!
WE'LL HAVE TO CUT ACROSS THROUGH THE CARGO HOLD, DOC.
HOW, YORICK?
THEIR HEROIN SUPPLY IS LOCKED LIKE FORT KNOX, AND DEADEYE DICKLESS JUST BLEW UP EVERY WOMAN WHO MIGHT HAVE HAD A KEY.
ANYONE GOT A BOBBY PIN?

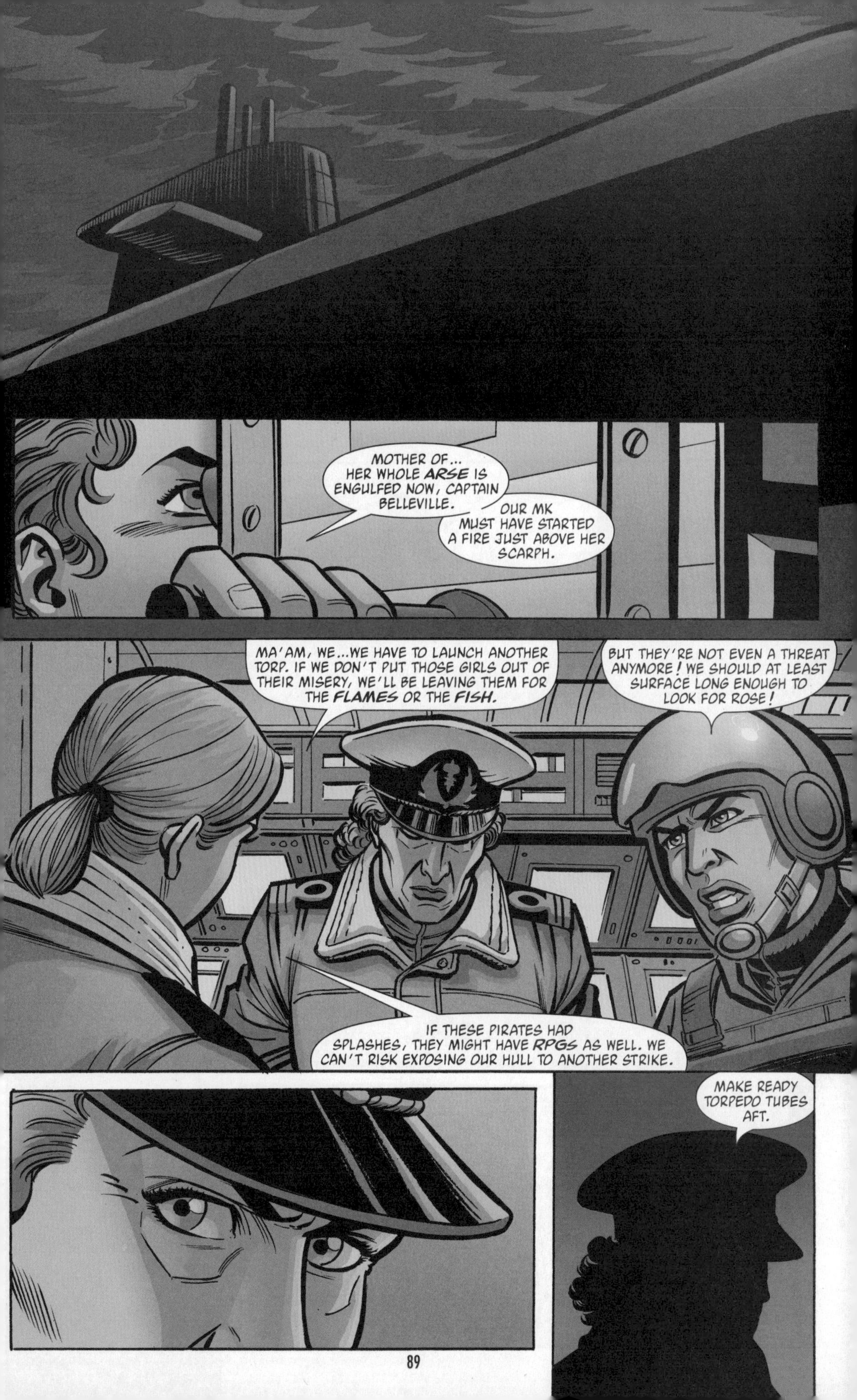
MOTHER OF... HER WHOLE ARSE IS ENGULFED NOW, CAPTAIN BELLEVILLE.
OUR MK MUST HAVE STARTED A FIRE JUST ABOVE HER SCARPH.
MA'AM, WE...WE HAVE TO LAUNCH ANOTHER TORP. IF WE DON'T PUT THOSE GIRLS OUT OF THEIR MISERY, WE'LL BE LEAVING THEM FOR THE FLAMES OR THE FISH.
BUT THEY'RE NOT EVEN A THREAT ANYMORE! WE SHOULD AT LEAST SURFACE LONG ENOUGH TO LOOK FOR ROSE!
IF THESE PIRATES HAD SPLASHES, THEY MIGHT HAVE RPGS AS WELL. WE CAN'T RISK EXPOSING OUR HULL TO ANOTHER STRIKE.
MAKE READY TORPEDO TUBES AFT.

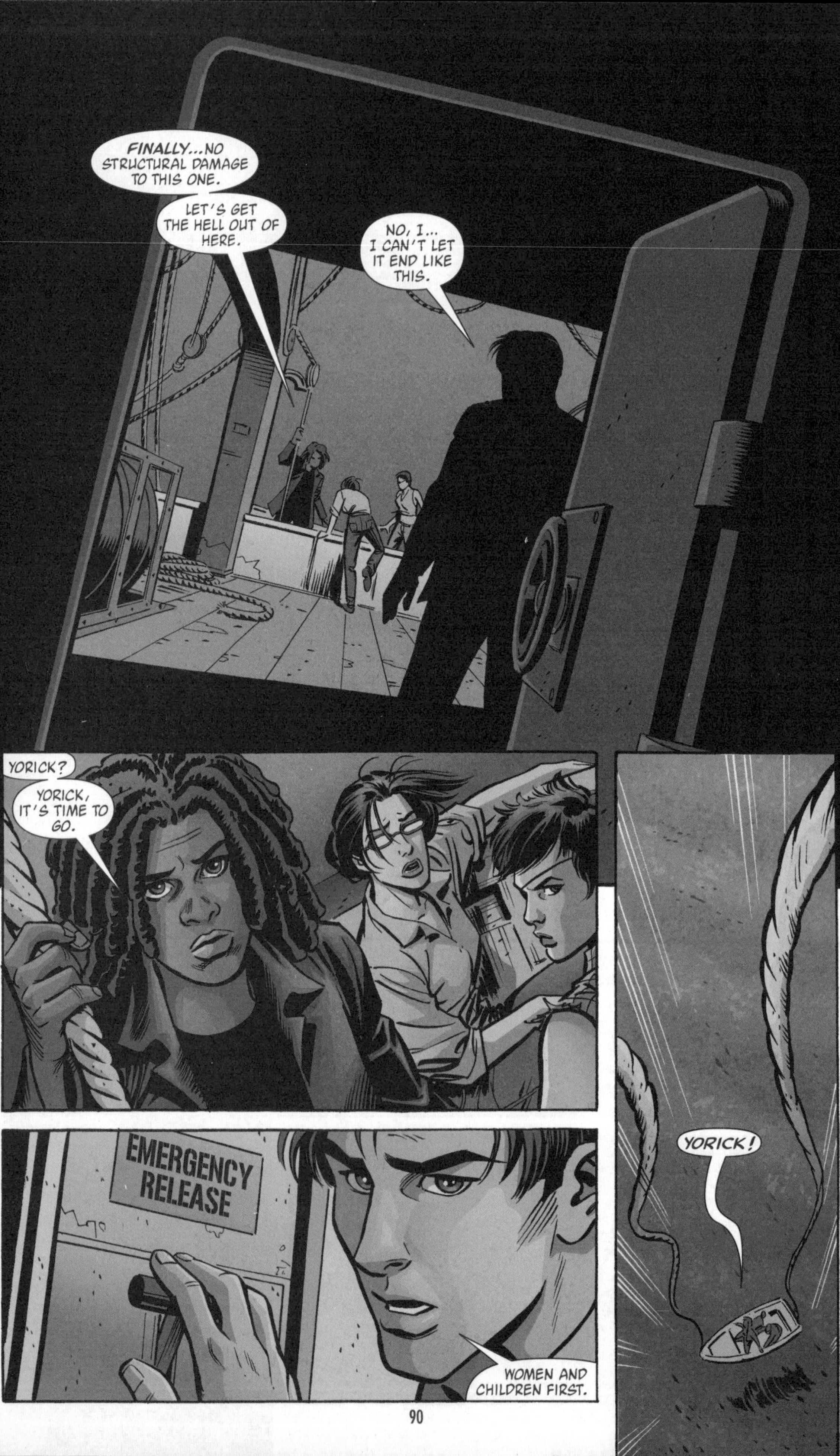
FINALLY...NO STRUCTURAL DAMAGE TO THIS ONE.
LET'S GET THE HELL OUT OF HERE.
NO, I... I CAN'T LET IT END LIKE THIS.
YORICK?
YORICK, IT'S TIME TO GO.
EMERGENCY RELEASE
WOMEN AND CHILDREN FIRST.
YORICK!

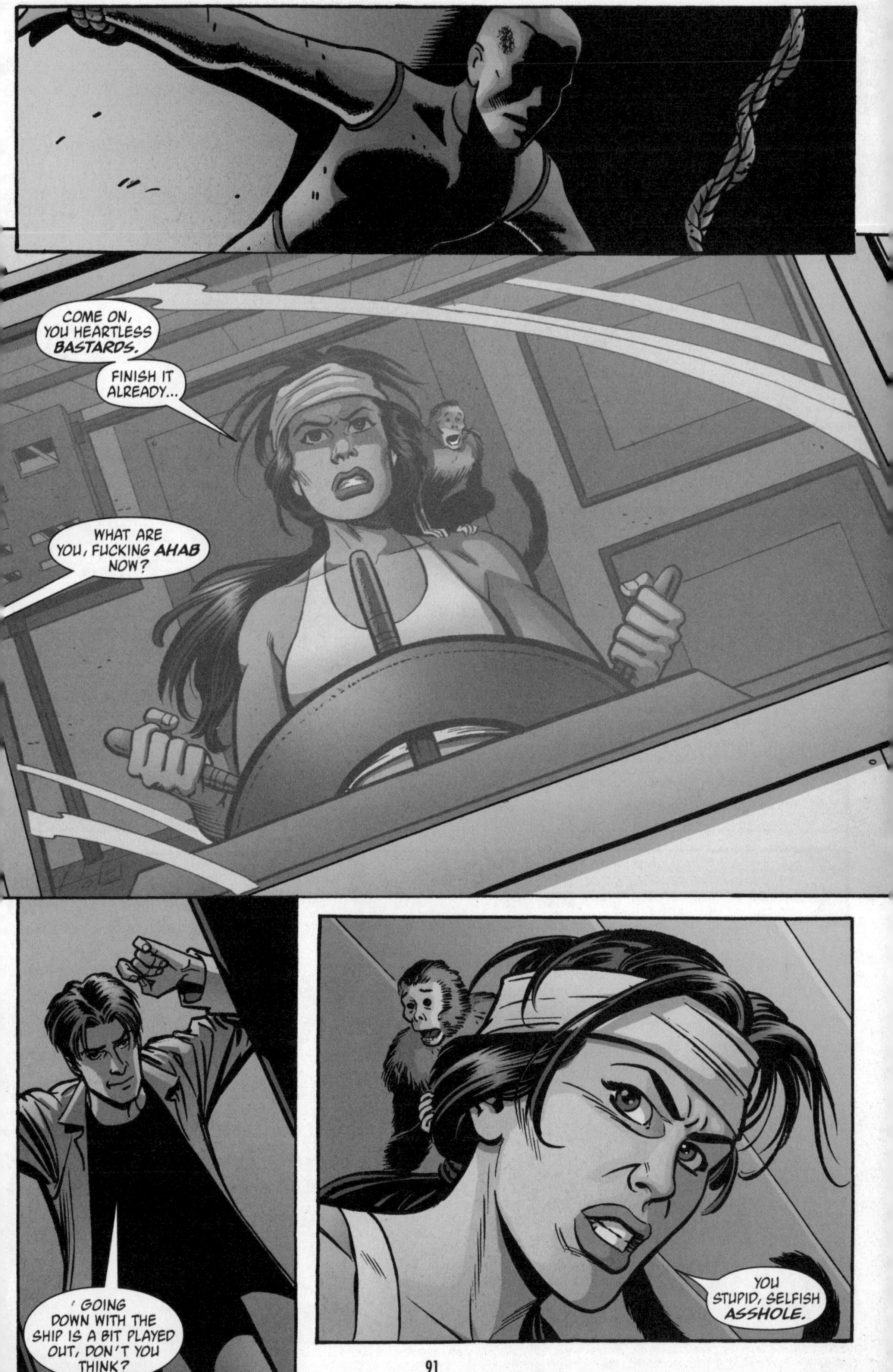
COME ON, YOU HEARTLESS *BASTARDS.*
FINISH IT ALREADY...
WHAT ARE YOU, FUCKING *AHAB* NOW?
'GOING DOWN WITH THE SHIP IS A BIT PLAYED OUT, DON'T YOU THINK?
YOU STUPID, SELFISH *ASSHOLE.*

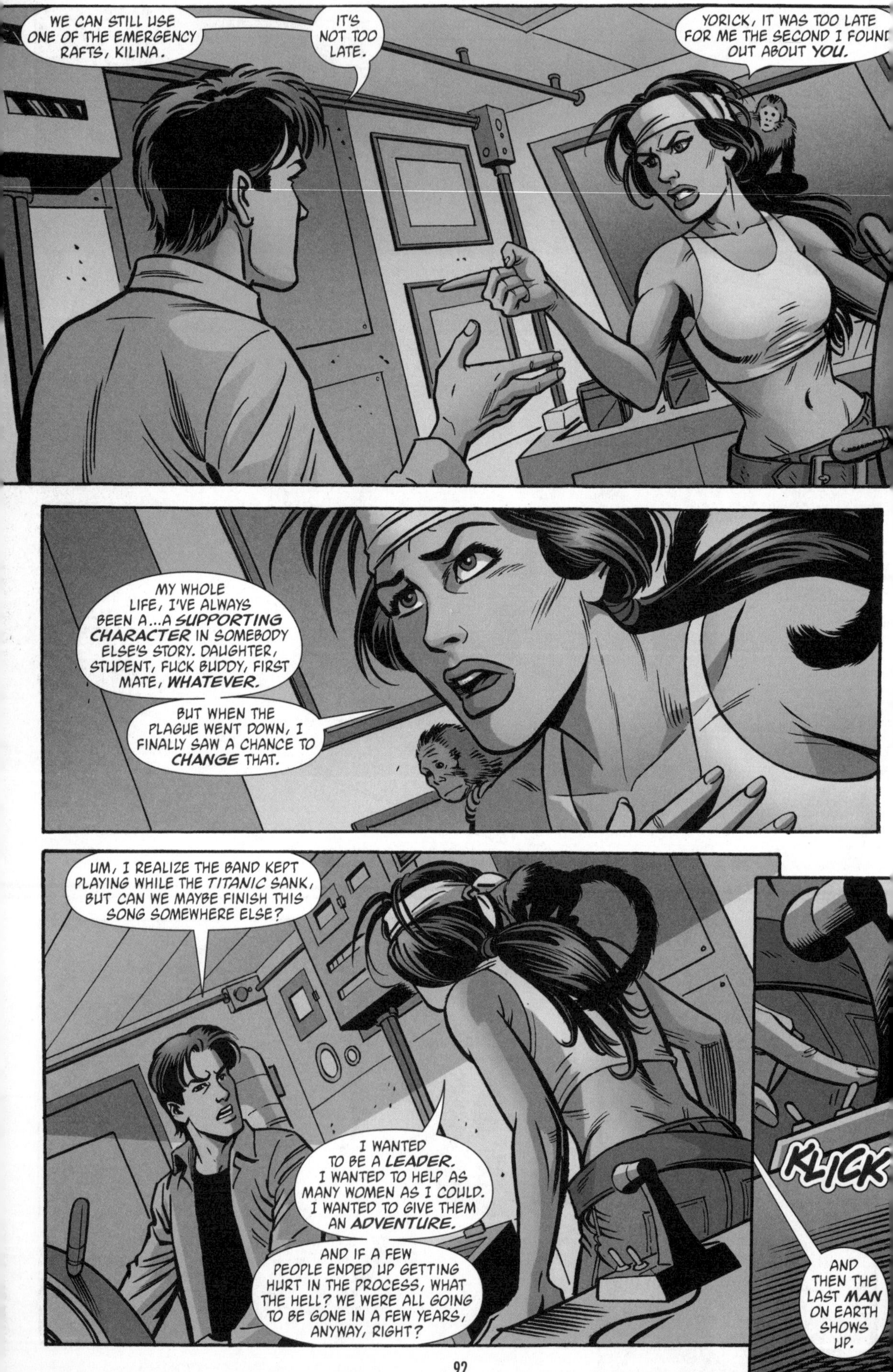

WE CAN STILL USE ONE OF THE EMERGENCY RAFTS, KILINA.
IT'S NOT TOO LATE.
YORICK, IT WAS TOO LATE FOR ME THE SECOND I FOUND OUT ABOUT YOU.
MY WHOLE LIFE, I'VE ALWAYS BEEN A...A SUPPORTING CHARACTER IN SOMEBODY ELSE'S STORY. DAUGHTER, STUDENT, FUCK BUDDY, FIRST MATE, WHATEVER.
BUT WHEN THE PLAGUE WENT DOWN, I FINALLY SAW A CHANCE TO CHANGE THAT.
UM, I REALIZE THE BAND KEPT PLAYING WHILE THE TITANIC SANK, BUT CAN WE MAYBE FINISH THIS SONG SOMEWHERE ELSE?
I WANTED TO BE A LEADER. I WANTED TO HELP AS MANY WOMEN AS I COULD. I WANTED TO GIVE THEM AN ADVENTURE.
AND IF A FEW PEOPLE ENDED UP GETTING HURT IN THE PROCESS, WHAT THE HELL? WE WERE ALL GOING TO BE GONE IN A FEW YEARS, ANYWAY, RIGHT?
KLICK
AND THEN THE LAST MAN ON EARTH SHOWS UP.

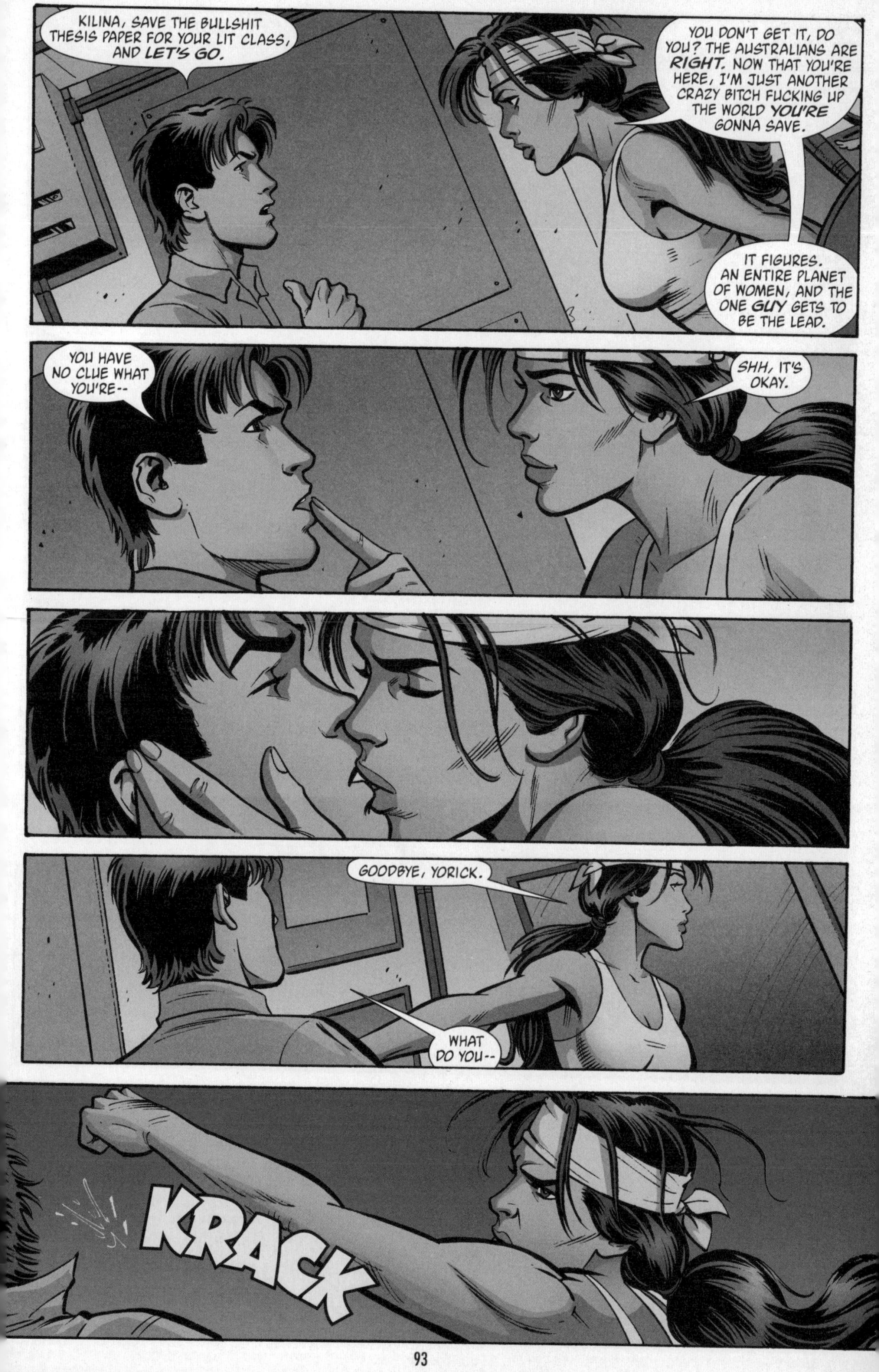
KILINA, SAVE THE BULLSHIT THESIS PAPER FOR YOUR LIT CLASS, AND LET'S GO.
YOU DON'T GET IT, DO YOU? THE AUSTRALIANS ARE RIGHT. NOW THAT YOU'RE HERE, I'M JUST ANOTHER CRAZY BITCH FUCKING UP THE WORLD YOU'RE GONNA SAVE.
IT FIGURES. AN ENTIRE PLANET OF WOMEN, AND THE ONE GUY GETS TO BE THE LEAD.
YOU HAVE NO CLUE WHAT YOU'RE--
SHH, IT'S OKAY.
GOODBYE, YORICK.
WHAT DO YOU--
KRACK

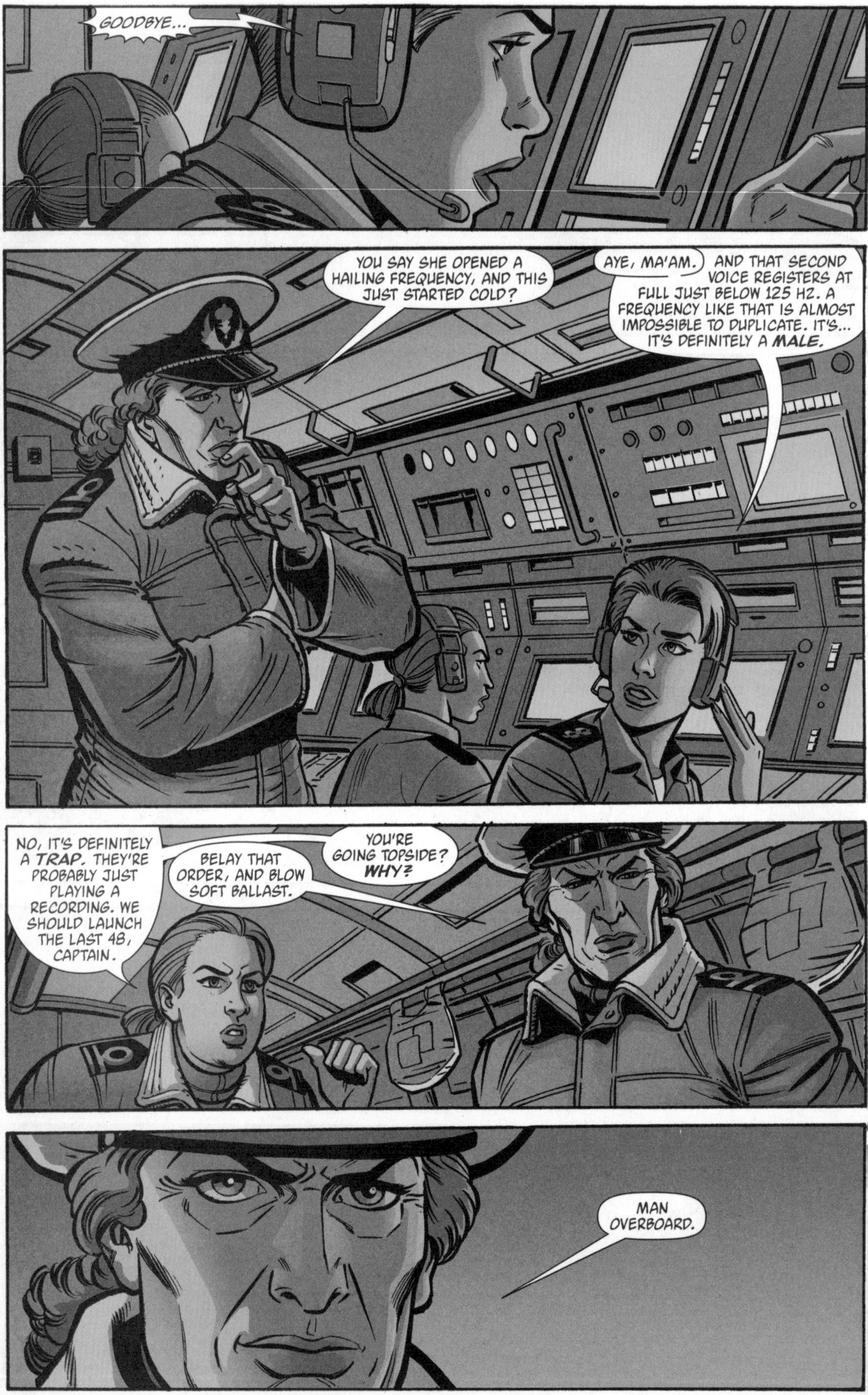
GOODBYE...
YOU SAY SHE OPENED A HAILING FREQUENCY, AND THIS JUST STARTED COLD?
AYE, MA'AM.
AND THAT SECOND VOICE REGISTERS AT FULL JUST BELOW 125 HZ. A FREQUENCY LIKE THAT IS ALMOST IMPOSSIBLE TO DUPLICATE. IT'S... IT'S DEFINITELY A **MALE.**
NO, IT'S DEFINITELY A **TRAP.** THEY'RE PROBABLY JUST PLAYING A RECORDING. WE SHOULD LAUNCH THE LAST 48, CAPTAIN.
BELAY THAT ORDER, AND BLOW SOFT BALLAST.
YOU'RE GOING TOPSIDE? **WHY?**
MAN OVERBOARD.

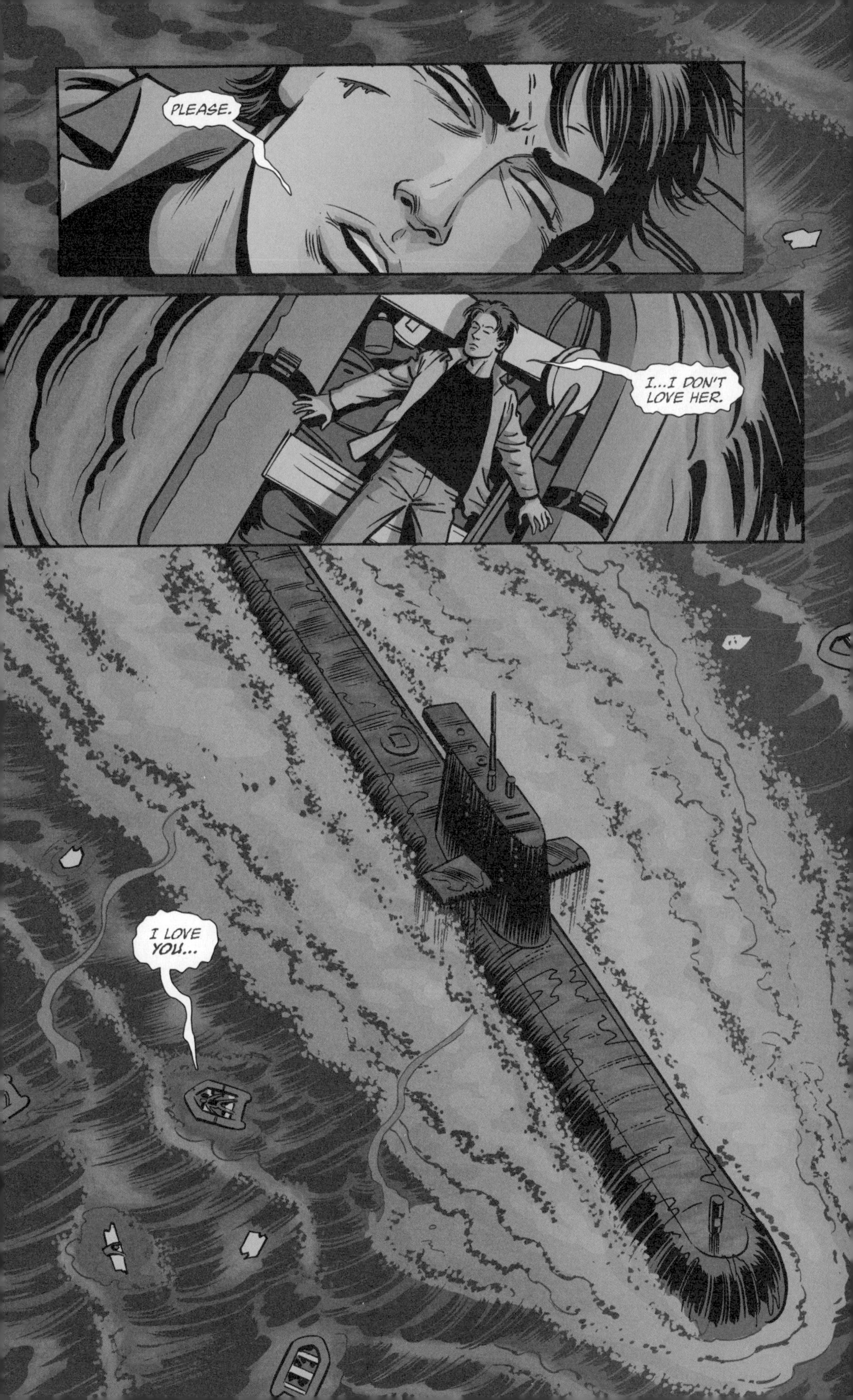
PLEASE.
I...I DON'T LOVE HER.
I LOVE YOU...

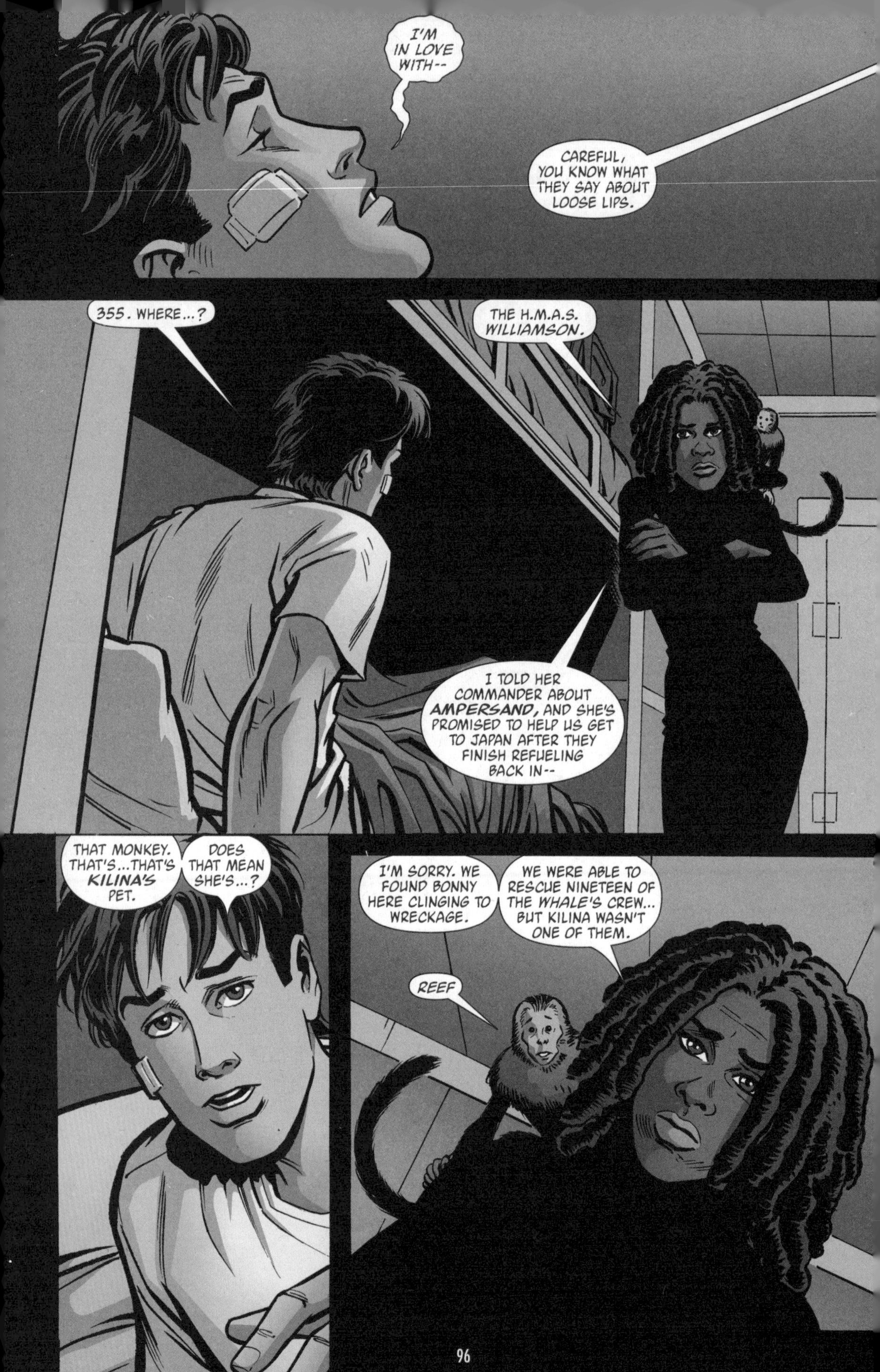

I'M IN LOVE WITH--
CAREFUL, YOU KNOW WHAT THEY SAY ABOUT LOOSE LIPS.
355. WHERE...?
THE H.M.A.S. WILLIAMSON.
I TOLD HER COMMANDER ABOUT AMPERSAND, AND SHE'S PROMISED TO HELP US GET TO JAPAN AFTER THEY FINISH REFUELING BACK IN--
THAT MONKEY. THAT'S...THAT'S KILINA'S PET.
DOES THAT MEAN SHE'S...?
I'M SORRY. WE FOUND BONNY HERE CLINGING TO WRECKAGE.
WE WERE ABLE TO RESCUE NINETEEN OF THE WHALE'S CREW... BUT KILINA WASN'T ONE OF THEM.
REEF

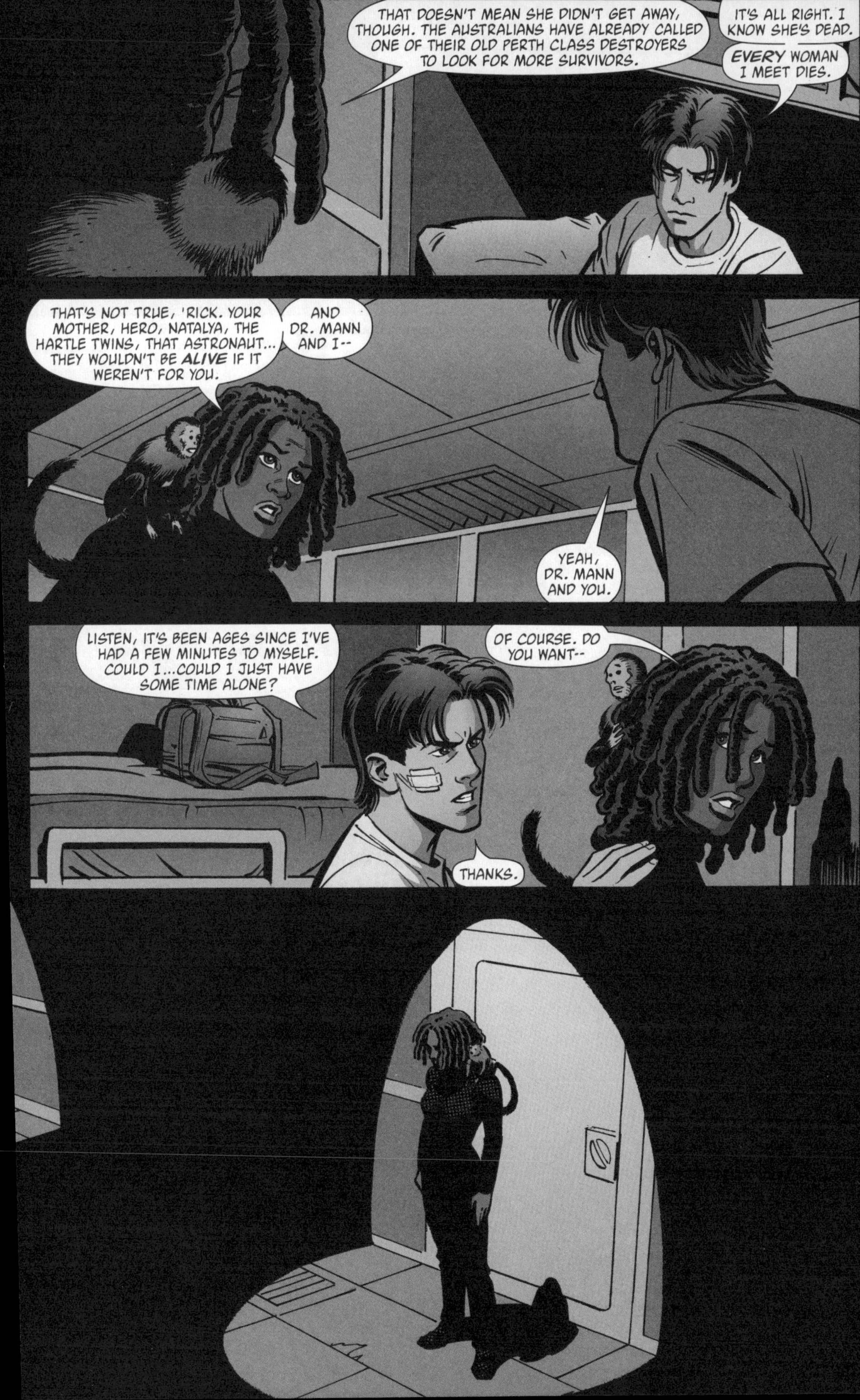

THAT DOESN'T MEAN SHE DIDN'T GET AWAY, THOUGH. THE AUSTRALIANS HAVE ALREADY CALLED ONE OF THEIR OLD PERTH CLASS DESTROYERS TO LOOK FOR MORE SURVIVORS.
IT'S ALL RIGHT. I KNOW SHE'S DEAD.
EVERY WOMAN I MEET DIES.
THAT'S NOT TRUE, 'RICK. YOUR MOTHER, HERO, NATALYA, THE HARTLE TWINS, THAT ASTRONAUT... THEY WOULDN'T BE *ALIVE* IF IT WEREN'T FOR YOU.
AND DR. MANN AND I--
YEAH, DR. MANN AND YOU.
LISTEN, IT'S BEEN AGES SINCE I'VE HAD A FEW MINUTES TO MYSELF. COULD I...COULD I JUST HAVE SOME TIME ALONE?
OF COURSE. DO YOU WANT--
THANKS.

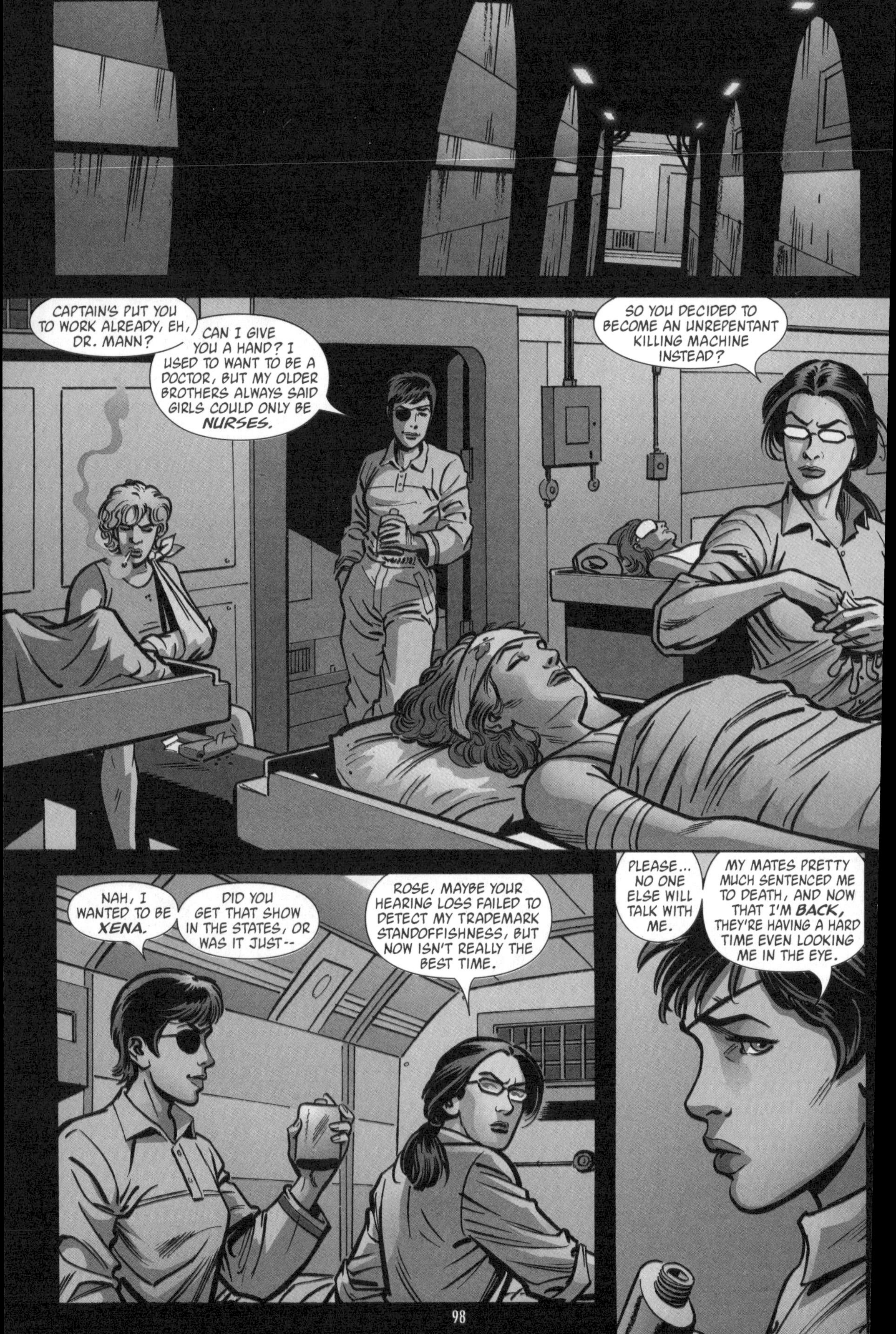
CAPTAIN'S PUT YOU TO WORK ALREADY, EH, DR. MANN?
CAN I GIVE YOU A HAND? I USED TO WANT TO BE A DOCTOR, BUT MY OLDER BROTHERS ALWAYS SAID GIRLS COULD ONLY BE **NURSES.**
SO YOU DECIDED TO BECOME AN UNREPENTANT KILLING MACHINE INSTEAD?
NAH, I WANTED TO BE **XENA.**
DID YOU GET THAT SHOW IN THE STATES, OR WAS IT JUST--
ROSE, MAYBE YOUR HEARING LOSS FAILED TO DETECT MY TRADEMARK STANDOFFISHNESS, BUT NOW ISN'T REALLY THE BEST TIME.
PLEASE... NO ONE ELSE WILL TALK WITH ME.
MY MATES PRETTY MUCH SENTENCED ME TO DEATH, AND NOW THAT I'M **BACK,** THEY'RE HAVING A HARD TIME EVEN LOOKING ME IN THE EYE.

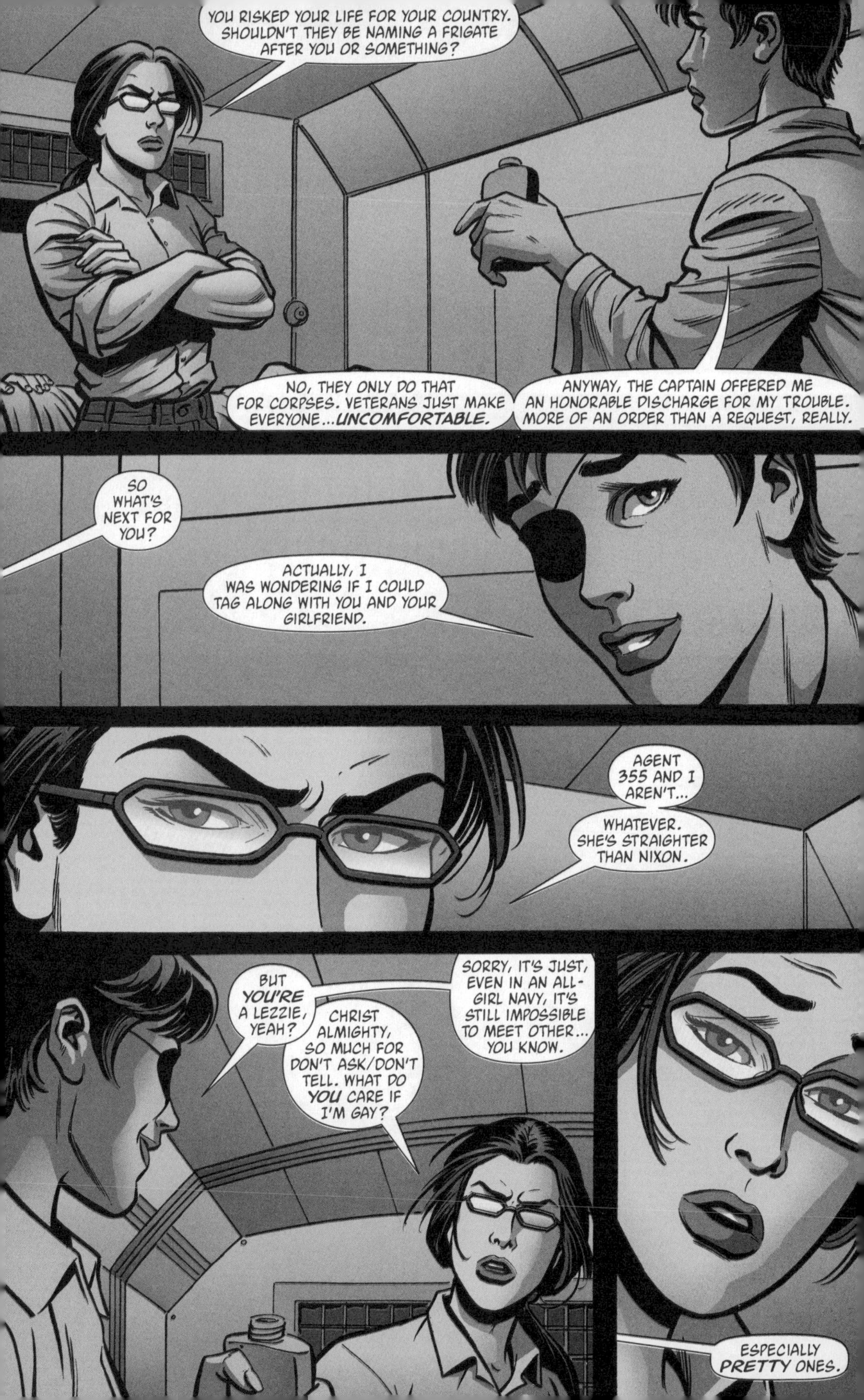
YOU RISKED YOUR LIFE FOR YOUR COUNTRY. SHOULDN'T THEY BE NAMING A FRIGATE AFTER YOU OR SOMETHING?
NO, THEY ONLY DO THAT FOR CORPSES. VETERANS JUST MAKE EVERYONE... UNCOMFORTABLE.
ANYWAY, THE CAPTAIN OFFERED ME AN HONORABLE DISCHARGE FOR MY TROUBLE. MORE OF AN ORDER THAN A REQUEST, REALLY.
SO WHAT'S NEXT FOR YOU?
ACTUALLY, I WAS WONDERING IF I COULD TAG ALONG WITH YOU AND YOUR GIRLFRIEND.
AGENT 355 AND I AREN'T...
WHATEVER. SHE'S STRAIGHTER THAN NIXON.
BUT YOU'RE A LEZZIE, YEAH?
CHRIST ALMIGHTY, SO MUCH FOR DON'T ASK/DON'T TELL. WHAT DO YOU CARE IF I'M GAY?
SORRY, IT'S JUST, EVEN IN AN ALL-GIRL NAVY, IT'S STILL IMPOSSIBLE TO MEET OTHER... YOU KNOW.
ESPECIALLY PRETTY ONES.

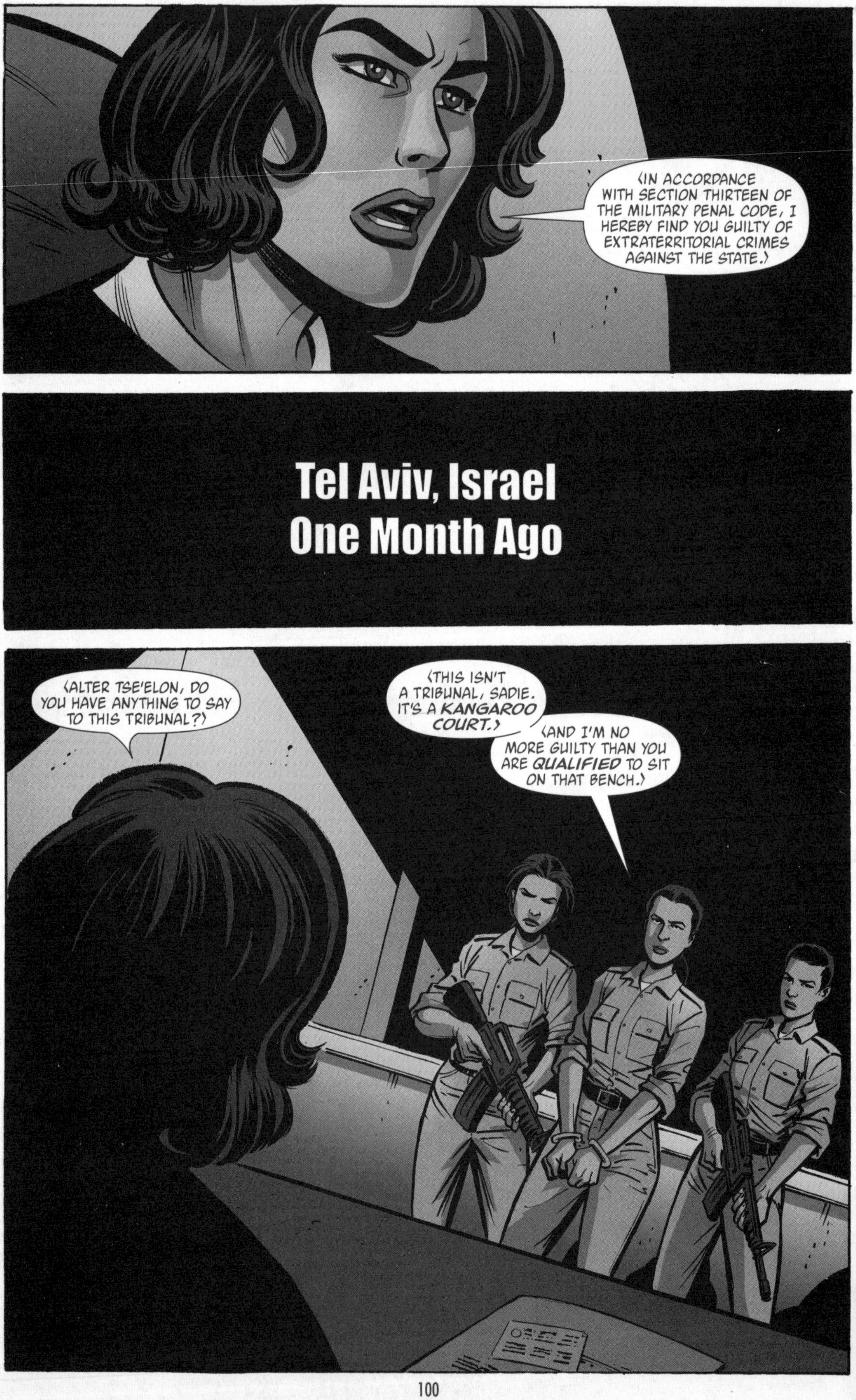
‹IN ACCORDANCE WITH SECTION THIRTEEN OF THE MILITARY PENAL CODE, I HEREBY FIND YOU GUILTY OF EXTRATERRITORIAL CRIMES AGAINST THE STATE.›
Tel Aviv, Israel
One Month Ago
‹ALTER TSE'ELON, DO YOU HAVE ANYTHING TO SAY TO THIS TRIBUNAL?›
‹THIS ISN'T A TRIBUNAL, SADIE. IT'S A KANGAROO COURT.›
‹AND I'M NO MORE GUILTY THAN YOU ARE QUALIFIED TO SIT ON THAT BENCH.›

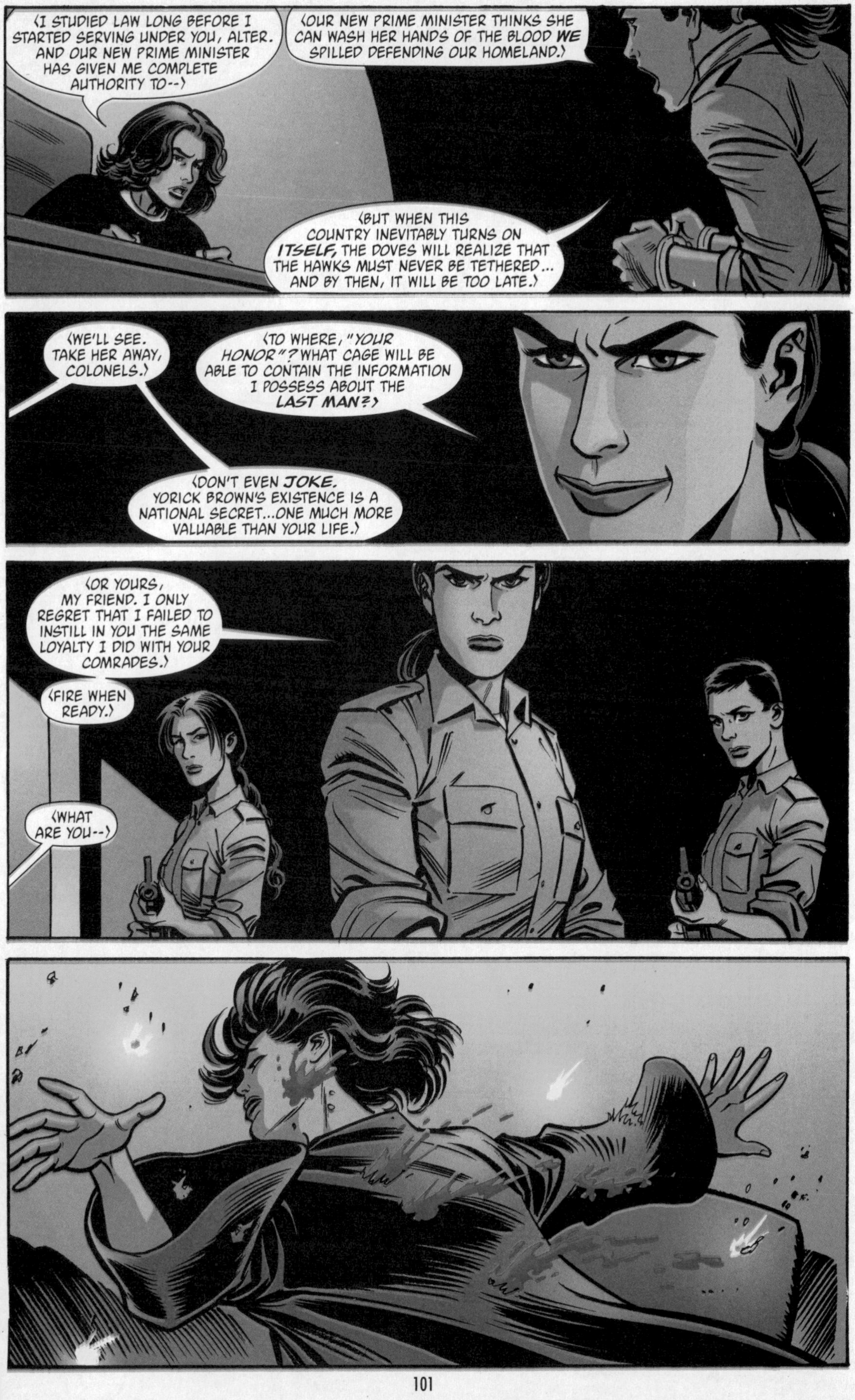
‹I STUDIED LAW LONG BEFORE I STARTED SERVING UNDER YOU, ALTER. AND OUR NEW PRIME MINISTER HAS GIVEN ME COMPLETE AUTHORITY TO--›
‹OUR NEW PRIME MINISTER THINKS SHE CAN WASH HER HANDS OF THE BLOOD WE SPILLED DEFENDING OUR HOMELAND.›
‹BUT WHEN THIS COUNTRY INEVITABLY TURNS ON ITSELF, THE DOVES WILL REALIZE THAT THE HAWKS MUST NEVER BE TETHERED... AND BY THEN, IT WILL BE TOO LATE.›
‹WE'LL SEE. TAKE HER AWAY, COLONELS.›
‹TO WHERE, "YOUR HONOR"? WHAT CAGE WILL BE ABLE TO CONTAIN THE INFORMATION I POSSESS ABOUT THE LAST MAN?›
‹DON'T EVEN JOKE. YORICK BROWN'S EXISTENCE IS A NATIONAL SECRET...ONE MUCH MORE VALUABLE THAN YOUR LIFE.›
‹OR YOURS, MY FRIEND. I ONLY REGRET THAT I FAILED TO INSTILL IN YOU THE SAME LOYALTY I DID WITH YOUR COMRADES.›
‹FIRE WHEN READY.›
‹WHAT ARE YOU--›

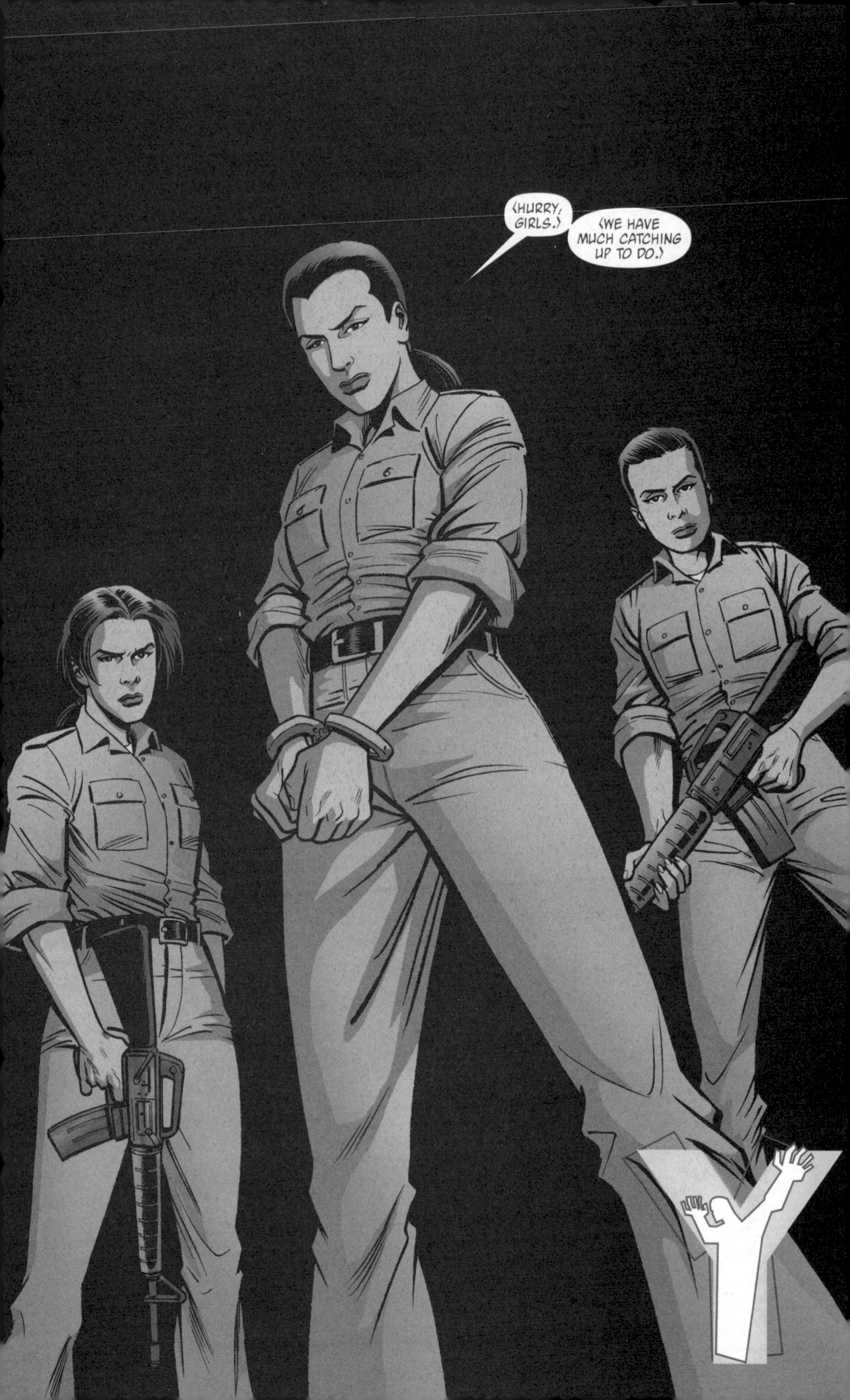
‹HURRY, GIRLS.›
‹WE HAVE MUCH CATCHING UP TO DO.›

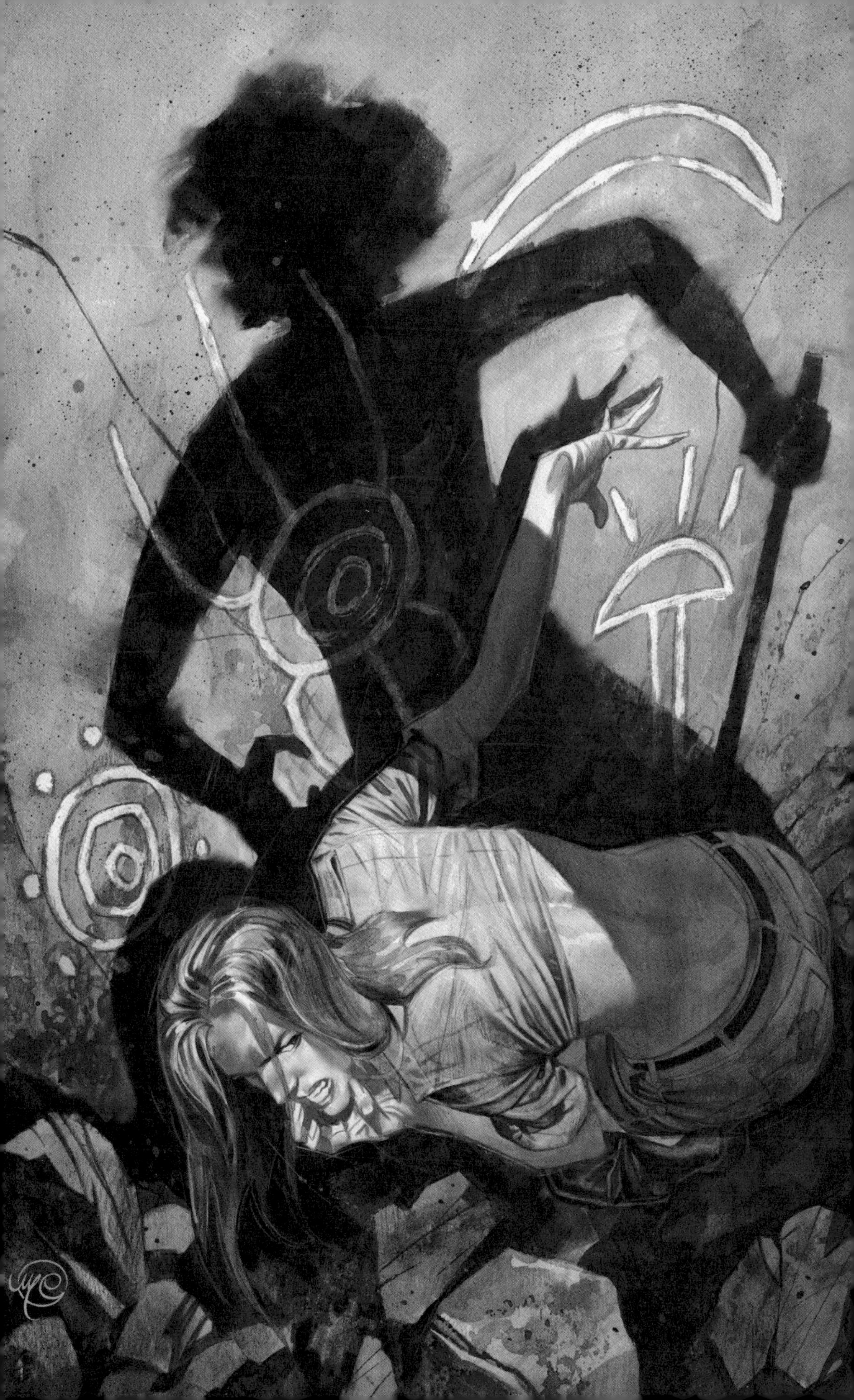

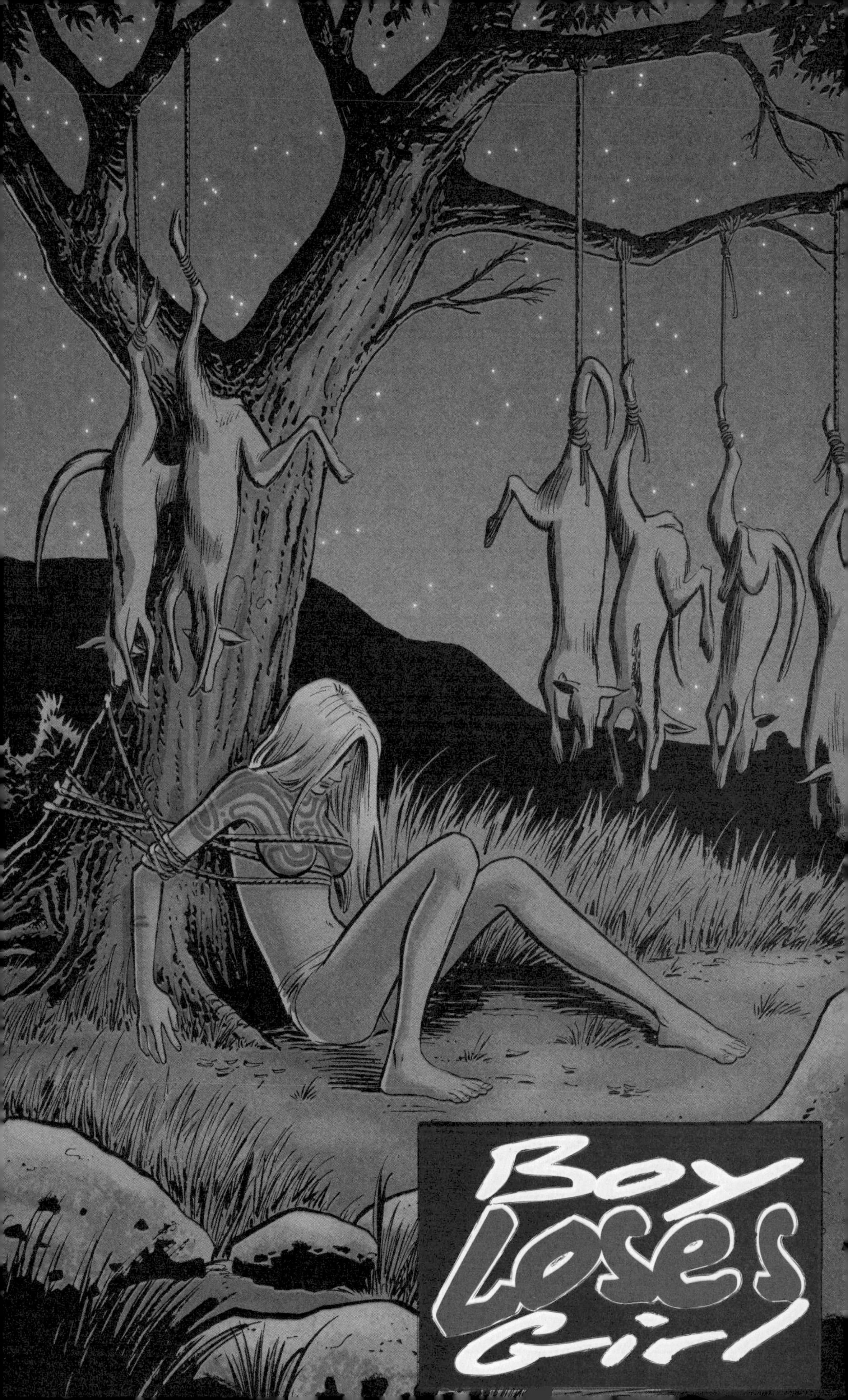
Boy
Loses
Girl

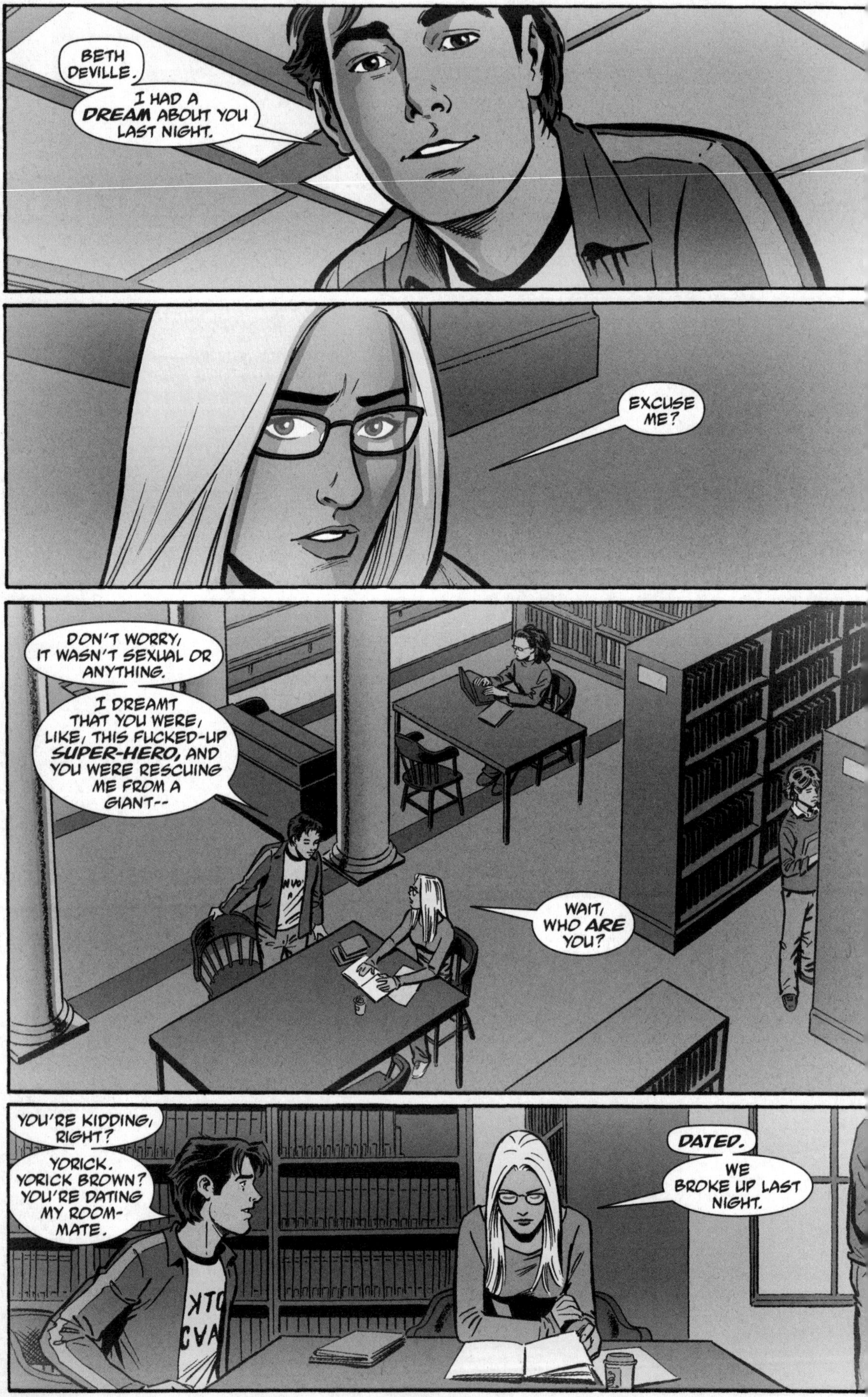
BETH DEVILLE.
I HAD A DREAM ABOUT YOU LAST NIGHT.
EXCUSE ME?
DON'T WORRY, IT WASN'T SEXUAL OR ANYTHING.
I DREAMT THAT YOU WERE, LIKE, THIS FUCKED-UP SUPER-HERO, AND YOU WERE RESCUING ME FROM A GIANT--
WAIT, WHO ARE YOU?
YOU'RE KIDDING, RIGHT?
YORICK. YORICK BROWN? YOU'RE DATING MY ROOM-MATE.
DATED.
WE BROKE UP LAST NIGHT.

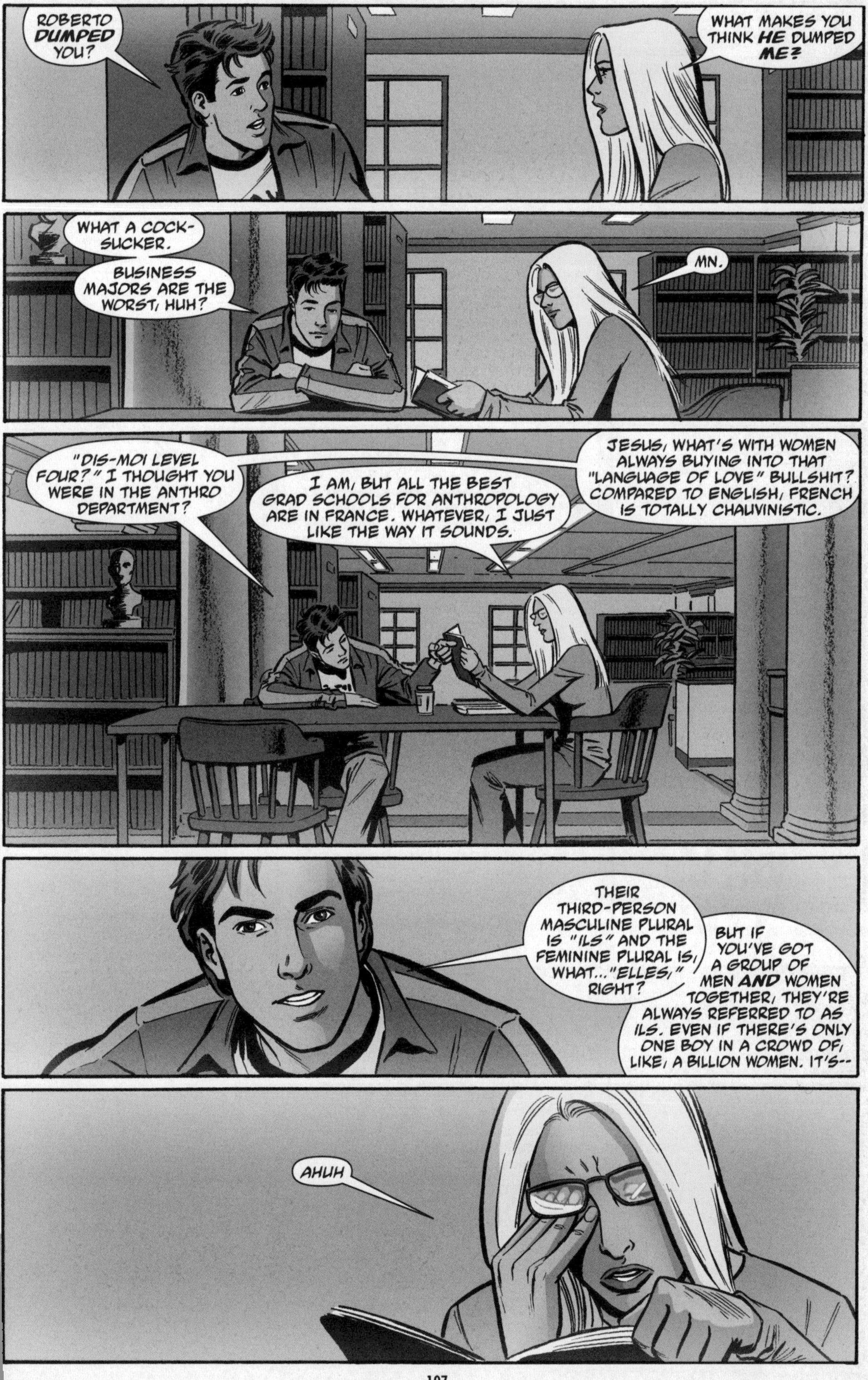

ROBERTO DUMPED YOU?
WHAT MAKES YOU THINK HE DUMPED ME?
WHAT A COCK-SUCKER.
BUSINESS MAJORS ARE THE WORST, HUH?
MN.
"DIS-MOI LEVEL FOUR?" I THOUGHT YOU WERE IN THE ANTHRO DEPARTMENT?
I AM, BUT ALL THE BEST GRAD SCHOOLS FOR ANTHROPOLOGY ARE IN FRANCE. WHATEVER, I JUST LIKE THE WAY IT SOUNDS.
JESUS, WHAT'S WITH WOMEN ALWAYS BUYING INTO THAT "LANGUAGE OF LOVE" BULLSHIT? COMPARED TO ENGLISH, FRENCH IS TOTALLY CHAUVINISTIC.
THEIR THIRD-PERSON MASCULINE PLURAL IS "ILS" AND THE FEMININE PLURAL IS, WHAT..."ELLES," RIGHT?
BUT IF YOU'VE GOT A GROUP OF MEN AND WOMEN TOGETHER, THEY'RE ALWAYS REFERRED TO AS ILS. EVEN IF THERE'S ONLY ONE BOY IN A CROWD OF, LIKE, A BILLION WOMEN. IT'S--
AHUH

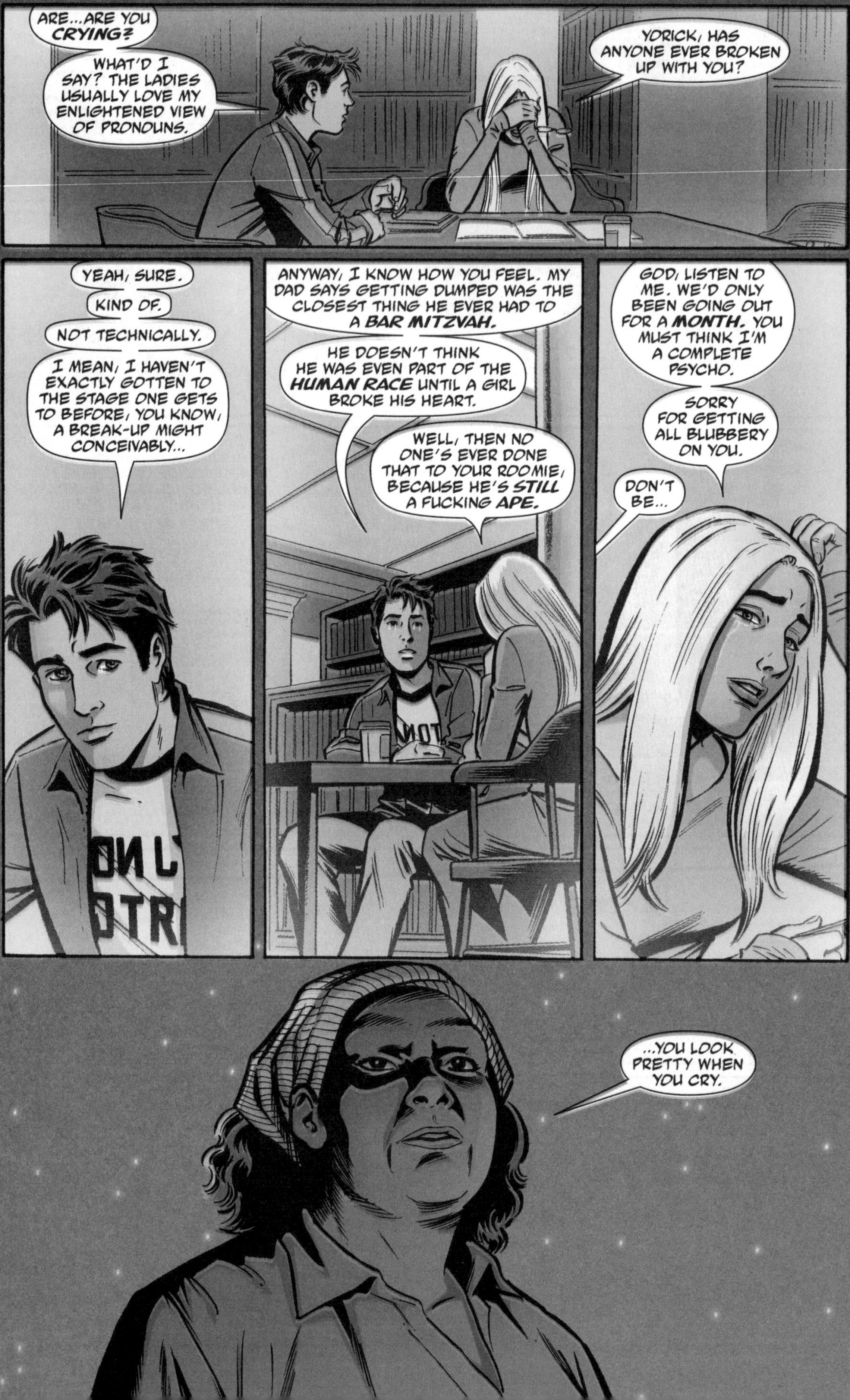
ARE...ARE YOU CRYING?
WHAT'D I SAY? THE LADIES USUALLY LOVE MY ENLIGHTENED VIEW OF PRONOUNS.
YORICK, HAS ANYONE EVER BROKEN UP WITH YOU?
YEAH, SURE.
KIND OF.
NOT TECHNICALLY.
I MEAN, I HAVEN'T EXACTLY GOTTEN TO THE STAGE ONE GETS TO BEFORE, YOU KNOW, A BREAK-UP MIGHT CONCEIVABLY...
ANYWAY, I KNOW HOW YOU FEEL. MY DAD SAYS GETTING DUMPED WAS THE CLOSEST THING HE EVER HAD TO A BAR MITZVAH.
HE DOESN'T THINK HE WAS EVEN PART OF THE HUMAN RACE UNTIL A GIRL BROKE HIS HEART.
WELL, THEN NO ONE'S EVER DONE THAT TO YOUR ROOMIE, BECAUSE HE'S STILL A FUCKING APE.
GOD, LISTEN TO ME. WE'D ONLY BEEN GOING OUT FOR A MONTH. YOU MUST THINK I'M A COMPLETE PSYCHO.
SORRY FOR GETTING ALL BLUBBERY ON YOU.
DON'T BE...
...YOU LOOK PRETTY WHEN YOU CRY.

WHAT?

I SAID, HOW THE HELL ARE WE SUPPOSED TO GET OUT OF HERE?

THE GUIDES ARE GONE, HALF OUR CLASS IS DEAD, THE SAT-PHONE SUDDENLY DOESN'T WORK FOR SHIT, AND OUR RATIONS ARE FUCKING TOXIC!

SETTLE, MARGO. WE DON'T KNOW THAT THE FOOD KILLED THEM.

WELL, THAT'S BLOODY REASSURING, BOSS. MAYBE IT'S JUST EBOLA.

NO, IT WAS THE ABOS.

WATCH YOUR MOUTH.

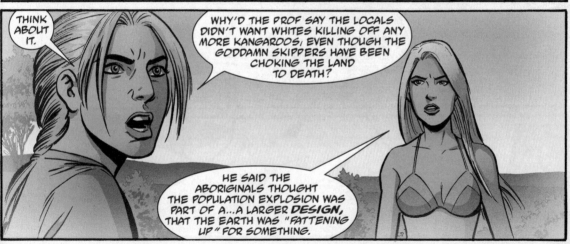

THINK ABOUT IT.

WHY'D THE PROF SAY THE LOCALS DIDN'T WANT WHITES KILLING OFF ANY MORE KANGAROOS, EVEN THOUGH THE GODDAMN SKIPPERS HAVE BEEN CHOKING THE LAND TO DEATH?

HE SAID THE ABORIGINALS THOUGHT THE POPULATION EXPLOSION WAS PART OF A...A LARGER DESIGN, THAT THE EARTH WAS "FATTENING UP" FOR SOMETHING.

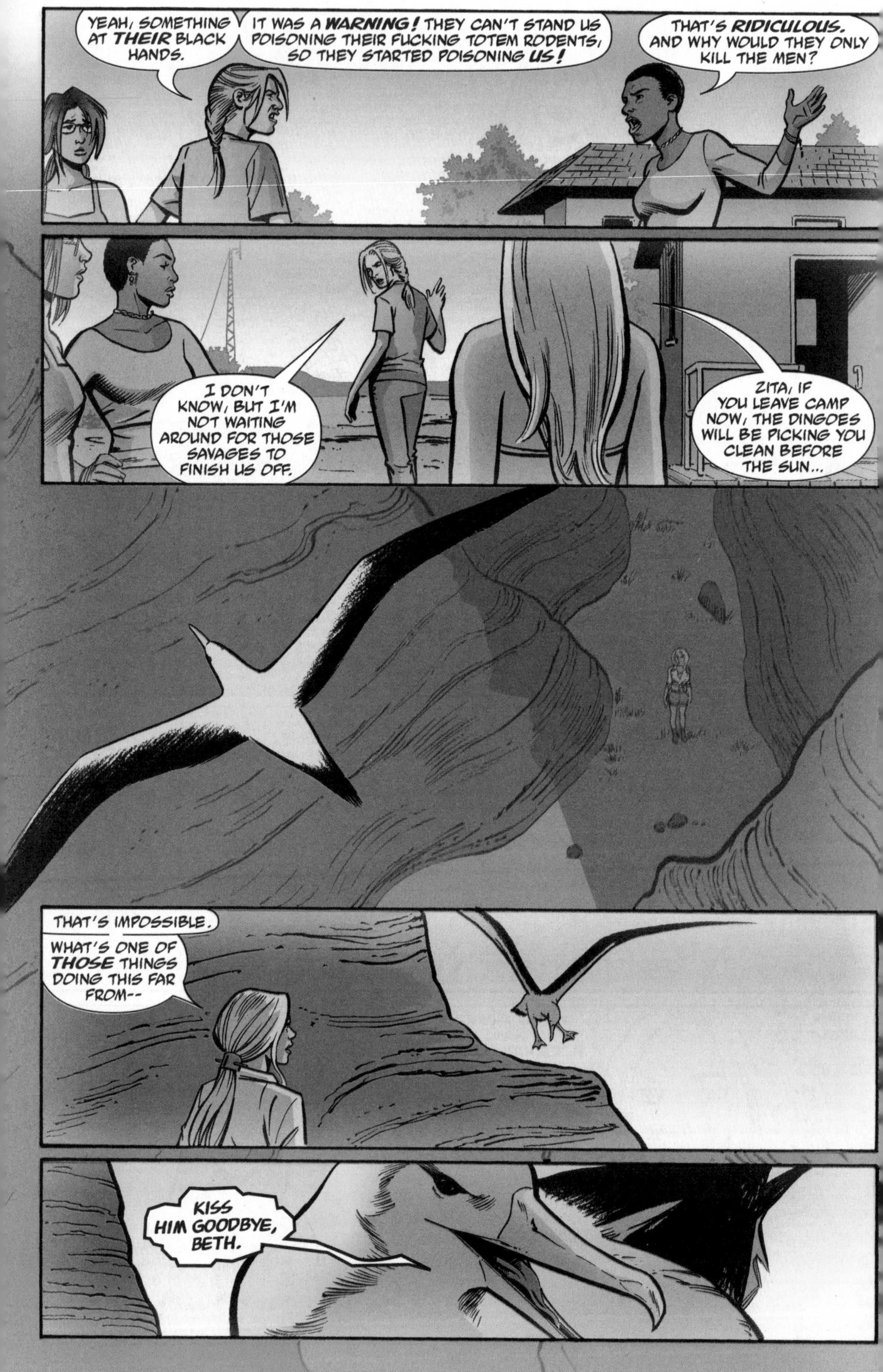
YEAH, SOMETHING AT THEIR BLACK HANDS.
IT WAS A WARNING! THEY CAN'T STAND US POISONING THEIR FUCKING TOTEM RODENTS, SO THEY STARTED POISONING US!
THAT'S RIDICULOUS. AND WHY WOULD THEY ONLY KILL THE MEN?
I DON'T KNOW, BUT I'M NOT WAITING AROUND FOR THOSE SAVAGES TO FINISH US OFF.
ZITA, IF YOU LEAVE CAMP NOW, THE DINGOES WILL BE PICKING YOU CLEAN BEFORE THE SUN...
THAT'S IMPOSSIBLE.
WHAT'S ONE OF THOSE THINGS DOING THIS FAR FROM--
KISS HIM GOODBYE, BETH.

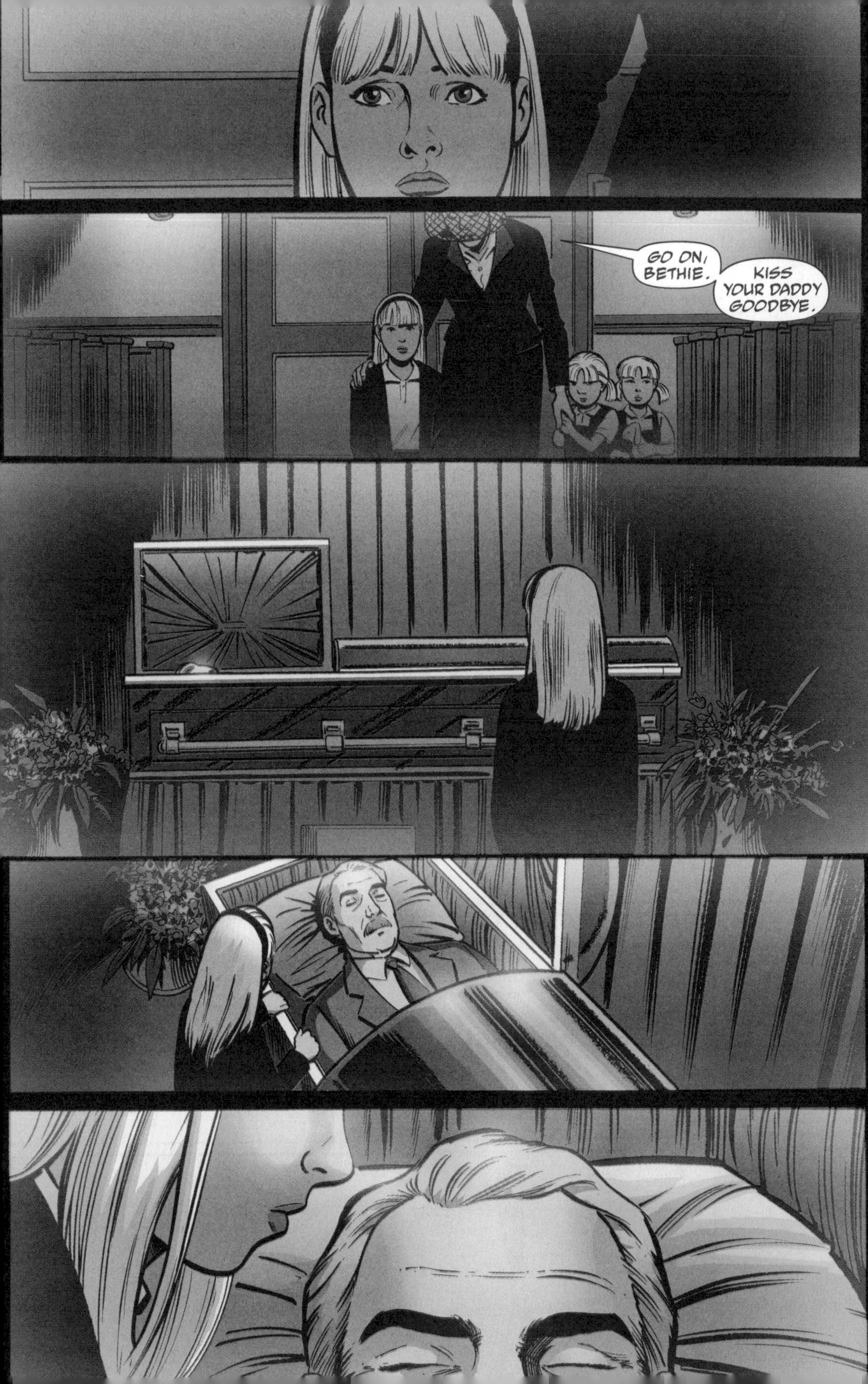
GO ON, BETHIE.
KISS YOUR DADDY GOODBYE.

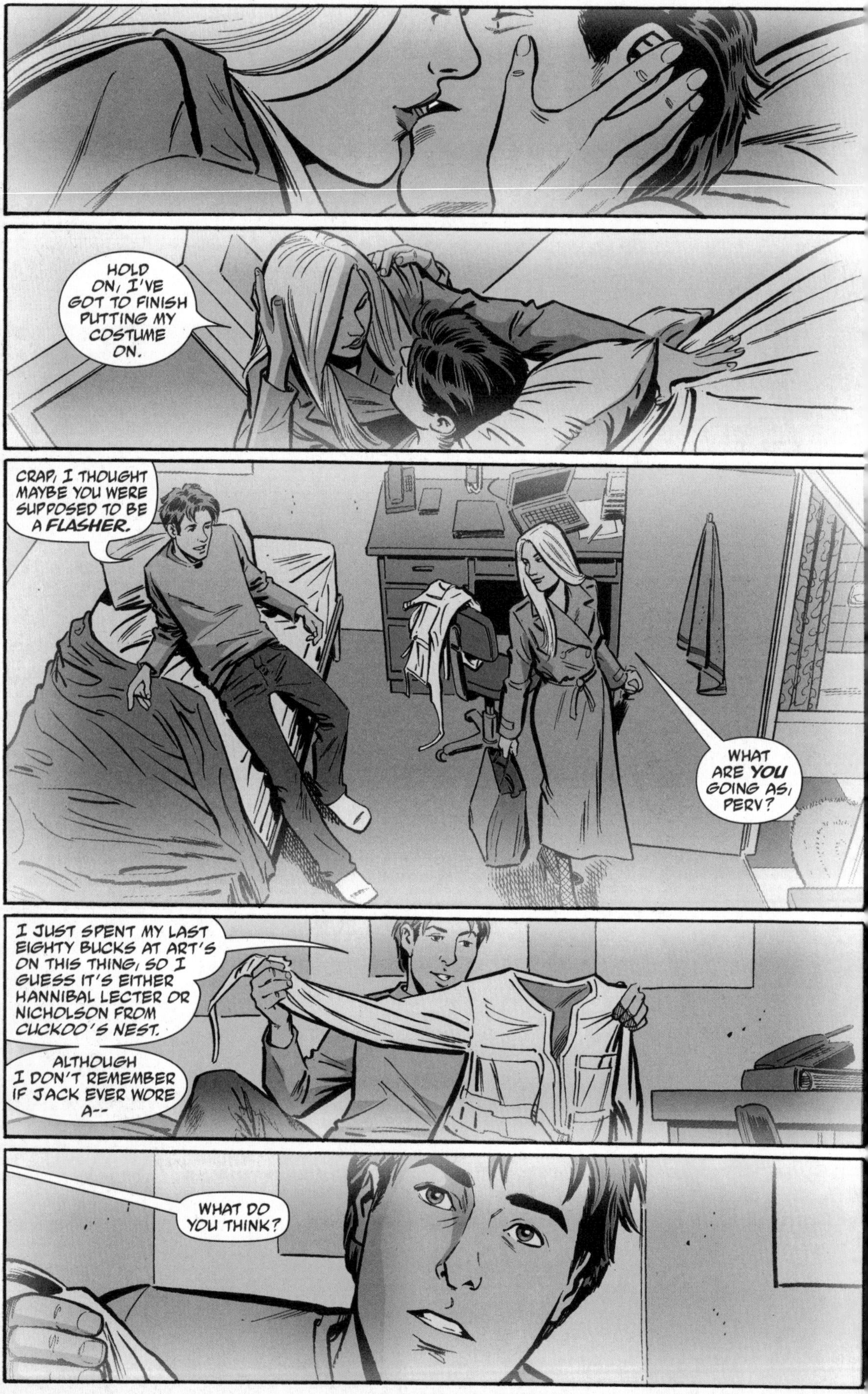
HOLD ON, I'VE GOT TO FINISH PUTTING MY COSTUME ON.
CRAP, I THOUGHT MAYBE YOU WERE SUPPOSED TO BE A FLASHER.
WHAT ARE YOU GOING AS, PERV?
I JUST SPENT MY LAST EIGHTY BUCKS AT ART'S ON THIS THING, SO I GUESS IT'S EITHER HANNIBAL LECTER OR NICHOLSON FROM CUCKOO'S NEST.
ALTHOUGH I DON'T REMEMBER IF JACK EVER WORE A--
WHAT DO YOU THINK?

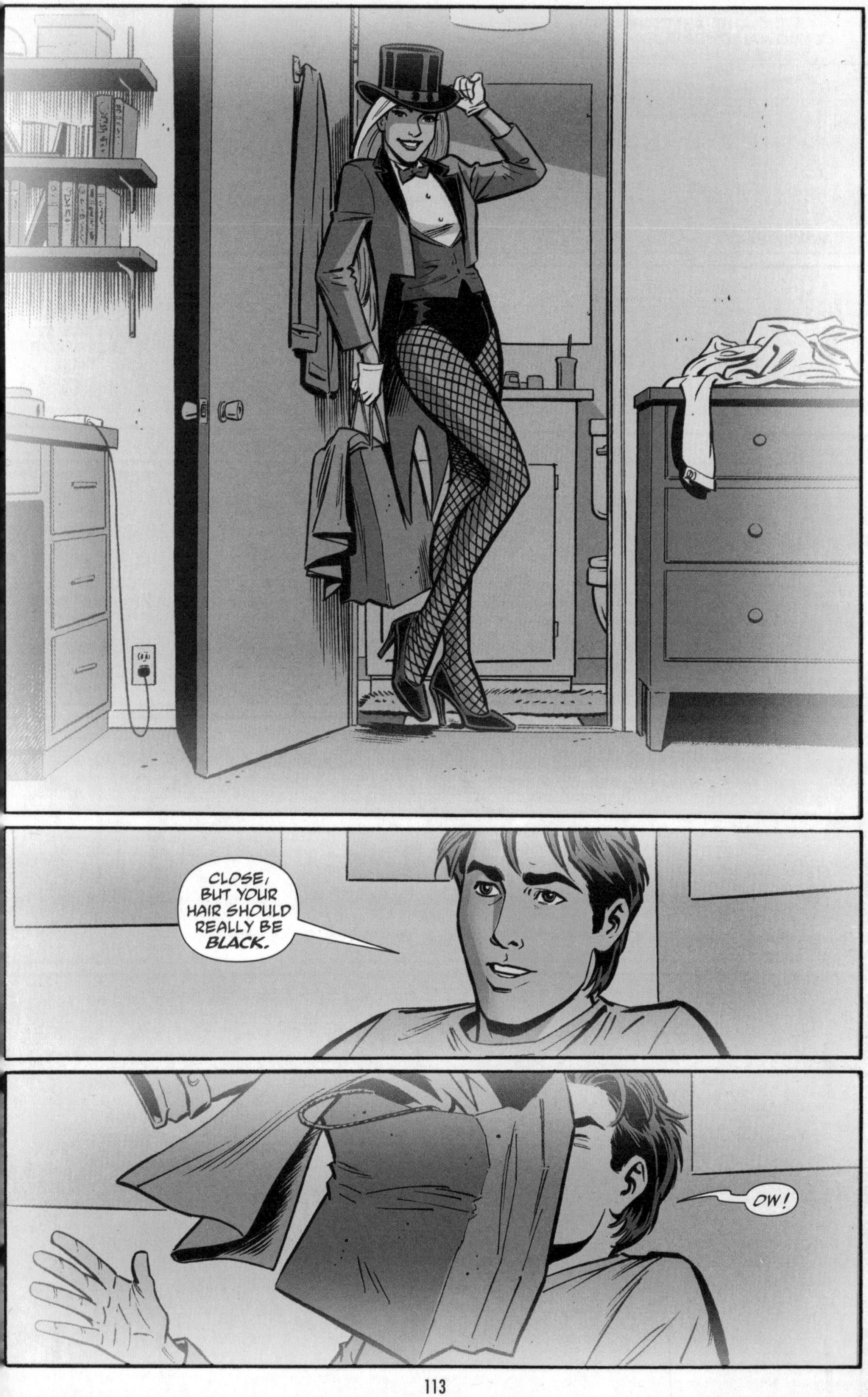
CLOSE, BUT YOUR HAIR SHOULD REALLY BE BLACK.
OW!

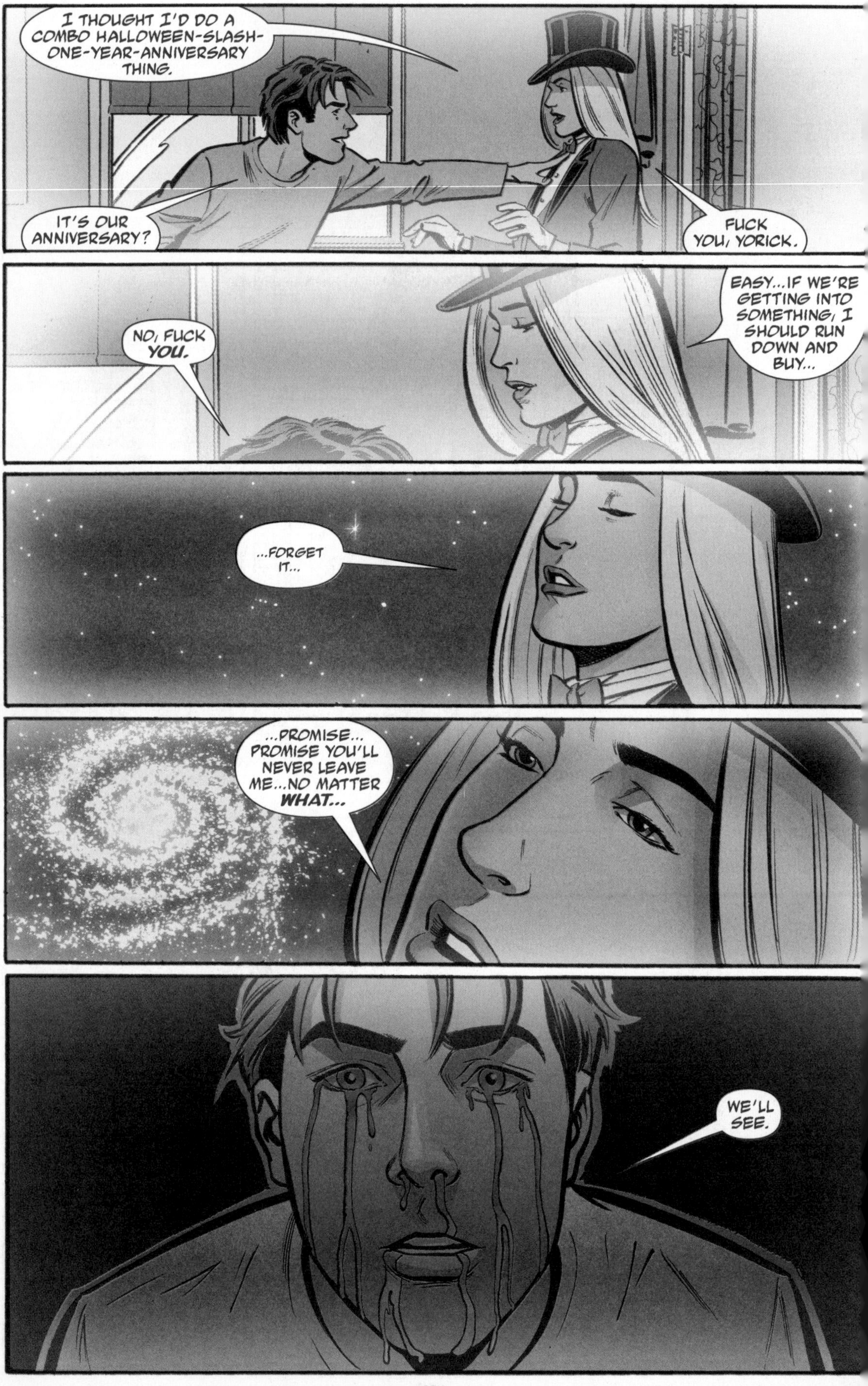
I THOUGHT I'D DO A COMBO HALLOWEEN-SLASH-ONE-YEAR-ANNIVERSARY THING.
IT'S OUR ANNIVERSARY?
FUCK YOU, YORICK.
NO, FUCK *YOU.*
EASY...IF WE'RE GETTING INTO SOMETHING, I SHOULD RUN DOWN AND BUY...
...FORGET IT...
...PROMISE... PROMISE YOU'LL NEVER LEAVE ME...NO MATTER *WHAT...*
WE'LL SEE.

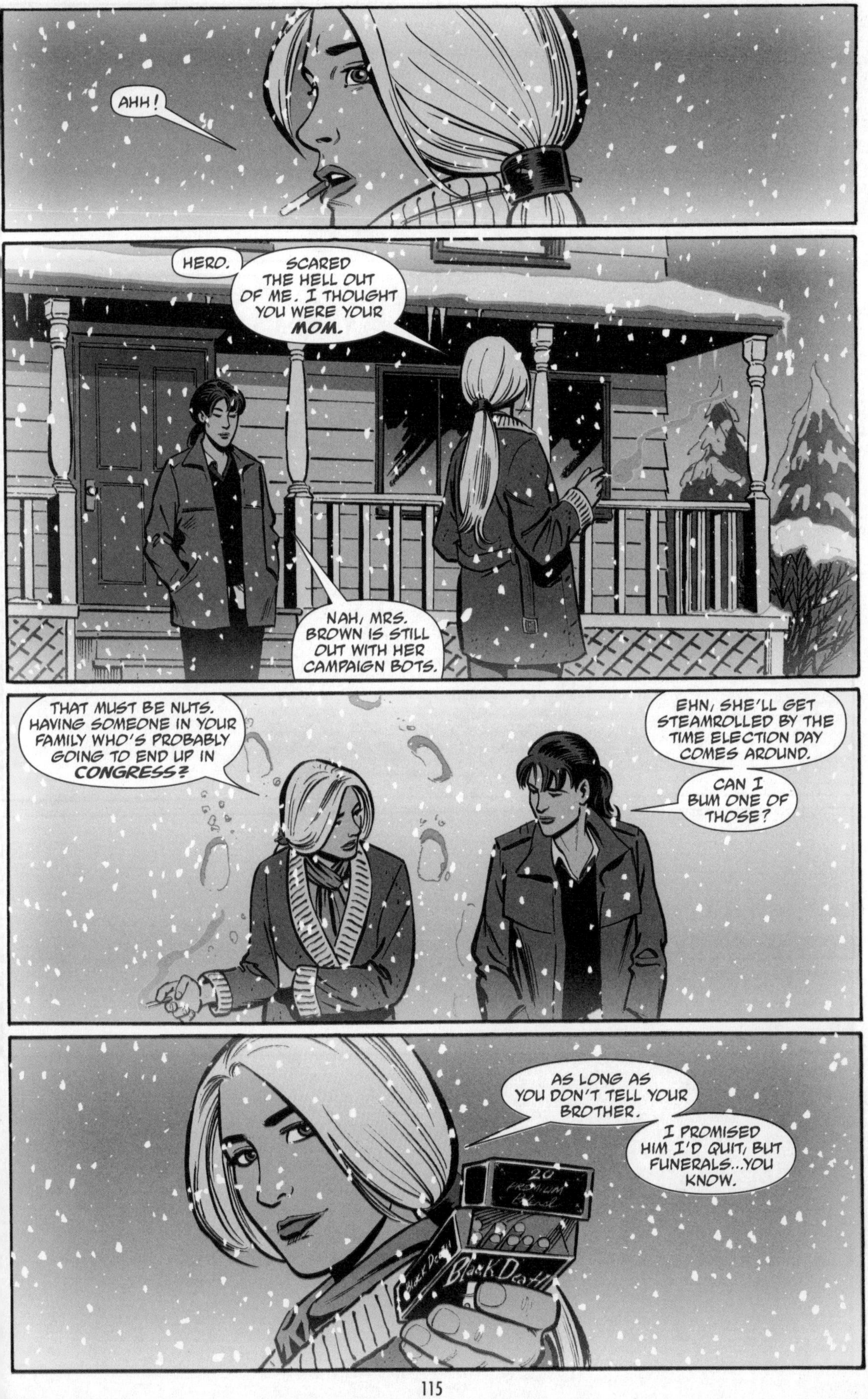
AHH!
HERO.
SCARED THE HELL OUT OF ME. I THOUGHT YOU WERE YOUR MOM.
NAH, MRS. BROWN IS STILL OUT WITH HER CAMPAIGN BOTS.
THAT MUST BE NUTS. HAVING SOMEONE IN YOUR FAMILY WHO'S PROBABLY GOING TO END UP IN CONGRESS?
EHN, SHE'LL GET STEAMROLLED BY THE TIME ELECTION DAY COMES AROUND.
CAN I BUM ONE OF THOSE?
AS LONG AS YOU DON'T TELL YOUR BROTHER.
I PROMISED HIM I'D QUIT, BUT FUNERALS...YOU KNOW.
20 PREMIUM Blend
Black Death

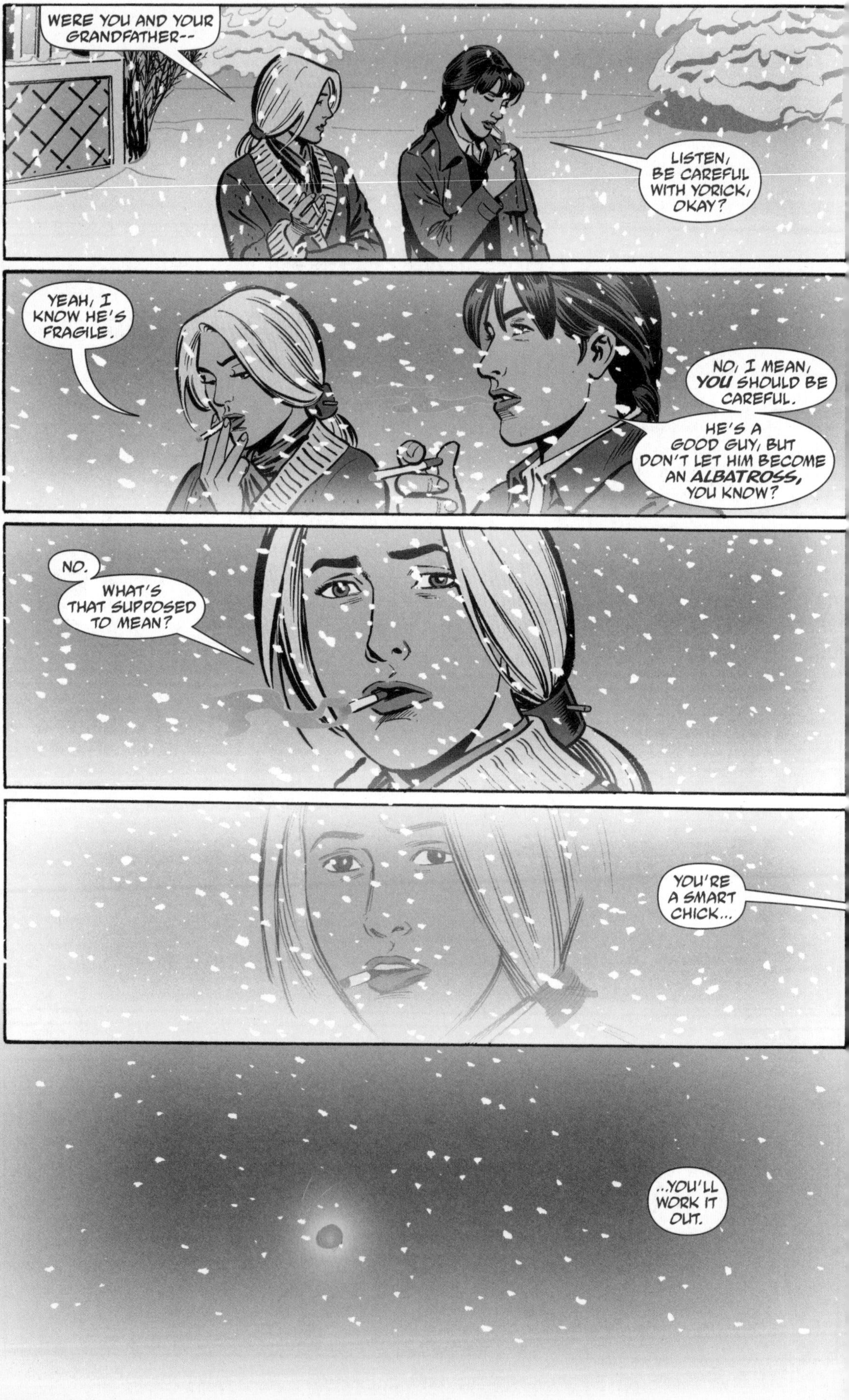

WERE YOU AND YOUR GRANDFATHER--
LISTEN, BE CAREFUL WITH YORICK, OKAY?
YEAH, I KNOW HE'S FRAGILE.
NO, I MEAN, **YOU** SHOULD BE CAREFUL.
HE'S A GOOD GUY, BUT DON'T LET HIM BECOME AN **ALBATROSS,** YOU KNOW?
NO.
WHAT'S THAT SUPPOSED TO MEAN?
YOU'RE A SMART CHICK...
...YOU'LL WORK IT OUT.

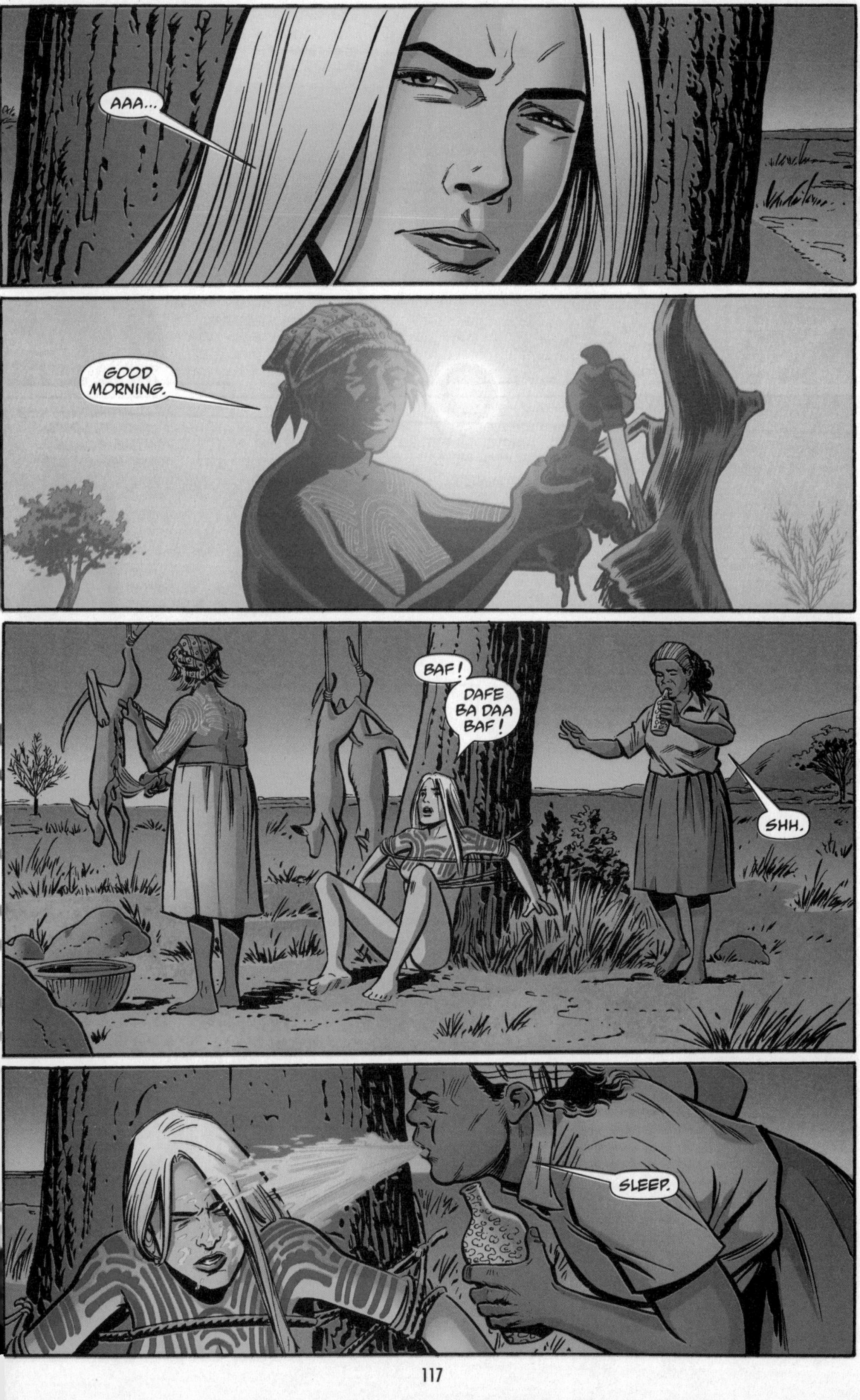
AAA...
GOOD MORNING.
BAF!
DAFE BA DAA BAF!
SHH.
SLEEP.

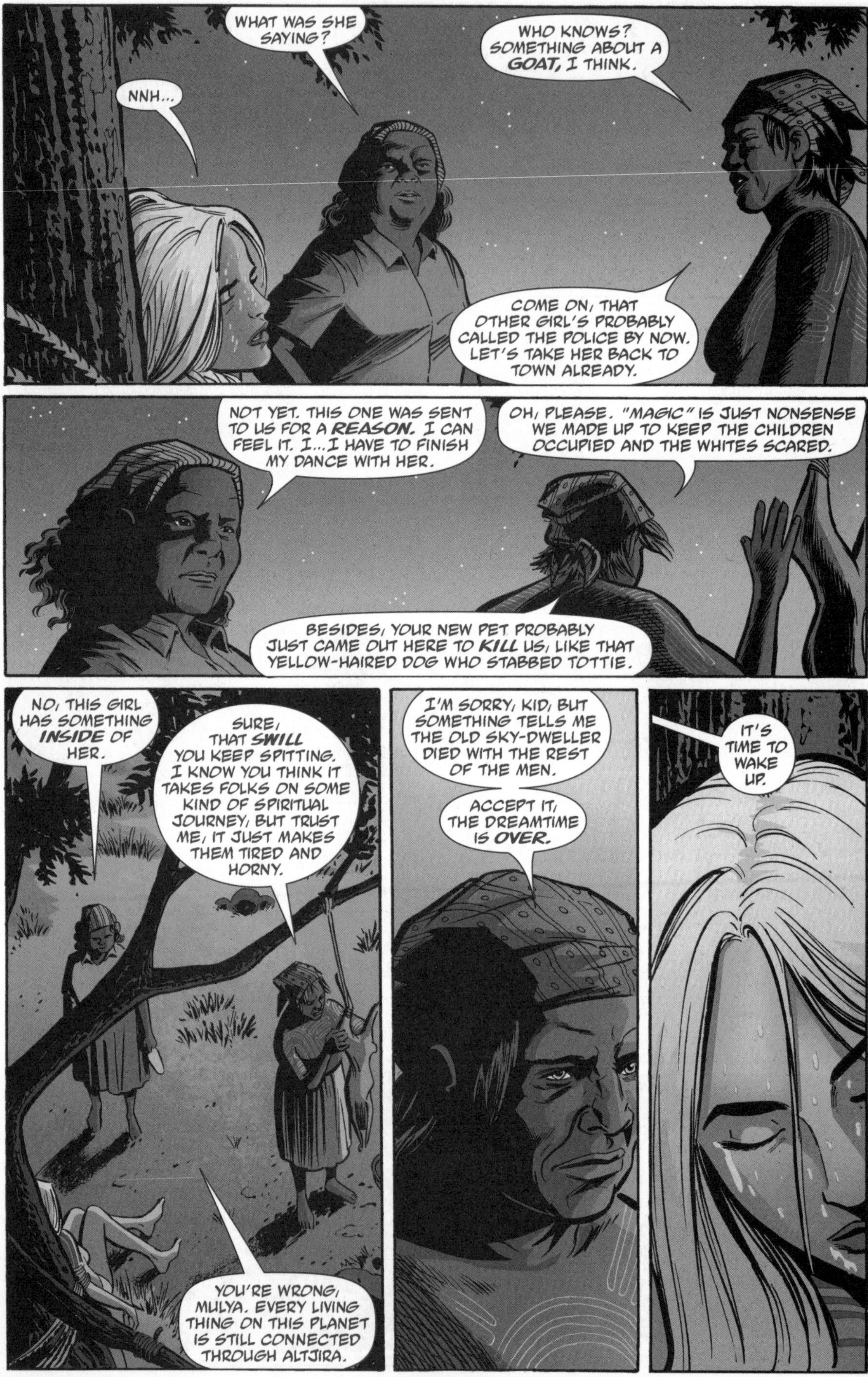
WHAT WAS SHE SAYING?
NNH...
WHO KNOWS? SOMETHING ABOUT A GOAT, I THINK.
COME ON, THAT OTHER GIRL'S PROBABLY CALLED THE POLICE BY NOW. LET'S TAKE HER BACK TO TOWN ALREADY.
NOT YET. THIS ONE WAS SENT TO US FOR A REASON. I CAN FEEL IT. I...I HAVE TO FINISH MY DANCE WITH HER.
OH, PLEASE. "MAGIC" IS JUST NONSENSE WE MADE UP TO KEEP THE CHILDREN OCCUPIED AND THE WHITES SCARED.
BESIDES, YOUR NEW PET PROBABLY JUST CAME OUT HERE TO KILL US, LIKE THAT YELLOW-HAIRED DOG WHO STABBED TOTTIE.
NO, THIS GIRL HAS SOMETHING INSIDE OF HER.
SURE, THAT SWILL YOU KEEP SPITTING. I KNOW YOU THINK IT TAKES FOLKS ON SOME KIND OF SPIRITUAL JOURNEY, BUT TRUST ME, IT JUST MAKES THEM TIRED AND HORNY.
YOU'RE WRONG, MULYA. EVERY LIVING THING ON THIS PLANET IS STILL CONNECTED THROUGH ALTJIRA.
I'M SORRY, KID, BUT SOMETHING TELLS ME THE OLD SKY-DWELLER DIED WITH THE REST OF THE MEN.
ACCEPT IT, THE DREAMTIME IS OVER.
IT'S TIME TO WAKE UP.

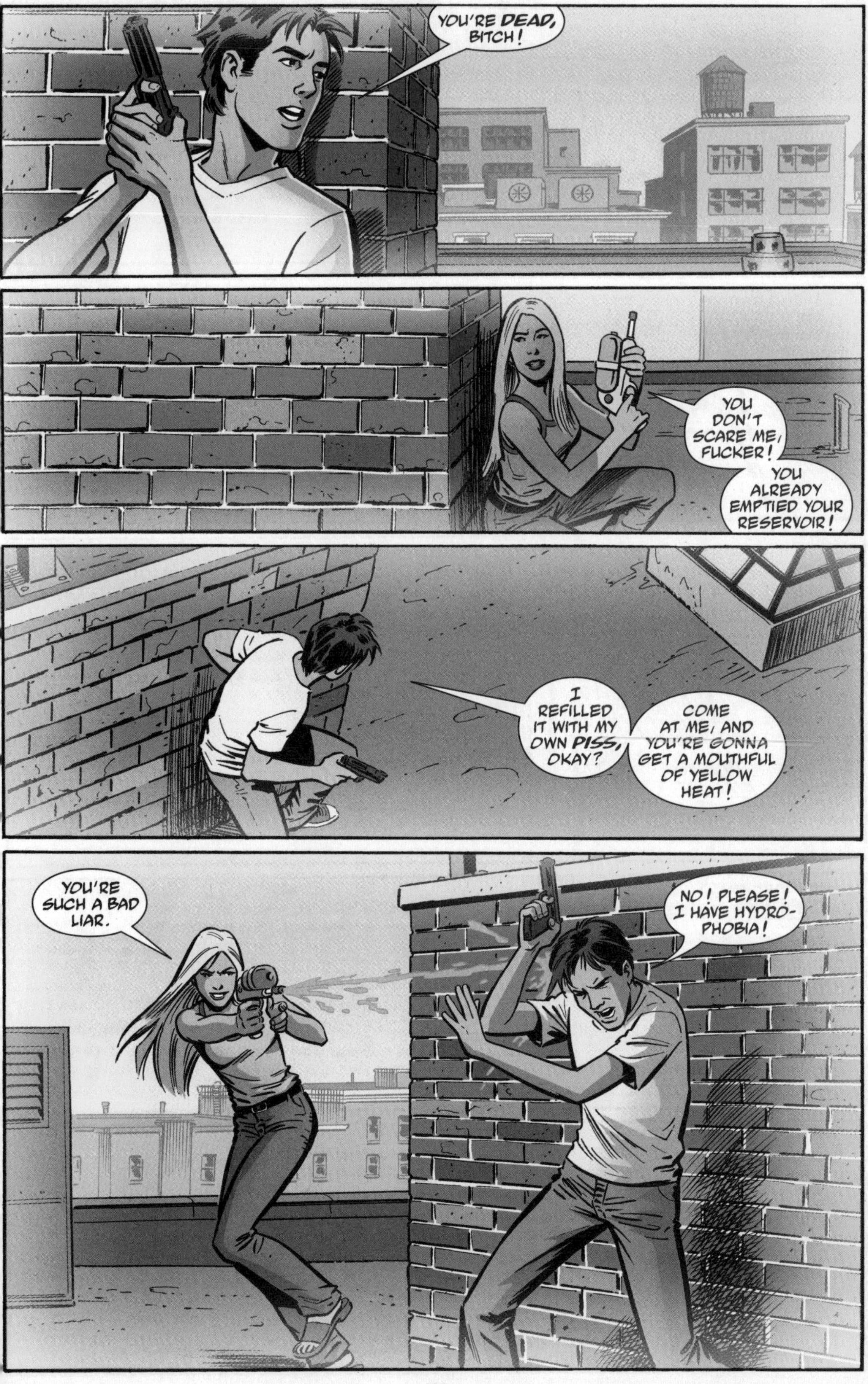
YOU'RE DEAD, BITCH!
YOU DON'T SCARE ME, FUCKER!
YOU ALREADY EMPTIED YOUR RESERVOIR!
I REFILLED IT WITH MY OWN PISS, OKAY?
COME AT ME, AND YOU'RE GONNA GET A MOUTHFUL OF YELLOW HEAT!
YOU'RE SUCH A BAD LIAR.
NO! PLEASE! I HAVE HYDRO-PHOBIA!

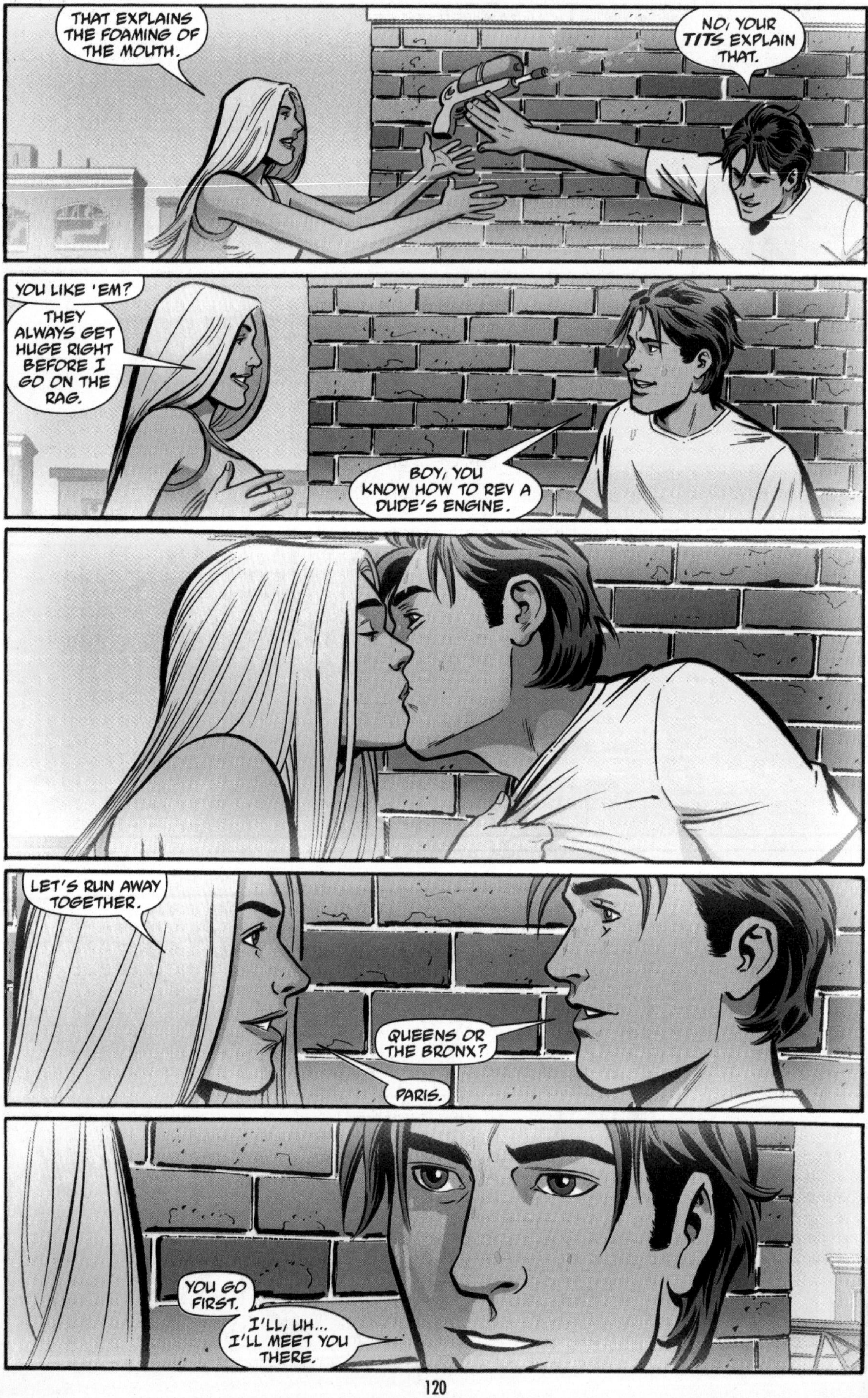
THAT EXPLAINS THE FOAMING OF THE MOUTH.
NO, YOUR TITS EXPLAIN THAT.
YOU LIKE 'EM?
THEY ALWAYS GET HUGE RIGHT BEFORE I GO ON THE RAG.
BOY, YOU KNOW HOW TO REV A DUDE'S ENGINE.
LET'S RUN AWAY TOGETHER.
QUEENS OR THE BRONX?
PARIS.
YOU GO FIRST.
I'LL, UH... I'LL MEET YOU THERE.

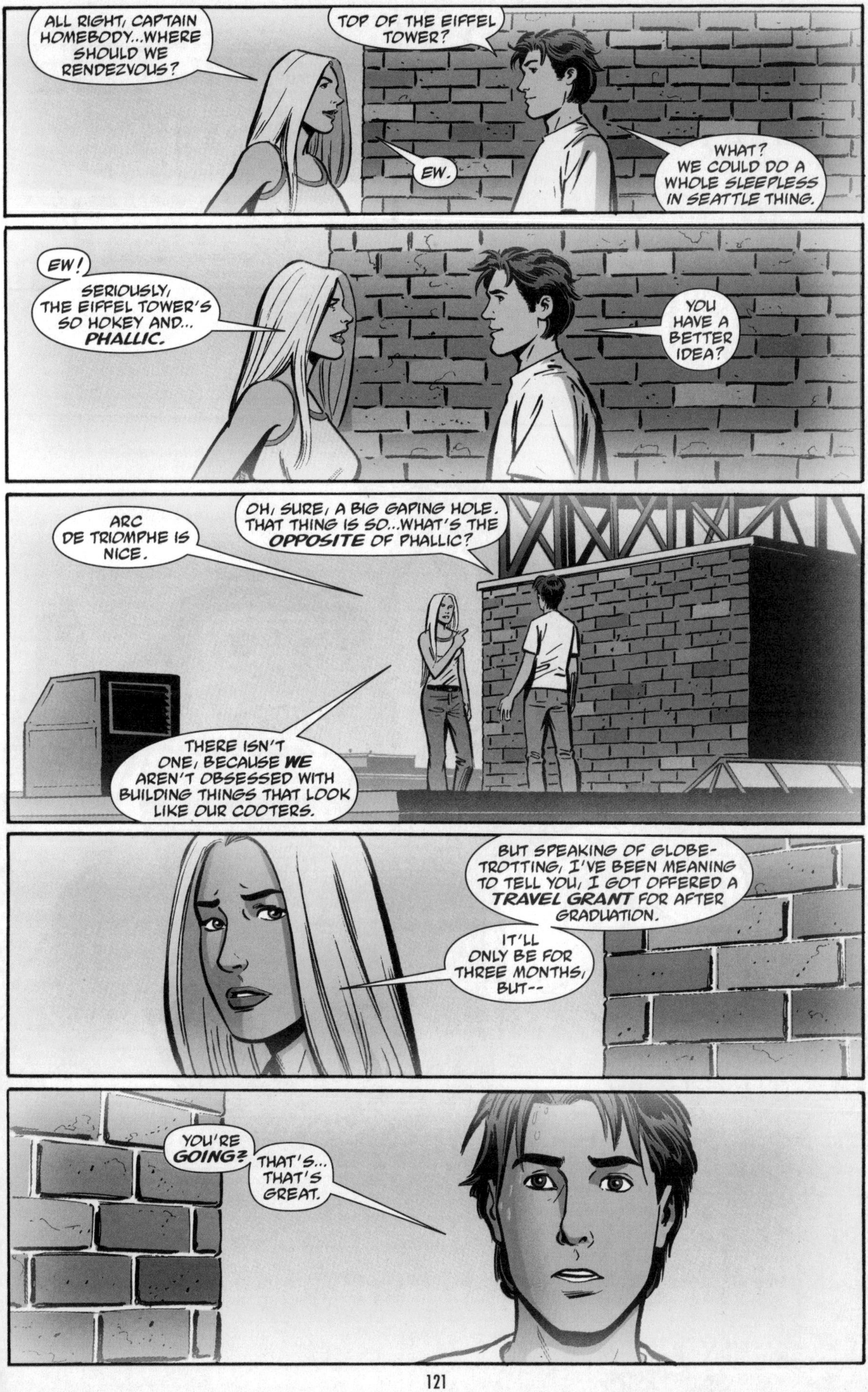
ALL RIGHT, CAPTAIN HOMEBODY...WHERE SHOULD WE RENDEZVOUS?
TOP OF THE EIFFEL TOWER?
EW.
WHAT? WE COULD DO A WHOLE SLEEPLESS IN SEATTLE THING.
EW!
SERIOUSLY, THE EIFFEL TOWER'S SO HOKEY AND... **PHALLIC.**
YOU HAVE A BETTER IDEA?
ARC DE TRIOMPHE IS NICE.
OH, SURE, A BIG GAPING HOLE. THAT THING IS SO...WHAT'S THE **OPPOSITE** OF PHALLIC?
THERE ISN'T ONE, BECAUSE **WE** AREN'T OBSESSED WITH BUILDING THINGS THAT LOOK LIKE OUR COOTERS.
BUT SPEAKING OF GLOBE-TROTTING, I'VE BEEN MEANING TO TELL YOU, I GOT OFFERED A **TRAVEL GRANT** FOR AFTER GRADUATION.
IT'LL ONLY BE FOR THREE MONTHS, BUT--
YOU'RE **GOING?**
THAT'S... THAT'S GREAT.

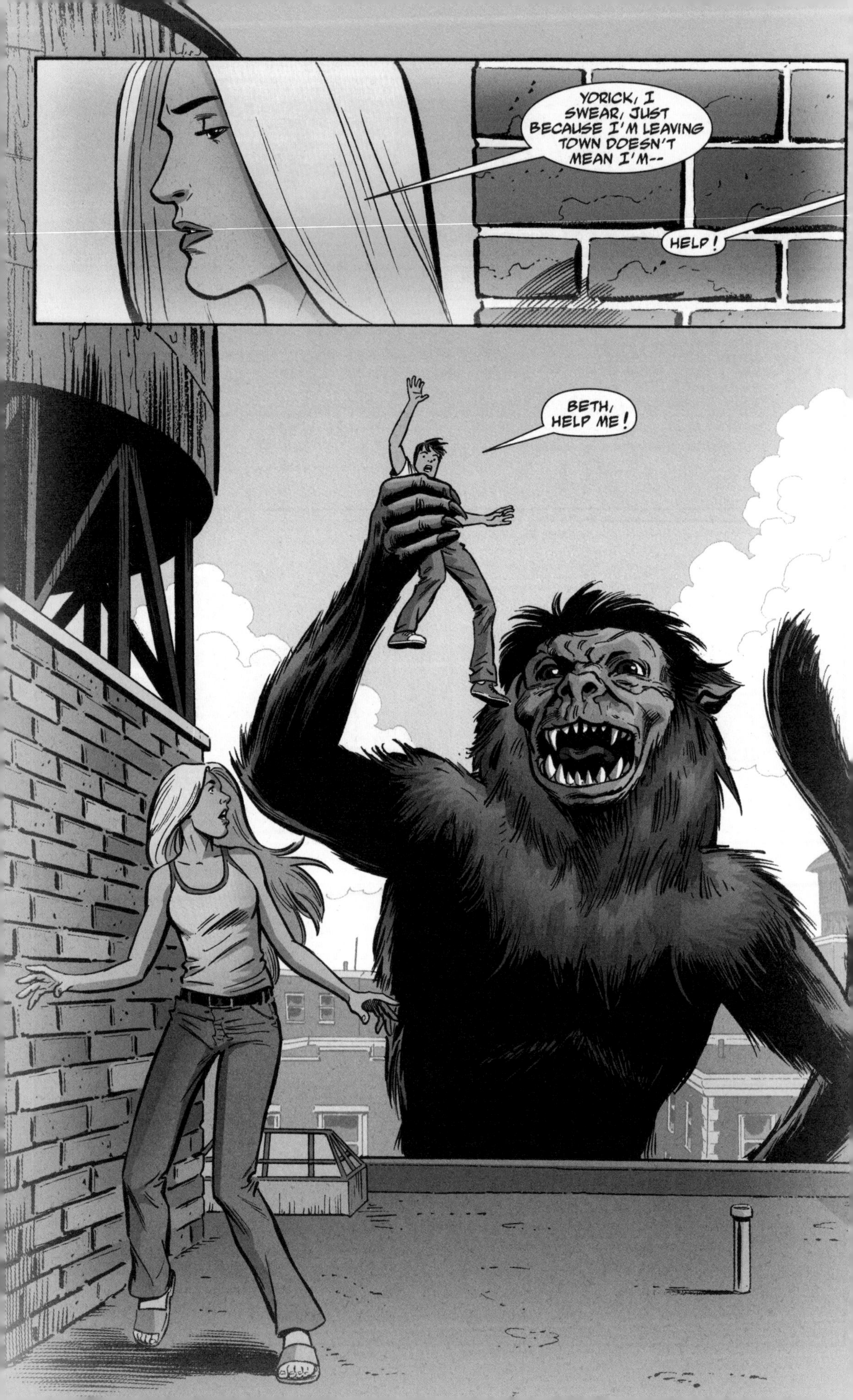
YORICK, I SWEAR, JUST BECAUSE I'M LEAVING TOWN DOESN'T MEAN I'M--
HELP!
BETH, HELP ME!

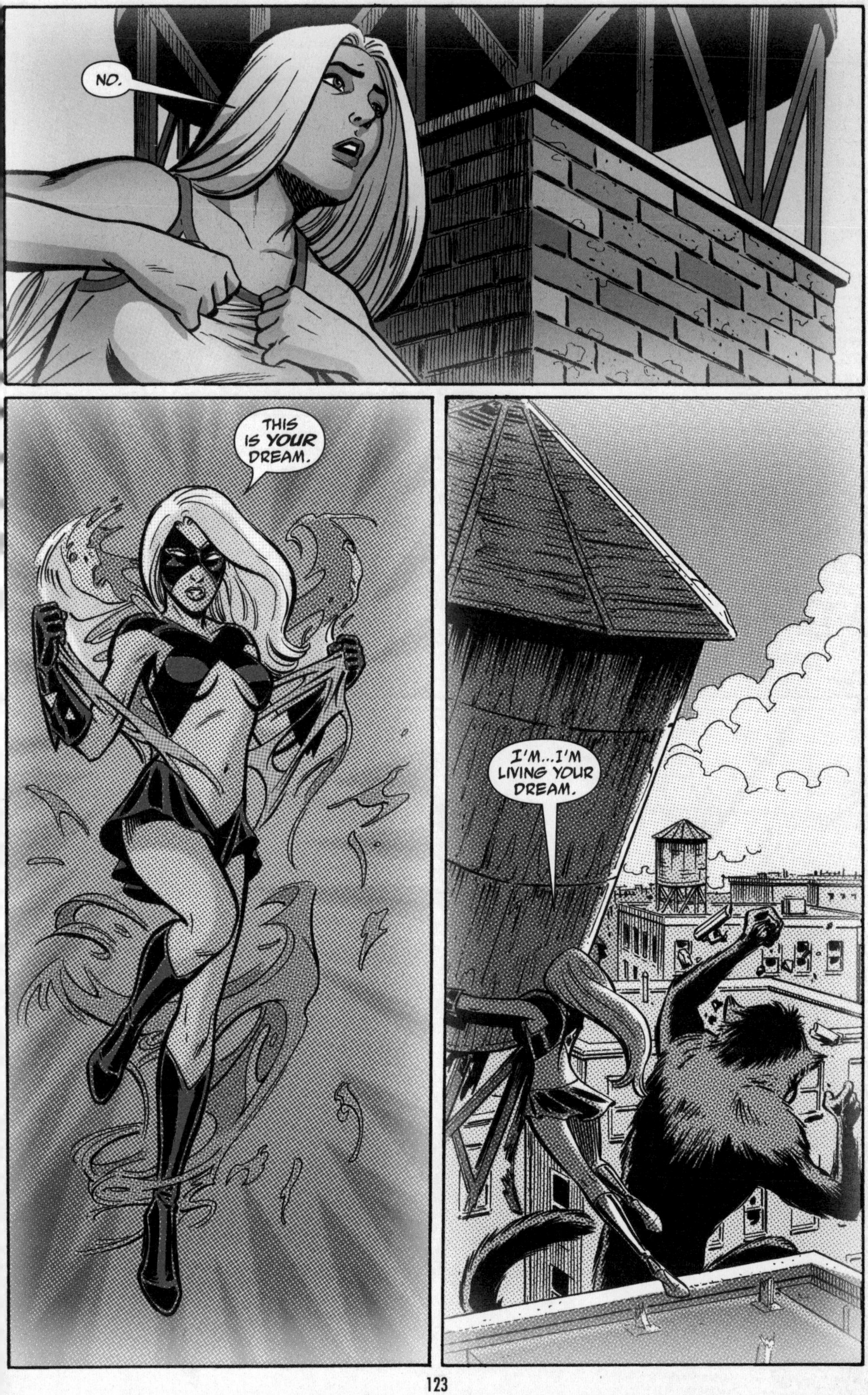
NO.
THIS IS YOUR DREAM.
I'M...I'M LIVING YOUR DREAM.

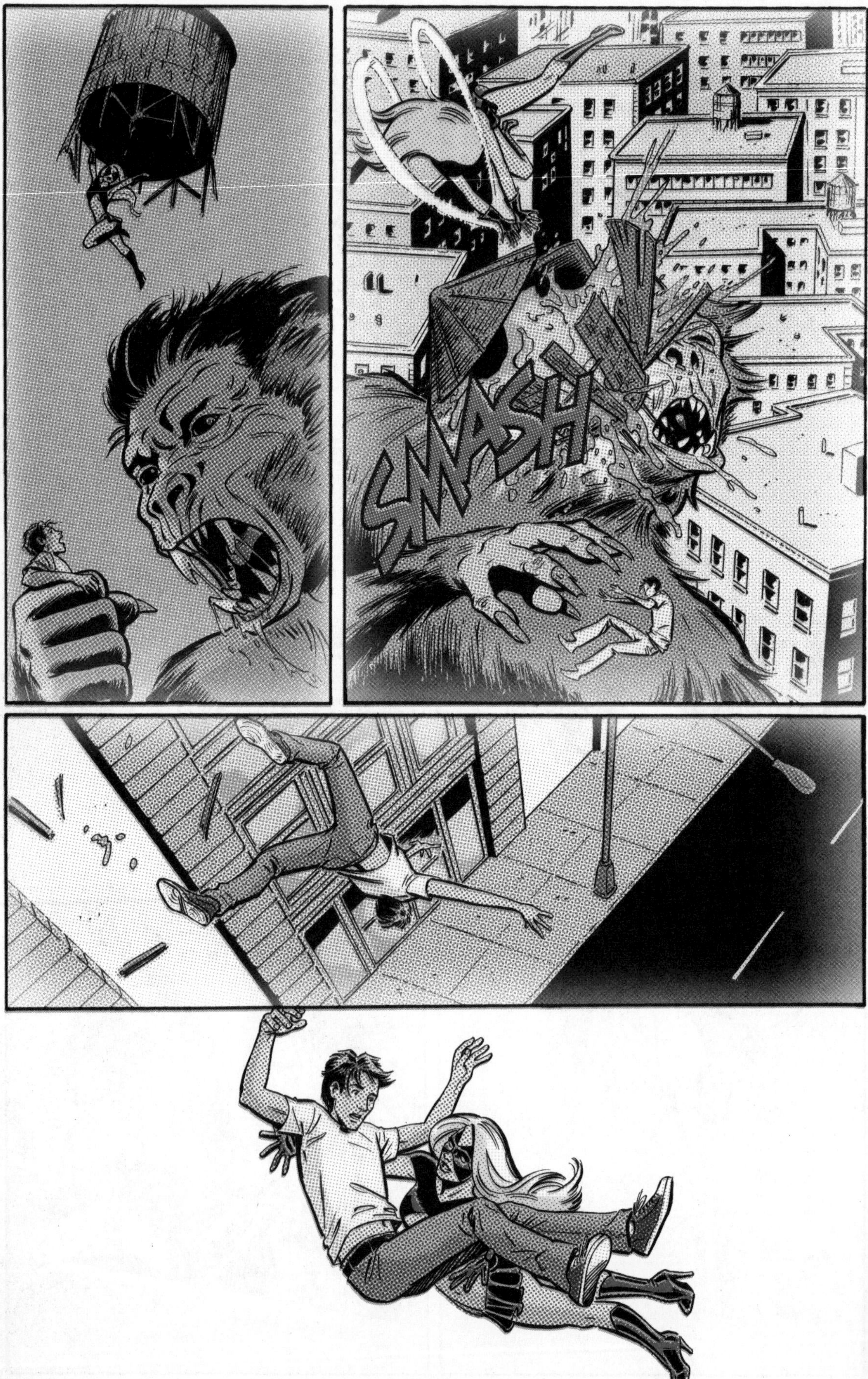
SMASH

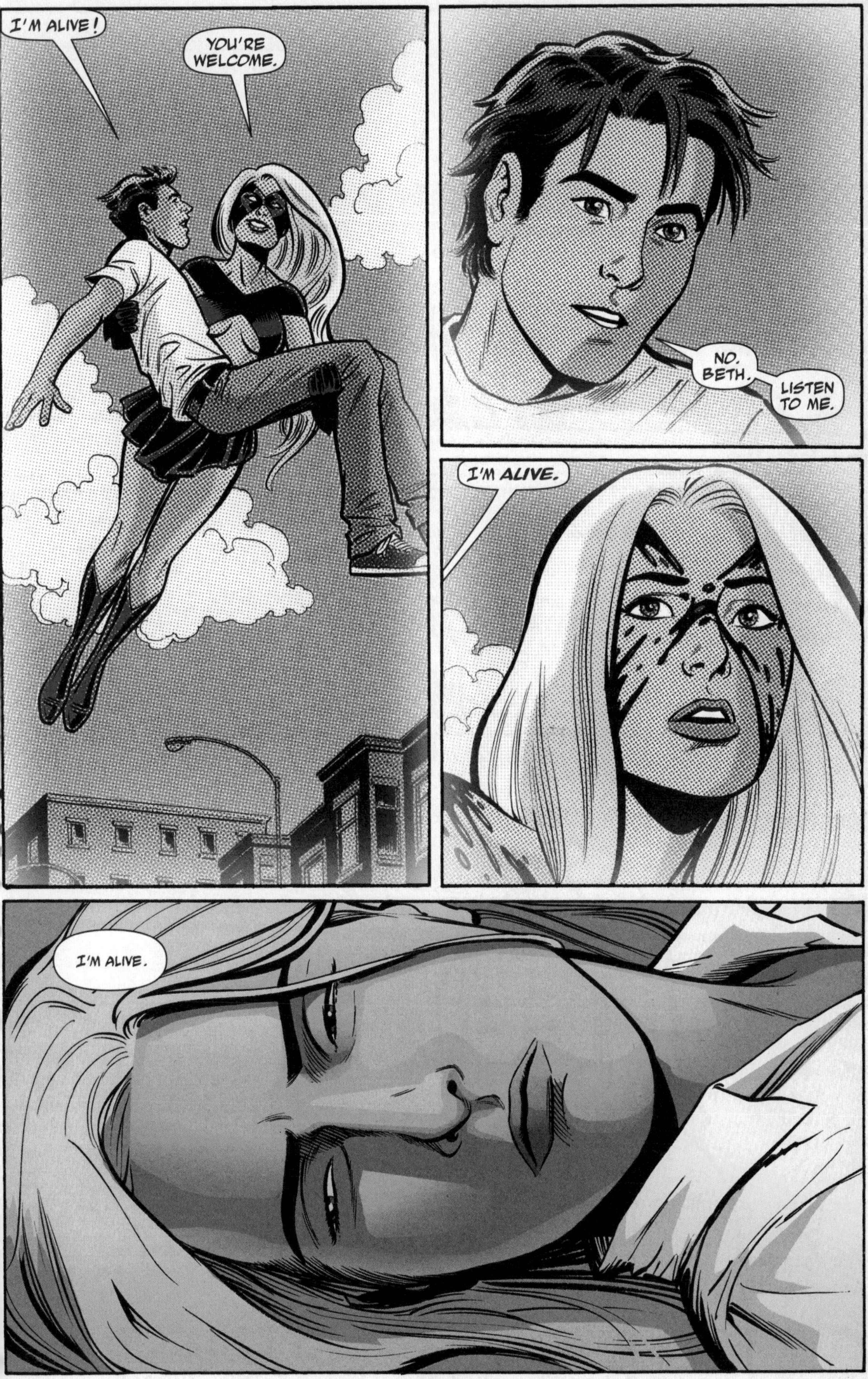

I'M ALIVE!
YOU'RE WELCOME.
NO. BETH.
LISTEN TO ME.
I'M ALIVE.
I'M ALIVE.

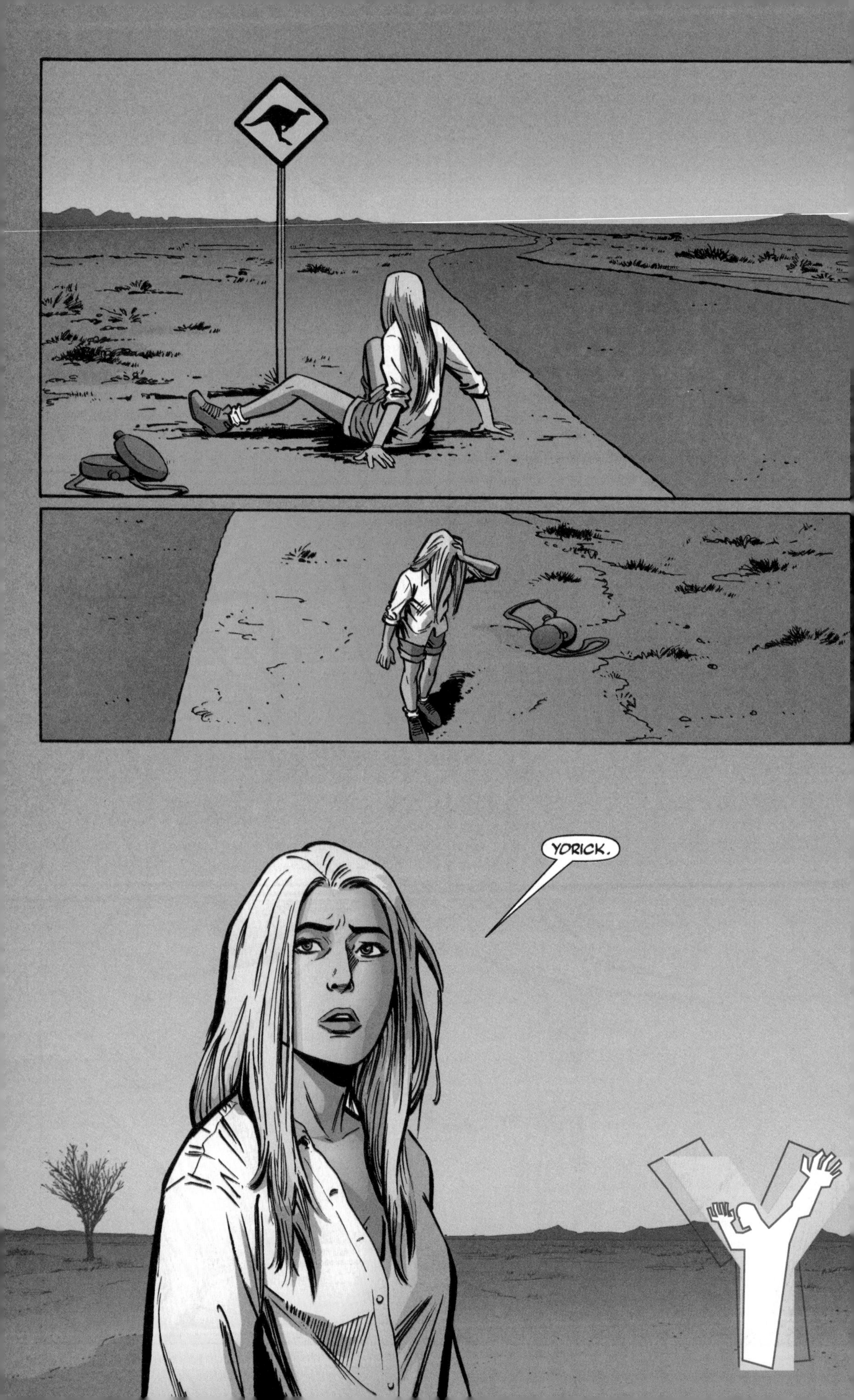
YORICK.

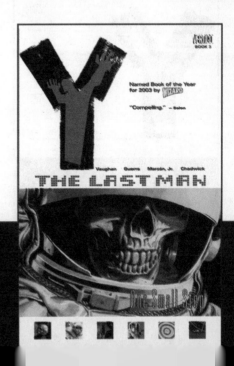